LEARNING BUSINESS STRATEGY

JOHN LOK

Contents

Preface *vii*

Prologue *xi*

1. Online Knowledge Task Strategy 1
2. Knowledgeable Jobs Will Raise Productivity And Efficiency 3
3. Why Employers Need To Considerate Labor Morality 7
4. Can A Useful Indicator Measure Low Income Living Standard Of Labor's Efficiency And Performance And Productivity 9
5. How To Apply " Standard Growth Enhancing Policy" To Improve Low Income Level Householders Living Of Standard To Raise Productivity 10
6. Why Economists Need To Concern Ethic To Raise Productivity 12
7. Why Ethic Relates To Labor Behavior 19
8. Outsource Strategy 27
9. Labor Morality Strategy 30
10. The Historical Development Of Behavioral Economics To Entrepreneur's Advantage 32
11. Experimental Control Method Measures Consumption Behavior 34
12. Judgement And Choice Influences Behavioral Consumption 36
13. Expected Utility Theory Estimates Behavioral Consumption 39
14. How Behavioral Game Theory Influences Shareholder's Individual Investment Behavior 42
15. How To Apply Behavioral Economic Principles To Make Any Business Strategy 47
16. Behavioural Economy And Business Strategy Relationship 53
17. How Labour Behavior Influences Efficiency 56
18. How Utility Maximization, Equilibrium And Efficiency Concepts Influence Employee's Individual Behavior 64
19. Costs And Benefits Analysis Concept Measures Consumer's Individual Or Employee's Individual Behavior 66
20. Preferences Over Risky And Uncertain Outcomes Of Individual Behavior Economic Theories 70

Contents

21. What Is Behavioral Game Theory 73

22. How Entrepreneur Applies Behavioral Economic Strategy To Do Decision 78

23. Consumer Psychology And Economy Environment Close Relationship 84

24. Body Shop Case Study 87

25. Case Study Change In The Marketing Environment On Sales Of Ready Meals To Supermarket, Such As Walt Mark 98

26. Case Study Of Ryanair Airline 104

27. How Can Ethnographic Research Predict Consumer Emotion 111

28. Marketing Research Methods 122

29. England Wine Bar Segmentation Case Study 132

30. P&g Body And Skin Product Marketing Strategy Case Study 139

31. Mobile Phone Company Marketing Strategy Case Study 151

32. England Nhs Public Hospital Patient Price Structure Of Marketing Strategy Case Study 160

33. Tesco Supermarket Value Chain Strategy Case Study 170

34. Chapter 34 187

35. A National Chain Of Restaurant Mobile Advertising Strategy 188

Preface

Preface

This book concerns my recommendation how entrepreneur chooses to achieve whose marketing or/and economy or / and human resource strategy to achieve to raise organizational more efficiency and effectiveness. I shall indiate why some UK and US some large business organizations whose weakness and strengths to cause whose organizations inefficient and I shall give recommendation how they can change their marketing or/and economy or/and human resource (organizational behavior) strategy to achieve more efficiency or effectiveness.

I shall apply behavioral economy theory: choice to explain why UK and US some entrepreneur can apply choice concept to solve clients' shopping choice to choose to buy their products or consume their service. Cases include: hospital, supermarket, television, mobile phone etc. different products or services. Readers can make judgment how and why the entrepreneur can attract consumers to choose to consume their services or products. In organizational behavioral part, managers can apply choice concept to predict how and why their employees choose to do the kind of behaviors in any organizations. Organizations include: school, bank, baseball team, financial etc. different organizations. Readers can make judgement to feel how and why the organization employee chooses to do the kind of behavior in the organization.

Entrepreneur labor economy strategy

In the entrepreneur first labor economy strategy, I shall explain how the entrepreneur attempts to use whose labor strategy methods to solve any challenges during who faces any challenges to achieve more efficiency in the labor environment. I shall indicate evidences to let my readers to predict how entrepreneur can attempt to achieve any new or fresh knowledgeable jobs, such as online office workers, online freelance electronic book authors, online survey researcher, online business researcher etc. internet channel office jobs which will be caused efficiency as well as their labors will feel more interest to work popularly in the future. So, I shall indicate why entrepreneurs need to concern this online job style because nowadays employees prefer to work free time and no overtime often , so if employers hope their employees feel more interest to work or raise more efficiency , then they will need to concern how to raise their labor efficiency.

Finally, I shall explain why entrepreneurs ought to consider the ethics to labor to judge whether how to do right decisions to keep the fairness productivity and the welfare and benefits to whose employees. I also indicate why labor ethics and productivity and even economic growth which has close relationship, so why economists and employers who need to concern ethics to labor to judge to make any social benefits of decisions to raise whose moralty to serve their employers honestly to avoid they do immoral or illegal behaviors to influence their employers' image to damage their business good image in society.

Entrepreneur behavioral economic strategy

In entrepreneur behavioral economic strategy, I shall indicate the entrepreneur how to apply behavioral economy concepts and assumptions to assist them to choose to do the reasonable judgement behavior and moral behavior when to decide labor welfare and raise productivity in intention. It is important to any economists or entrepreneurs who know how to learn how to do the right behavior to satisfy whose employees‘ emotion to raise productivity.

How behavioral economics can provide more realistic psychological foundations to any entrepreneur. This Chapter is intended to provide an introduction to the approach and methods of behavioral economics, and to some of its major findings, application, and promising new directions to any entrepreneur. I shall explain how the process of behavior economic field develops, then I shall show what methods are used to measure behavioral economy to let the entrepreneur to choose to do more reasonable behavior to satisfy their employee's any needs. Next, I shall indicate what the main two categories of behavioral economy are as well as I shall explain what risky and uncertain outcomes of individual behavior economic theories are as well as what behavioral game theory is ,such as entrepreneur can attempt to apply to solve any business challenges.

Finally, I shall explain behavioral economic principles of policy makers or decision makers as well as I shall also analyze whether behavioral economy and psychology which has close relationship to let entrepreneur to understand. For example, I shall explain what the concept is that behavioral economics can provide more realistic psychological foundations. This chapter is suitable to any economists or policy makers or individual consumption makers or students or working people who have interest learn how to apply behavioral economy to judge to do the most reasonable or the most right economic activities in everyday life.

Entrepreneur marketing environment strategy

This is any entrepreneur marketing environment strategy choice. These different marketing environment strategies concern sample of large companies case studies and indicated how the entrepreneur attempts to apply marketing theoretical bases which are often borrowed from the disciplines of economics and psychology to give opinions to solve these large companies' problems.

Practical application of any marketing strategy theory is provided through case studies. This chapter tries not to present prescriptive solutions to any marketing problems, but encourages discussion about causes and effects. This chapter is arranged in four thematic discussion. The first discussion begins by identifying the fundamental building blocks of marketing. The second thematic discussion focuses on consumers, and on understanding the complex factors that lead to buying decisions. The third thematic discussion focuses on how these sample companies use knowledge about consumers and the broader marketing environment to develop a competitive advantage. The final thematic discussion seeks to integrate the previous chapters and provides an overview of the marketing management process in the context of an increasingly globalized marketing environment.

I shall indicate these sample large companies, such as Body Shop, Ryanair airline, Walt Mark food supermarket , Nestle , England NHS public hospital etc. which had encountered what problems had cause difficulties to compete to their competitors as well as I shall recommend what solutions are the best to let them to solve these problems. Thus, these problems were the fact that these sample large companies had encountered.

key words: Corporate social responsibility , marketing oriented sales oriented, production oriented, ecological concerns , ethnographic research ,cognitive information processing, demographic segmentation

Prologue

CONTENTS OF TABLE

Chapter 1 Online knowledgeable task strategy p.3-20
Chapter 2 Why does knowledgeable jobs will raise productivity and efficiency p.21-35
Chapter 3 Why employers need to considerate labor morality p.36-47

Chapter 4 Can a useful indicator measure low income living standard of labor's efficiency and performance and productivity p.48-60
Chapter 5 How to apply " standard growth enhancing policy" to improve low income level householders living of standard to raise productivity p.61-70

Chapter 6 Why economists need to concern ethic p.71-80

Chapter 7 Why ethic relates to labor behavior p.81-91
Chapter 8 Outsource strategy p.92-106
Chapter 9 Labor morality strategy107-119
p.107-119

Chapter 10 The historical development of

behavioral economics to
entrepreneur's advantage
Chapter 11 Experimental control method measures consumption behavior
Chapter 12 Judgement and choice influences behavioral consumption
Chapter 13 Expected utility theory estimates behavioral consumption
Chapter 14 How behavioral game theory influences shareholder's individual investment behavior
Chapter 15 How to apply behavioral economic
principles to make any business
strategy
Chapter 16 Behavioural economy and business
strategy relationship

Chapter 17 How labour behavior influences efficiency

Chapter 18 How utility maximization, equilibrium and efficiency concepts influence employee's individual behavior

Chapter 19 Costs and benefits analysis concept
measures consumer's individual or
employee's individual behavior

Chapter 20 Preferences over risky and uncertain outcomes of individual behavior economic theories.

Chapter 21 What is behavioral game theory

Chapter 22 How entrepreneur applies behavioral economic strategy to do decision

Chapter 23 Consumer psychology and economy environment close relationship

Chapter 24 Body shop facial product sale

Chapter 25 Walt Mark Supermarket

Chapter 26 Ryanair airline & Easy Jet airline & budget airline

Chapter 27 Ethnographic research

Chapter 28 Quantitative and qualitative approaches

Chapter 26 England wine bar segmentation

Chapter 27 P&G (Procter & Gamble) body and skin product marketing strategy

Chapter 28 Mobile phone company marketing strategy case study

Chapter 29 England NHS public hospital patient price structure strategy

Chapter 30 Tesco supermarket supply for fruit
and vegetables supply chain strategy

Chapter 31 A national chain of restaurant mobile advertising strategy

Bibliography

CHAPTER I

Online knowledge task strategy

Entrepreneur will face knowledge productivity environment change and labor need challenges. Nowadays, enterprise competition is serious. Entrepreneur needs to change employees' productivity methods to raise employee efficiency. In what way has globalization affected employers choose online work to provide to local or overseas to raise productivity? Is online work still a useful working place environment for local and overseas employers to raise productivity in a globalized online age, such as online electronic books‘ authors, online office administration or online surveys or online researchers etc. kind of online jobs supplying?

Our age is entering an online business environment, such as online electronic air tickets sale, online electronic books publishing, online advertising and online shopping and website design service promotion , online university education etc. different kind of online businesses from internet. It seems online channel can increase global online job chances to affect that our live and our job nature to be changed every day. For example, online electronic book publishing business will be popular, many different countries' readers who like to buy electronic books to study, due to these online electronic book shops, e.g. Amazon, lulu, book Rix, book tango etc. electronic book stores which can provide free charge to deliver cheaper paper books to any overseas countries‘ readers' homes and which paper book prices are more cheaper to compare to book shops‘ paper books process after who have paid to buy any electronic books or paper books from these online book stores websites. Moreover, these readers can read these book stores' electronic books from online publishing sellers‘ websites to download these electronic books to study at homes or any libraries etc. computer provision of places easily and conveniently. So readers do not need to walk to any book shops to buy any paper books and who also do not need to bring any heavy paper books back to homes conveniently. Hence, electronic publishers can provide electronic book authors' job chances to write their books and type to computers to register to be online authors to publish whose electronic or paper books to earn loyalty income at home very easily. Also, the globalizing online job nature can change the customized office work style. It won't need staffs go to office to work from 9:00 AM to 6:00 PM. In general office workers need to spend eight to ten working hours with five or six working days within per week commonly. Hence, online office workers don't need to pay transportation fee and lunch cost, due who can work at their home when who turn on their computer to enter whose employers' websites to work and make email communication to connect between them conveniently. So, I feel the online electronic book authors and online office administration jobs which will be popular further occupations to be provided from global online job structure style and many labors will like to work online, then who can raise productivity conveniently when who work at home in the future. Beside, due to online (internet) is very popular and cheap cost to be needed to spend expenditure from employer.

So, internet will build the relationships between workplaces and every staff role identity and everyday life and online working environments can connect them to work in the process of globalization in the future. Also, our everyday life and work is entering in a globalizing world. It emphasizes on time and space compression and the importance of virtual space and experience in our daily lives of many people, the working style seems spent online working time to change how our social traditional work roles and our traditional office working places-based environments to home online working environments further long time in the future. So, employers ought plan to prepare online working methods to let their employees to raise productivity.

In conclusion, Online knowledgeable job concept can raise productivity and efficiency because many office jobs can be accepted to apply online technological working in order to reduce staff numbers and to raise fast speed job efficiency as well as labors shall be prefer to work in online environment in the work.

CHAPTER II

knowledgeable jobs will raise productivity and efficiency

Entrepreneur needs to predict when and why consumers will begin to dislike online shopping because it is possible consumers will choose any fresh or new technological consumption if it had another kind of popular technological consumption to replace online shopping. Social science can explain knowledgeable jobs will be useful and popular and assisting labors to raise productivity to work at home online working environments. It seems knowledgeable online job and undiscovered new technological consumption which will have possible close relationship and influence to any consumer's consumption of method.

Within social science, in such discipline is sociology and human psychology and geography which indicates internet technology have changed to online working place environment, sense of working place, online employee role identity, everyday online work and life style, website global working communication and email online communication working interconnections. It seems internet brings access to social, economic and political resources to effect change to both individual and social working conditions, such as employers accept to attempt to use internet to assist office staffs to work at home, e.g. many book publishing businesses like to attempt to publish electronic books from online book store, instead of book shops channel to sell paper books. So these online book stores give chance to authors to publish electronic books or online paper books from online sale channel to earn loyalty income. For example, Amazon online electronic bookstore can publish electronic books and online paper books to sell all one day 24 hours to any countries' readers from its website, so when any countries' readers can enter its website to choose any different kind of subjects of electronic books to buy by visa card conveniently. Such as fiction, psychology, economy, science, law, architecture, medicine, commerce, management etc. subjects. So, any country's reader who does not need to buy air tickets to go to the country's book shop to buy the paper book, who only needs to pay visa card to buy the electronic or online paper books from Amazon publishing's website to buy any countries' electronic and paper books and then the overseas reader can choose either to download it from whose home computer or pays more price to deliver the online paper book to post to whose country conveniently. Hence, this online bookstore sale method will be popular and many free work authors will choose to work to raise the productivity of more quality electronic books numbers from this internet channel.

However, the consequences of global change are far from uniform with globalizing influences and adapted as new technological, economic and online working cultural experiences are incorporated by any countries' staffs of any cities, towns and rural areas into their everyday work lives from long distance easily. Since one company can employ different countries' staffs to work from internet working channel at their homes. For example, a America company can employ overseas countries' staffs to work at the same time together by sending job duties from email communication channel among them when the America company has any job arrangement to notify to any staff to finish it any time, then the overseas staff finish the job and who can send whose finished documents to whose America employer any time. It seems the overseas staffs whose working hours can be flexible and those working hours have no regular office working hours to be fixed time table, so they do not need to work in any fixed working time table every working days, who can send their finished office documents to whose employers after who have finished their documents by either email communication channel or office online website downloads office download any time conveniently.

It will be a new working style position that online working globalization is in a new stage. We are living in an age of very rapid and fluid flow of information, ideas, products and people which are having an effect of a variety of scales. I shall indicate evidences to explain why employers will be encountered online knowledgeable jobs to raise productivity in a globalizing world by sociology concept in the future one day. I shall focus on research into the connections between our everyday online life style, online working place and online working role identity.

The first is that everyday online life is the manifestation of social existence and always involves either distant or direct interaction with other people. Such as we can use internet email channel to communicate with overseas friends or strange people, even employers or employees can also use email to exchange to receive and send their office documents by email or company website any time conveniently. Good example includes such things are as online participation in work, employment, cultural events, and recreation, shopping and communication from internet channel. It is related to employees are working in whose home working places and their home working place are possible to connect their overseas employers' offices and however, readily these may be separated in far distant conceptual terms, such as an online working environment. The employee's home is such whose employer's office, who can work at home from online channel conveniently. When who receives whose employer's email about what job duties who needs to do every day. Then, who sees his employer's email, then either if who did not understand how to do whose job duties clearly, who can send email back to ask whose employers to explain how who needs to do whose office job duties by email communication channel again easily. Even after who finish whose office job duties on that day or another day, then who can send finished office job duties to whose employers by email conveniently. In this view, online working places and sense of online working places are produced by different countries' large enterprise employers and overseas employees interacting together.

At the same time, employees and employers whose sense are contacted by employees' individual role identity from email or office website communication channel any time. Thus, traditional office working environment is constrained and enabled by different countries' working histories and cultures and social class backgrounds and economic conditions and job opportunities, working positions of power and working geographical locations and development of local change and distant social interaction. In the future, online working place will be changed from traditional socially significant to online social relationship; underlying this sense of online working place will be the notion that some employers and employees themselves ought feel that life.

Moreover, online working place is the possibility of non controlling employees' working time, due to working hours are flexible and employers' working places sizes are very limited to supply to many staffs to work in a limited office working place in the same working time. It seems online home environment will be very popular, due to every employee will use whose home to work to finish whose office documents at home every day any time very conveniently as well as employers won't need to spend much expenditure to pay for large sizes of office rent when the employer needs to rent more than one room office at more than one floor in one building. Hence, company's website expenditure can reduce the employers' office rent seriously.

Moreover, employees can be dominated by feelings towards changing general office working place to online working at home as well as changing fixed working time table to flexible working time table, e.g. the staff can see whose employer's email to know what office job duties who needs to do tonight, so who will finish whose office documents and will send whose finished office documents to whose employer by email tomorrow. So, home online working environment is seen as an ideal home working place, and home online working environment which is quiet, safe and it has certain valued facilities and home online working environment is such as the type of residents in the employee's living building. This sense of living and online work place will be held by residents who will be employed in professional/ managerial/ technical etc. occupations. Hence, local employees won't catch any transportation to go to office as well as overseas employees won't also catch planes to go to whose employer's country's office to work, due to who can use online email communication or office website communication channels to work together conveniently.

However, working facilities will be one online computer working commodity which is purchasable, useable and exchangeable and saleable to any employees are located at home and employers are located at office, and after a flexible working time table is discarded easily by employer, due to whose website or office email can receive any employee's individual finished office documents by every employee's individual email communication any time very conveniently. Moreover, home online working place is also like a stage on every employee's life is lived out. The employee will feel that whose life and working time is lived at home together at the same time. Similar to feel commodity sense of home and the working place which are the same location, but it is distinguished from it by the establishment of arriving strange and far distant of the employee's local or overseas employer's office when the employee's working place is family interacting to the employee's house or home.

Our world is entering globalization, people are connecting in an increasing number of ways. It is clear also that is the face of globalization, the ways of our everyday working life is either constituted which are still shaped by local expenditure of working place or is by where the firm's overseas employees love locally, regionally and nationally or is by the access who have limited to office resources and home office online working locations opportunity changing from general office working environment to home online working environment. Roberston (1992) shows is that" this is not just about economic processes, but about social and cultural issues are as well. In the early part of the 21 ST century, it is necessary to see this as a set of processes that encompass economic, political, social, cultural and environmental changes."

In conclusion, online knowlegeable job method can raise efficiency and productivity because many clients accept online shopping or anyundiscovered technological consumption of methods.

CHAPTER III

Why employers need to considerate labor morality

Entrepreneurs need to consider low income level worker life challenges and how employers themselves moral behaviors to treat their employees. Because their moral behaviors will influence their employees‘ performance and efficiency and producticity .

Is globalization influenced to new online knowledgeable jobs to raise efficiency and productivity? One of the key areas of debate among theorists is the extent to which globalization is a new phenomenon or stage in a process. When it began and the path that it has followed and thus how new it is. Such as internet is used in communication aspect in early, e.g. hospital or war email communication channel. Then, many businessmen discovered online electronic commerce is also one online sale and purchase method. So, it will cause online office workers or online freelance online jobs, e.g. electronic book authors working style or electronic book reading cultural existed in our society in common possibly in the future.

However, I recognize globalization is a misleading concept since what is described as globalization has been happening for the 500 years history ago. Rather what is new is that human are entering an age of transition, such as online knowledgeable workers or knowledgeable nature of different jobs will be caused from online working environment popularly.

There are key processes of globalization: the economic, often is seen as the central process, the political, social, cultural and online working environment. Every natural economy needs to maintain the rate of growth, employment, welfare provision and minimum wage balance levels, so it will cause knowledgeable jobs provided, such as online organized labors, it also will change the traditional office organizational environment to cause online new organizational home work environment popularly in the future.

Hence, economic and political has close connection, political and cultural has also close connection, cultural and social has also close connection, social and working environment has also connection. After all these connections cause globalization finally, then the new online knowledgeable working environment, such as online jobs will be required by global office employees popularly in the future. It will bring many online workers supply to the employment market in the future.

As capital in the new globalized economy has a limited attachment to working place, production centers, such as offices, factories or farms which locate any where it is competitively advantages to do so, and economic activity moves to where labor is cheapest or raw materials is the least expensive. It can be raised demand to online knowledgeable workers demand in global competitive employment environment directly. For example, cultural, social, global expansion of Mc Donald’s and other fast food chains will be entered to the online sale channel. Hence, environmental globalization raises human awareness, includes a new view of the natural and the social worlds to environmental protection message.

These message source is from online channel popularly nowadays. Online organizing environment and living will influence our everyday working worlds. Due to many industrial cities and life will be not needed by global employers. However, industrial cities concentrate on demanding in developing countries, e.g. China, India, Korea etc. countries. So, developed countries, such as America, England, Japan etc. countries' employers will need many online knowledgeable employees to help them to work from online work place environment popular in the future. Later, knowledgeable online working environment will be popular to developing countries when which economy had developed mature in the future. So, it is possible online jobs will raise low income level householders' living of standard because online can create more job chance for this group people as well as it can bring more efficiency and productivity to employers.

CHAPTER IV

Can a useful indicator measure low income living standard of labor's efficiency and performance and productivity

Nowadays, developing countries, such as India, China, Hong Kong, etc. and developed countries, such as America, England etc. which are facing social challenges. For example, many low income level labors whose income level can't be raised and inflation is also high in society. Although, these developing countries' economy is growing, but which can not raise the low income level householders' income level to let them have afford to buy one house in minimum in whose country, even these low income level family have no enough income to buy foods to eat and cloths to wear easily.

Also, the developed countries' economy had arrived the mature growing stage, but which also can not give any benefits to whose low level income level income householders group. Hence, governments have responsibilities to find methods to solve these challenges, such as: How to reduce poor occurrence? How much does economic growth help the poor? How can social policy help? Can a country have a sizeable low-wage sector of house to provide to the poor? What role can public service social spending better for the poor?

Justice is the distribution of income and wealth is fairest. Any country's government needs play a large role in determining it's citizen's abilities to do common occupation, what job choices are preferences to them, how to raise employment of motivation and what social circumstances are to cause households have no poor occurrence to cause many low level income jobs to do to earn income in society.

In order to reduce the unfair income distribution between rich and poor people. Why it is important to improve unfair income treatment between rich and poor people to any countries? However, in a rich and growing economic country, such as America, England etc. , which are difficult to justify stagnant living standards for those at the floor bottom low income people nowadays. Although, these developed countries' economy are growing, but which can not give benefits to this low level income households group.

However, I suggest any country ought favor not simply a satisfactory level of living standards for the poor people, but it ought consider how to improve or review poor people living standards every year. Analysts typically set the poverty line at 50 or 60 percent of the median income within each country. In general, poverty means to level of resources insufficient to achieve a minimal acceptable standard of living as well as people tends to experience poverty as relative is to living standards by comparison in any country's citizen's own society. If the absolute incomes or living standards for the poor grow less rapidly than those of households in the middle income level in the country. So, it seems that it is not fair economic growth in these developing countries and income seems to be a useful indicator to measure living of standard.

CHAPTER V

How to apply " standard growth enhancing policy" to improve low income level householders living of standard to raise productivity

Is income a useful indicator of living standards? Income is a resource that allows any country's households to acquire the sort of things e.g. food, housing, medical care, transportation, education, entertainment etc. needs. So, which are needed for a minimal decent standard of living. Income also is comparatively easy to measure. However, causing poor factors might have many reasons, such as illness, temporary unemployment, a large amount of bonus reduction, overtime long time working hours, family members unemployment, even economic decline (falling down), so these factors can reduce jobs supply to any countries to cause poor occurrence.

However, any countries' income measures seldom include the value of government service and in kind benefit, such as pension, unemployment assistance etc. as well as some low income households have assets (savings in bank, and owned home). So, it seems income is not an accurate measure to the actual living standard to the low income people numbers in the countries effectively. If income is not an accurate measure to actual living standard, then it can not improve the low income level householders of living standard and productivity level will be reduced because these low income level labors can not get reasonable salaries and unfair welfare to work from whose employers. Otherwise, the high income level labors can get increased salaries and fair welfare to work from whose employers. When these both low and high income level labors work in same company, the low income level labors will feel angry to work unhappy, then it is possible that who will decrease their productivity.

The poor people numbers will be reduced possibly. How to evaluate the actual poor people numbers decreasing? In think when the degree to the country which economic growth boosts the income level of low and households to rise their general savings amounts to the income level of middle households. Then, the country's poor people numbers will be decreasing, due to this group of the numbers of incomes level of low households has been decreasing and it's numbers has been increasing to the income level of middle group, then productivity will also raise to every employers in any country.

In general, economic growth is assumed that poor households get more jobs, work more hours and/or receives higher wages. Hence, when one country measure economic growth, which can apply the relationship between per capita GDP and low income households of numbers between the past year and current year to measure the rising or falling numbers per capita GDP in the low and income households group, for example, in Sweden, Denmark, Norway, the Netherlands and Finland countries which net transfers are received by low income level households increased significantly between 1979 year and 2007 year. But, average earnings, were flat in Demarks country, when in Sweden and Finland countries which declined sharply during those countries' deep recessions in the early

1990 year. Otherwise, in the United Kingdom, the period was from 1979 year to 1995 year, it saw no changes in transfers pension or retirement savings from United Kingdom government and a slight drop in earnings, but from 1999 year to 2005 year, social earning increased slightly, but more important was a large rise in net government pension and retirement saving transfers, which resulted in a sizeable increase in low income level incomes group. When net government pension or retirement savings transfers to citizen increased this was caused by economic growth. In general, economic growth allows policy makers to boost inflation-adjusted benefit levels for pension or retirement saving transfer to citizen programs, which will increased the incomes of pension or retirement saving benefit recipients. With GDP rising, government social benefit pension or retirement saving transfers as a share of GDP tended to remark more or less constant.

However, in some countries, the rise in pension of retirement saving net transfers was achieved in part by reduction of income or profit taxes for low income households or low business profit households, since the 1970 year, most of the world's rich nations, such as America, united Kingdom have not significantly increased the share of their GDP that goes to pensions or retirement savings transfer for the low income level poor households. It seems that if any country hoped the low income level of householders numbers will be increase, which ought need to upgrade their low income level to go up middle income level in society, then its economic growth will be raising. How economic growth can boost incomes for the poor households. It seems economic growth has made rising low income level of households is more likely, but several countries are exceptions. They experienced growing per capita GDP, but little or no improvement in the income of low income level of households, such as Hong Kong has seven million people who are living in a small city.

Although, it was encountering economic growth from 1970 year in beginning, but the low income level of households had little or no improvement, it was possible that the numbers of Hong Kong low income level of households are more than the middle or high income level of households seriously. So, the HK economic growth seems not improve low income level of households to assist this low income level of households to raise whose income to be risen to the middle income level of households group. The reason is possible that the failure of some governments to increase public transfers as the economy grows is a key part of reason. But why did not more economic growth reach the low income level of poor households in the form of rising market income? For example, in HK, whether economic growth is likely to directly benefit the poor group's employment hours reduction and rising hourly wage levels. However, I discovered that HK economic growth produced no increase in the wage or salary market rate of low level of income households and without employment hours reduction and without rising hourly wage levels. So, HK economic growth seems to raise more job supply in the employment market, but it seems without employment hours reduction. Otherwise, it's economic growth rises employment hours, but without rising hourly wage. Hence, it seems low income level householders of numbers and economic growth have close relationship to any country, so employers need to concern their labors numbers of low income level to raise their income to be middle income level in society.

CHAPTER VI

Why economists need to concern ethic to raise productivity

Entrepreneur needs to concern business ethic to whose employees because employees' negative emotion will influence whose performance and productivity to be poor. I recommend this economic policy to reduce poor occurrence, such as growth on average benefit the poor as much as anyone lives in the country's society, such as "standard growth enhancing policy" should be at the center of any poverty reduction strategy. I believe economic growth is the most powerful instrument for reducing poverty, due to many businessmen have enough money to invest to their countries to do any kind of businesses, then the jobs supply will be raised any many people can get any jobs supply number is more than job seekers number, then it is no doubt, the unemployment numbers will be reduced. When many people have new jobs to do and who can earn enough wages to prepare to save more money in bank.

What has been the impact of economic growth on employment hours and wages? In fact, work hours are matter a great deal for the incomes of poor group of households in developed countries, such as United States or United Kingdom or developing countries, such as Hong Kong, China etc. countries. For example, HK economic growth has a large influence to raise employment hours more than rising wage levels, such as HK general working hours are risen up to 10 to 12 hours or more per week working days to low income level of households, but the low income level of households group has not been rising wage level generally. So, I feel HK economic growth could not give any benefits to the low income level of households, such as without reduction employment hours and without raising wage level to the low income level of households in HK. Also, HK's economic growth only raises many jobs supply in HK society. Otherwise, America economic growth can give benefits to low income level of households, such as reduction employment hours, rising wage level to low income level of households and raising jobs supply in America society. Hence, the developed countries, such as America , England which economic growth can give more benefits to low income level of households. Otherwise, the developing countries, such as India, China, Korea which economic growth can not give more benefits to the low income level of households and these developing countries will cause disadvantages to this low income level of poor group in society. It is possible that the developing countries' low income level of households often need to increase to spend more working hours to assist whose employers to develop whose employers' business, due to their employers do not want to increase to employ extra workers or staffs to assist whose business development, who need whose current employees to raise more extra working hours to work to raise work efficiency when these developing countries are encountering the economic growth stage.

For example, HK employers do not concern moral issues about abnormal working hours influence. The outcome is either Hong Kong labors work long time working hours abnormally who can not rise Hong Kong economic growth or who can rise Hong Kong economic growth in long time. Generally, Hong Kong employers choose to pay less salary expenditure to need many extra labors to work abnormal working hours to help them to rise productivity, but who don't concern that long time working factor will influence unhealthy to current workers due to who need to work long time working hours abnormally in long time and it seems to cause their workers will reduce productivity and inefficiency in long time.

Although, it is possible that HK labors can be increased extra abnormal working hours to work to rise Hong Kong employers' productivity and assist HK social economy will be grown up in short term, but it is also possible that it can't rise Hong Kong economic growth due to their unhealthy or sick increasing to cause productivity declining and inefficiency in long time. Thus, I shall find evidence to analyze whether Hong Kong labors need to work abnormal long time working hours. Otherwise, who will decline Hong Kong economic growth and reduce productivity and inefficiency in long time as well as I shall give suggestion to indicate whether either current workers work abnormal long time working hours or employers ought choose to employ more extra part time workers to assist current labors to rise their productivity to decide which is the best choice to raise HK economic growth and efficient productivity in long time.

Effects on Hong Kong employment of working time reduction is found to be difficult to predict. The results of Hong Kong macroeconomic simulations of the effects on employments of working time reduction rely heavily on certain basic assumptions, such as how many hours people will actually work or how productivity and pay levels will develop. Whether HK abnormal working hours will assist HK social economic growth or economic falling down in long term.

The reasons cause Hong Kong labors who need to work abnormal long time working hours. In fact, it isn't the reason that the Hong Kong high skillful labors market is shortage to supply for the nature of some occupations, e.g. hospital doctors and nurses, university teachers, law firm lawyers etc. professional occupations. HK has many high qualification university students graduation, it has enough labor supply to high labor market every year. The reason is that employers don't like to spend more salary to increase to employ extra labors to share current workers workload, such as low skillful and hardworking labors, such as cleaners, securities, waiters and high skillful professionals, such as hospital doctors and nurses, university teachers, lawyers etc. However, the low and high skillful labor market can be enough supply in Hong Kong, but Hong Kong employers need the current high and low both skillful workers who need to work more than 10 to 12 hours or more per working day commonly. It is possible that HK high and low educational labors will be caused unhealthy and lack enough sleep if who still need to work abnormal working hours time in long time. Although, who can rise productivity and efficiency in the short time, but it is possible that who can't rise productivity and inefficiency in the long time. Moreover, it will cause many young or middle or old ages high educational or low educational knowledgeable hardworking workers who will lose many jobs provided and who will be hard to find any jobs in HK labor employment market if HK employers don't choose to pay extra salaries to employ extra full time workers to share current labors' workload in the high and low salary occupations, due to they only choose to increase abnormal additional extra working hours to current workers to achieve to reduce employment expenditure and raise productivity. Hence, it is possible to influence HK social economy grows up slowly, even it's economy can go down seriously in long time.

I shall assume that working wage or salary of every individual labors can not be increased, even can be decreased as well as whose normal working hours can be increased abnormally in generally. This means that the Hong Kong individual worker's income will be decreased and general productivity raising is not affected generally, due to HK employers need current labors to work abnormal extra working hours to attempt to raise productivity daily, but their salary or wage have not increased more. However, HK employers need many workers to accomplish the same amount of work, even who don't like to employ extra labors to assist current workers to achieve long term productivity raising in their companies. These abnormal working hours labors will feel unfair treatment, due to they need to work abnormal working hours, but their salary or wage have not been increased.

In the first scenario of my hypothesis is about that HK labor employment market's general salary or wage has not been increased to the normal proportion of the increased extra abnormal working time(hours). Then, in HK labors market, due to the numbers of labors supply is more than the jobs supply because HK employers don't like to pay more salary or wage expenditure to employ extra labor, but they like to increase extra abnormal working hours to current workers to aim to achieve productivity. So it will cause many HK job seekers with adequate qualifications or with less qualifications who won't find any jobs easily, then the HK the numbers of unemployed people will be increased and their household incomes will decrease to cause many HK household do not like to spend easily. The result will cause a negative effect on HK social private consumption will be decreased and the businessmen' income will be decreased also. So, HK people private consumption decreasing will influence HK economy growth to be slow, even it will cause HK economy declining in the long time.

In the second scenario of my hypothesis is about that Hong Kong workers are fully compensated for the increasing extra abnormal working time(hours) by the abnormal additional working hours calculation. Although, Hong Kong companies' productivity will be raised, but which are not to the extent that it compensates Hong Kong enterprises for their increased wage or salary costs. In fact, Hong Kong enterprises, their costs are passed on to the clients, it causes Hong Kong's economic growth has an impact on international competitiveness to cause economic declining in possible when these enterprises need to raise their products' sale prices to balance their salary or wage cost raising to win their import competitors. Another effect is that Hong Kong individual labor's incomes decrease, which means that Hong Kong private consumption also falls in this scenario to influence HK economic growth seriously. Thus, the HK economic growth problem will be caused, due to these factors lead to a fall in Hong Kong social household private consumption. Consequently, it will cause many HK employers hope to raise Hong Kong productivity and they will raise the total amount of Hong Kong labor actually worked hours will be risen to such as extent as the increasing in normal working time(hours) from 8 or 9 hours per normal working day to 10 or 11 or 12 hours, even more extra abnormal hours per working day to the current labors. But they do not like to spend more salary or wage expenditure to employ full time extra labors, instead of increasing extra abnormal working hours to current labors to achieve productivity of raising, due to the cost will be increased if they choose to employ extra full time labors if they want to raise productivity. However, I feel they will raise productivity in the short term, but they will not raise productivity in the long term when they choose to raise their current labors abnormal working hours per working day.

The assumption will be made regarding to the relationship between the HK labor market's abnormal long time working hours factor and whether it can influence Hong Kong economic growth in long time for this research economic problem. For example, how many hours Hong Kong labor would actually work or how much workers have efficient productivity and efficiency and how much salaries or wages would be affected as a result of the increasing in working time(hours) in Hong Kong employment market.

I shall apply endogenous growth theory to Hong Kong labor market. As this theory indicates that this model also incorporated a new concept of human capital, whose capital is increasing rates of return. Research done in this area has focused on what increases human capital (e.g. education) or technological change (e.g. innovation) to influence HK economic growth. In macro economic environment, it indicates that economic growth means the increase in the market value of the products and services produced by the country's economy over time. It is conventionally measured as the percent rate of increase in real growth domestic product or real GDP. The growth of the ratio of GDP to population (GDP per capital, per capita income). Thus, an increase in growth is caused by more efficient use of inputs is referred to as intensive growth. GDP growth is caused only be increased in such as capital, population or territory is called extensive growth. Thus, in economy growth theory, typically refers growth off potential output, i.e. production is at full employment. However, HK unemployment ratio is still high to compare other developed or developing countries, although the labors supply are enough to HK employment market.

The working time is the period of time that an individual spends at paid occupation labor. Many countries regulate the work week by law, such as minimum daily rest periods, annual holidays and a maximum number of working hours per week. Working time may vary from person to person often depending on location, cultural, lifestyle choice and the profitability of the individual's livelihood.

Generally, most Hong Kong employers need labors work long time working hours abnormally. For example, low educational workers, such as security occupations of labors need to work per working day is twelve hours or more, restaurant waiters and dish cleaners also need to work ten to twelve hours or more per working day, bank counter cashiers or audit firm staffs also need to work over time from 10 to 12 hours or more per working day and who have no extra salaries for over time salaries payment commonly. Standard working hours or normal working hours refers to the legislation to limit the working hours per day, per week, per month or per year. If an employee needs to work overtime, the employer will need to pay overtime payments to employees as required in the law. Generally speaking, standard working hours countries word wide are around 40 to 44 hours per week (but not everywhere: such as France employers need labors work from 35 hours per week, North Korea employers need labors work up to 112 hours per week). Maximum working hours refers that the employee can't work than the level specified in the maximum working hours law. It seems that Hong Kong many employers had needed labors to work above standard working hours per week to compare to other developed countries, e.g. America, France, England, New Zealand etc. developed countries.

In conclusion, in my viewpoint, HK employers need to provide on job training to current labors to aim to raise their efficiency to productivity in the long time. Because when their labors had been trained to let them to learn how to use special skill to finish their job duties easily, then they will not need to spend much time (additional working hours) to finish their job duties per working day. On the one hand, HK employers need to measure to compare what benefits are in favor of standard working hours to whose employees. The benefits include, such as promoting work life balance and enjoy family life, increasing time for leisure and rest, beneficial to health and employees can have more time to pursue further studies as well as employers do not need to pay higher salaries to longer working hours employees or overtime pay boost income as most HK companies pay time and a half to some employees only. On the other hand, HK employers need to measure to compare what benefits are against standard working hours to employers, such as employing many part time working hours employees to assist normal working hours full time employees rather than needing full time employees work abnormal hours daily, lowering or cancelling year and bonus etc. Moreover, HK employers may also use various measure to offset the increased cost of running businesses, such as lowering average hourly annual compensation. However, when HK employees are forced to work part time jobs, who may need to acquire additional employment to maintain their standard living. Even, HK employers only force employees to work overtime in some situations. Appropriate standard working hours can vary across different industries based on the type of work performed. Such as some HK certain professional positions are difficult to define in terms of appropriate working hours. Issues can arise with employers expecting employees to work extra hours "off the clock" in order to keep costs down. Thus, I believe that HK labors abnormal working hours time issue ought be decreased and HK employers ought employ extra workers assistance to share current labors' workload to help them to raise productivity and efficiency and HK economy will grow fast in the long time. Finally, my research aims to find that the number of hours worked is a more responsive measure of the state of the labor market than employment in HK. Comparing the number of hours worked to indicators of the wider economy shows that it is likely to be demand from HK firms (employers) which is driving the numbers of hours, rather than individual job applicant supply to HK employment market. My analysis also show that the HK appears to have developed a long working hours culture to compare other developed countries, such as America, England, Canada etc. In fact, in the presence of HK firms may even invest to find which are more profitable to able to reduce their every employee's abnormal working hours daily rather than normal number of working hours of their every employee.

Finally, I shall recommend some methods to rise the living standard to low income level households group in any countries. On the income policy, I recommend governments ought implement the progressive tax policy, so the income taxes tend to be progressive to the middle and high income level of households. It aims to achieve the low income level group and the middle and high income level groups whose income level to be balanced. Whereas taxes on payroll and consumption usually are regressive, due to payroll and consumption taxes are more useful than income taxes for increasing revenues taxes on income and payroll are the least conductive to economic growth, so payroll taxes can raise growth of employment in possible. Because the low income level of households have no more effort to spend to buy any expensive products or foods generally, so who can pay less taxes when who spend less. Otherwise, because the middle or high income levels of households have more effort to spend to buy any expensive products or foods generally, so who need pay more taxes when who spend more. It is possible to reduce the level amount of difference of savings between the low income level of households and the middle income level of households. Finally, I conclude that the method of taxes on payroll and consumption usually are regressive and the method of income taxes tend to be progressive to the middle and high income level of households, which are possible to raise the low income level of households of living standard for long term if governments could attempt to achieve these two policies to apply to the low income level group and the middle income level groups both, such as income tax and payroll or consumption tax policies both. It aims to raise the better of standard of life to the low income level household and to assist the low income level household can be upgrade to the middle income level household group in the short time quickly.

Economists claim to be scientists or technicians who study fact, not values, who make scientific studies and predictions to decide why this matter is caused and to find the reasons. Often the public sector economists in USA predict the economic processes and find the facts of the world have not supported the economists' models wrongly. However, economists have ethical rules to control their behaviors to be judged any matter and to give the corrective and reasonable decisions to let public to know correctively. Hence, who can't attempt to mislead facts to present to let public to receive the wrongly message to achieve themselves unreasonable benefits and rewards. In fact, economist is similar to lawyer or accountant profession, who need to provide a "service" discipline to give corrective and reasonable judgement and facts and who can not attempt to mislead to publish whose economic research reports to let public to get wrong information frequently. I believe that the scientific of economics of the 20th century fully accepts the ethical separation. Economic theory is seen as a positive science which has to analyze and to explain the mechanisms of economic processes. Ethical valuations should not form part of the economist's research program. Modern economics stresses rational calculation, the base material objections and scientific neutrality on moral issues. I think whose idea is concerned micro economy is based on assumptions of rationally selfish behavior. Whether what is concerned to current ethical crisis in economics? Economic matters have been debated throughout human history. I feel economic ethical matters which can be concerned in aspects, such as wealth accumulation, lending, business and commerce economic issues, journals or reports or books publishing. Due to any economic matters happen in economic processes which will be recorded in history, then economists will analyze why these issues are caused and find what reasons which cause the economic issue happening is discussed by theology, ethics and politics issues are as view points. So, the moral and ethics is needed to concern to any economists when who need to do any economic research nowadays.

Economy is concerned to human will face limited resources to use or spend, so economy theory indicates to be researched what methods how human chooses to allocate resources to achieve the efficient and effective result. Economy aims to achieve human rationality to control the desire to acquire material products in order to allow better satisfaction of the true human need. Many economists concern for others now directly affects one's own welfare and commitment drives between personal choice and personal welfare and thus undermines modern economics ethic.

Individuals frequently display commitment, acting against their own welfare in favor of the group. This element of ethical behavior has been ignored by economists and needs to be brought into the analysis. Although ethical motivation are relevant to economists, but the capabilities approach is more concerned with social achievement. To a large degree, this is a theory of distributive justice that economy and political science and philosophy theories which have more relationship among of these three subjects theories.

CHAPTER VII

Why ethic relates to labor behavior

Entrepreneur needs to considers ethic issue can influence labor behavior indirectly. I shall give some current economists' judgement to indicate how well human are doing according to the capability standard to prove why employers need to concern moral behavior. The capability approaching requires that many means be provided to every person. This is an alternative to social achievement from economics approach, which uses the quantity of commodities available for consumption. The conventional measure of the standard of living (GDP/head) has been subject to sustained criticism in recent times, one source of the complaints is the capability theorists.

This capabilities approach is a new inter-disciplinary social science and there are still many problems with this approach to concern ethical issues of mainstream economics. However, some economists feel that ethical motivations exist and play a role in human's actual behavior. Human well being refers to living a full human life. It measures to show the things that demonstrate a good life being lived. So, human functioning achievements, must be the focus. Possession of a certain quantity of commodities, however, may be necessary in order to achieve human functioning. This provides social success in delivering well being across our society. Moreover, some scientists who also believe the standard of social success may be limited to basic functioning. Alternatively, a rich of human group may be accepted, but social success may be considered for only a small proportion of the population. So, for each theorist, we need to ask these following questions. Does the theorist present an ethical view of motivation? Does the theorist adopt a deep mind of human well being? In the assessment of social success, does the theorist concern human functioning achievements and means to promote functioning achievements?

I shall analyze on individual psychology, household psychology and social achievement three aspects to indicate labor morality and raising productivity and even economic growth has close relationship as below:

In economic view, household means a family which has female control functioning. On the individual and public policy means that support individual achievements. However, in concept analysis, I shall indicate three levels of analysis to economic ethic of human behavior. The lowest level is individual, it is individual psychology, human functioning and ethical motivation. The middle level is household, it is household management, moral education, character formation. The highest level is the city, it is social achievement (Public policy supports equipment needs for individual capability achievement and formative law). So, human's behavioral is an assumption of modern economics. From history viewpoint, our economic conditions are largely agricultural with some mining, manufacturing and commerce, there was limited scope for domestic and international markets; mutual give and take, lending and borrowing between households was widespread. Commonly, these activities are general human economic behavior of reasons to cause these business activities in our society.

Firstly, on individual psychology aspect, human's economy of behavior is in our society, human needs do this economy behavior because human needs have good life and education, the good life required leisure and the good use of leisure time to do leisure activities with friends. Otherwise, leisure required freedom from the duties of earning a living. It was commonly accepted that the good life is required to work to earn, such as labors, traders, professions, farmers etc. service or labor occupations their individual behavior is aim to achieve earning for good life and education. So, who need to spend some time to do economic activities to aim to earn some time for leisure and education.

Secondly, on household management psychology aspect, in general, managing revenues and expenditures is a part of household management. However, household management requires moderation on the desires for food, wine, sex and sleep. So, in labor economy relationship, household seems to be the frame of mind and habits needed for engineering to make sense. In old age, expenditure on subsistence continues, but no one will pay for the labor of the old. Saving for old age, therefore is sensible. However, if one is habituated in youth to lazy, one will find it hand to change later. Nevertheless, these habits are unsustainable in old age, when one can't be labor and generate income. Hence, in labor economy view, moderation is an essential element of good household management. Although, wealth is also important, but more important is the knowledge or skill of household management. However, if one has no leisure and is unable to develop his capabilities (including bodily and non-bodily pleasures to easy to live with). Then, productivity will be reduce and inefficient work, due to the labor is hard to work, who feel himself/herself is such as a machine and who has no much time to rest often. Also the earning of friendship is also important, including certain market relationships in our modern societies. Clearly human's labor economy of behavior of household management in the broad sense is a comprehensive act and part of a way of human life. Hence, an ethical understanding is also needed, such as friendship relationship to complete household management in the middle level of household management between the city level and individual level. On functioning achievement and freedom to individual of labor economy behavior, it includes education, increased physical training etc. economic benefits to our individual in our society. Just as the city is a complex structure, so is human psychology to cause labor economy behavior. Justice in the city is defined as each class (and each individual within the class) doing its own job, justice in the individual is defined as each part of individual doing its own job. Hence, a good city has all of the individuals correctly assigned to the different classes and each individual and each class performs its appropriate job. Similarly, the good individual has each of labor's performing its job appropriately.

In the final social achievement aspect, it concerns micro. As the growth of the healthy city showed up to a certain point, economic development is required in terms of the city's physical size and population. So, modern economic principles are adopted (such as economic development and the division of labor). Nevertheless, our society must be justify to some degree to market relations. Various property rights and exchange justice must be enforced. These principles, however are limited by other ethical principles guiding the laws. Nevertheless, citizens are to be banned from engaging in most occupations. For example, the moral dangers of commercial activities are great. Moreover, market are limited to a specific location and regulated by market regulators. Although, duties are not imposed on foreign trade, prohibitions apply to various unnecessary imports and to exports of necessities. Hence, it will influence labor demand and job supply to influence the country's economic development in any time. To analyze labor economy, we need to know human nature and to establish the functions of human beings. These functions are shared with human beings, e.g. humans need to eat, drink. As a general rule, the passions that drive human to satisfy these needs, but it is of limited amount to supply.

So, these factors will influence labor's behavior between action, motivation and character. However, every organization is influenced to economic growth every year by its staff individual behavior, such as its staff individual has passions and emotions disposed toward bad action and decides to act well for other reasons, e.g. the staff feels fear of detection or punishment and then who will act well because of the staff's self control to avoid the firm will dismiss him/her in the firm. It seems the staff's passion, emotion will influence whose behavior to be good or bad to do whose work in whose firm. Hence, the firm needs have economic analysis to decide to dismiss the staff or not dismiss the staff if it discovered whose behavior is not acceptable to its firm and what it will be influenced from whose bad behavior in the short term and long term. If the staff is very important and if who left this firm, this firm will face business failure challenge because it has no any right applicant or another staff who can do this staff's job easily. Hence, in labor economy analysis, the firm needs to judge the benefits are much or the losses are much before which decide to dismiss the staff.

What are ethics? Ethics are a set of values or group of moral principles that are right and good a code or principles of behavior or conduct governing an individual or group. For example, when a engineer needs to do any researching jobs which concern to engineering, who needs to increase whose ability as engineer to responsibly confront moral issues raised by technological activity, not always in short term best interest, and long term into decision making ethics are imprecise, complex, and in a given situation may conflict. Who will have these questions to concern before who does his duties, such as does it pass the benefits /harm test? Whom does it harm? Whom does it benefit? Can these be justified, cost/ benefit analysis risk assessment? Does it treat everyone equally? equitable? If not, can the differences be justified? However, any employer needs to concern whose labor ethics issues, who have four aspects need to be considered, such as:

On the first concerning aspect, it is working condition ethics, whether the employer's act is moral right when it respects right relevant to a work environment or employment condition of situation. For example, whether the employer can provide whose employees have rights for life, liberty, pursuit of happiness, human rights and non-human rights, e.g. clean and safe working environment or fair salary and welfare, unreasonable normal working hours. On the second concerning aspect, it is duty ethics, whether the employer acts it is right when it conforms with ethics duties to whose employees, e.g. uphold promise, be fair treatment to job nature and duty, respect personal freedom, duty to protect the weak, duty to comply with employment laws, duty to do job to best of ability. On the third concerning aspect, it is utilitarianism ethic, whether the employer has right action consists in producing good consequences to whose employees, e.g. good intentions, outcomes, honesty, fairness, conscientiousness etc. On the final concerning aspect, it is the situational ethics, which means that depending on the specific circumstance, different rights, duties, values, etc. the right circumstance may be applied to whose labors, e.g. whether the workers work in the dirty and dark factory and who need to work abnormal working hours. It seems that if the working environment is not suitable to the employees to feel to work, it will influence the labors raise to work inefficient and poor performance.

So, employers need to concern their ethics to labor, it include moral development to labor, which are often classified such as, obedience or punishment, marketplace morality, conformity, law and order, social contract, universal human rights and integrity whole environment ethic moral development of issues. However, emotion is one important factor to influence labor's individual performance and productivity and efficiency to any employer. How emotional labor and ethic of care will influence productivity. Employers concern care which ought be more than labor itself. Labor's activity that is fundamentally about maintaining, continuing and repairing the working economic world, so that labor can live in it as well as possible. An ethic of labor care is more than a list of moral principles, the ethic of care labor elements, it includes attentiveness, responsibility, competence and responsiveness.

However, employers need to make distinctions between " caring for" and "caring about" to labor ethic. "Caring about" is directed toward less concrete objects/subjects. It is a general form of commitment to employees, when "caring for" focuses on a specific object/subject and responds to the particular, physical, spiritual, intellectual and emotional needs of labor. Caring labor is too inclusive of all kinds of economic activities. So employers ought not care relations too narrowly, but should include care is given by extended to employees' families, such as domestic workers and workers in hospitals and teachers etc. service labor occupations. So, labor care ethic relates to the work that employers do under the working conditions within which the employers' labor. Also, a labor care ethic is a deeply relational framework involving both labor care activities and practices as well as a habit of labor care mind. So, employers ought presume that dependent is valued, accepted and universal, it necessitates that care labor to every is shared equally and the society policy also needs to be promoted care labor values to let employers to concern this care labor issue. Care ethic means that empathy and responsiveness, among others, coming out of practices and experiences of " doing care". However, the important aspects of a care ethic that complicates our understanding of the reproduction of alienated labor under capitalism as well as in carrying out care labor, caring for the recipient is an expected part of that work.

In labour ethic view, employers ought attempt to answer this question. Does the expectation of such affective emotions necessitate a different formulation of compensation? In examining the relationship between an ethic of care and the alienation under capitalist relations of production. For example: What does make a "good work" ? Is a good worker someone who cares about whose work? How much should the worker care for the recipient of the labour? What does about the customer service representative who care about assisting someone? or does the retail salesperson care about helping someone look good? or does the carpenter care for the wood with which he is working? Whether the worker may or may not take time, be attentive, responsive and responsible. So, I suggest "caring about" and "caring for" the work and the recipient implies a relational experience with others. Many workers care about the outcome of their labour, whether a final product or service. They take pride in their work, they care about doing a good job, they take care of the people with whom who encounter in the process. In this way, workers make their work meaningful, who attempt to connect to it and to those who are "served" when carrying out the work.

Nowadays, human are encountering of an expended service economy, care and the emotional labour involved in such work. For example, luxury hotel workers are interactive service workers both consented to activity investing in the work, also luxury service is not only about what workers do; it is also about how they do it. Luxury service means that how workers make their jobs meaningful, become invested in them, and construct images of themselves as skilled and autonomous. For example, flight attendants who are the caring and emotional labour that is expected of these workers and it is the caring for the recipient, which allows workers to find meaning, creativity and feel connected to the work itself. I also think that labouring makes "real" something outside of the individual, the commodity as value is imposed external to the thing and to the labour itself. Under conditions of private property, the worker is disconnected from whose own creative powers and the objects of the labour become alien to the worker. So, I think employers ought not take away any labour whose individual's specific life, e.g. For long term abnormal working hours will reduce any labour's leisure and family private time.
However, I think labour can divide two kinds of physical labour and emotional labour. For example, the a factory worker works from whose own body and so who is a physical labour. Otherwise, a flight attendant works from whose own feelings and so who is a emotional labour. However, for the particular features of service -oriented labour, who needs to take "caring for" someone is central, necessarily alter these survival techniques. In care work, it is the consumers/recipients of care who expect that those who do caring work care about the work who do and care for the recipients of their care labour, e.g. hotel employees need to shoe genuine care and concern for guests' needs. So, care is the expected and central element of the labour and I think that health attendants and nurses home health carers etc. service workers who need provide more emotional service to whose clients, so who belong to emotional service labour seriously. For example, nursing profession, nurses are thought about as caring, moral creatures who show kindness and comfort to their patients. It is the doctors who are assumed to possess skills and knowledge. How care labour may be negatively affected, such as underpaid, overworked may happen in a situation where the care-giver is compensated unjustly and treated unfairly. Is it possible to argue that if care labour or any labour carried out in the context of a care ethic, the work that is done could be so much better for the whole of society and for the person doing the work and recipients of the work? In an ethic of care that predominates, would we simply value the labour of chid-care workers or home care attendants etc. workers? Would we reflect better compensation, better treatment and better working conditions because our relationship with ourselves and each other are acknowledged and values?

Hence, care activities are needed to focus on caring labour, e.g. nurses, personal attendants or home care workers and child care workers. That is, assuming the existence of a care ethic, such questions must be applied to any and all work activities that we do. Does every economic activity contain caring practices, even traditionally non care labour? I think caring about what we do and how we do it, we may help to improve our relations with others, thus reflecting an ethic of care. Does caring labour help to make invisible, reduce its harm to the self and society? It may be true that workers cared for their work, product or service, this would serve the needs of the employers quite well. How do we care for/about something but against the exploitation produced by capital labour relations? Is it good for society as a whole to care about what you do, care for the work you do, Does the product you make or the service you provide even if it enriches the owner and exploits the worker? What about the office cleaner who cleans the office effectively and efficiently in order to keep whose job that who desperately needs. Should the office cleaner care about doing a good job, care for the faceless people who doesn't know?

A care ethic both encourages this type of work ethic and at the same time, these relations are created and who serve are expected to care for and about the recipients of care, the customer is always right. However, structural inequalities between consumers and workers are normalized in the process. For the nurses and home care workers, the work becomes their own, who become attached to the work, connected to the process and the final outcome, and the work gives meaning to their live. At the same time, when workers don't care about whose work, when they don't care for their charges, or for the service who are offering. Should it, when may the labour be a child care provider neglecting the needs of the child? Or of the overworked social worker dismissing the needs of whose client in order to fill paperwork that who is directed to complete. Hence, I recommend employers need to concern about care is needed such as a practice, value, ethic activity to their labours. The elements of care, its affective emotional and relational qualities help to give meaning to the work for the worker. At the same time, it could be an ethic of care, where individuals view themselves as relational, identifying our connections to others and mutual responsibilities for each other become the necessary conditions for a working class politics.

Labour market equilibrium is an important issue to be concerned in law economy and ethic aspect. Workers prefer to work when the wage is high, and firms prefer to hire when the wage is low generally. Labour market equilibrium "balance out" the conflicting desires of workers and firms and determines the wage and employment observed in the labour market. If labour markets are competitive and if firms and workers are free to enter and leave; the equilibrium allocation of workers to firms is efficient; the sorting of workers and firms are accumulated by trading each other. In fact, labour markets are efficient plays a role by the public policy. Many government programs are often debated whether the particular policy leads to a more efficient allocation of resources or whether the efficiency costs are substantial.

Labour market equilibrium occurs when labour supply equals labour demand, generating the competitive wage(w) and employment (E). The wage (w) is the market clearing wage because any other wage level would create either upward or downward pressures on the wage. It would be too many jobs to supply, but the few available workers or too many workers competing for the few available job determined. Due to the competitive wage level is determined in this industry fashion, each firm in the industry hires workers up to the point where the value of marginal product of labour equals the competitive wage. Then, it seems the industry worker's wage level has arrived the maximum labour market wage level. So, employers ought not need to increase whose wage to attract more workers to choose to do whose industry often because it is not reasonable wage level increasing when the labour supply number is enough at the moment. Also the labour market of the industry has implied it's worker demand numbers has arrived the equal level of job supply numbers in the stage. What is caused to happen by worker surplus? When the difference between what the worker receives, that is the competitive wage(w) and the value of the worker's time outside the labour market gives the gains to workers. So, it will cause the excess workers have a value of marginal product that is less than their value of time. In effect, those workers are not being efficiently used by the labour market. So, firms ought to learn how to allocate the right number of persons to different positions that maximizes the total gains and firms ought need to learn how to form trade in the labour market in any efficient allocation way.

Search of labour economy, the central aim is to examine how a work perspective, countries can develop their skills base to increase both the quantity and the productivity of labour employed in the country. Inadequate education and skills of labour development can influence any countries' overall economic development in long term. So, governments need to achieve good policies to solve this issue. Due to skills and education development is central to improve productivity. Because productivity is an important source of improved living standards and growth. Other critical factors include macroeconomic policies maximize opportunities for poor employment growth, an enabling environment is for enterprise development and fundamental investments in education, health and physical to income level households. So, effective skills development systems which is needed to connect education to technical training, technical training to labour market entry and labour market entry to workplace to long life learning to concentrate on providing to low income level households.

Productivity growth can reduce production costs and increase returns on investments. Some of which provide greater income for business owners which some are given higher wages to labours. However, the productivity of individuals may be reflected in employment rates, wage rates, stability of employment, job satisfaction or employability across jobs or industries. The productivity of enterprises, in addition to output per worker may measure in terms of market share and export performance. The benefits to societies from higher individual and enterprise productivity may be evident in increased competitiveness and employment or in a shift of employment from low to higher productivity sector. So, employers can use this method to measure every employee's morality and job behaviour performance to judge whether their job ethic and job attitude whether which can adopt to continue to work in whose organizational environment. If the employer discovered the employee's morality and job behaviour performance and job attitude is not achieved to whose work performance standard, then who can decide to either reduce whose salary or dismiss him/her or not increasing whose salary for long term any decision. So, labour ethic issue is very important to influence economic growth to any countries.

Whether labour ethic has close relationship to economic growth. I feel this issues concerns any stage of the labour life cycle and organization life cycles, it includes the link between the design of economic theory and labour individual morality and job behaviour and performance. In fact, we need to suppose all research questions and labour economy is as mapping to particular stages of an individual's life cycle to labour economy ought be related to the accumulation of human (labour) capital, labour market entry and labour supply choices, behaviour within firms and household decision making. Prior years some researchers had been carrying on observing experiments to the women and men labour work and in whose nature environment for weeks, and then used various treatments, including manipulating the environment in such a way to increase and decrease rest periods. They got result long time working hours and not rest time, it will reduce labours(workers) of productivity. So, it implies the overall productivity and individual productivity will be reduced. Although, the employers have enough workers to work in the natural working environment at the same time, but due to who have no enough rest time to provide to them, then their workers' working performance and efficiency will be fallen. Nowadays, industrialized countries had began to consider how to plan similar welfare reforms, researching the economic reasons and consequences to labour economic issue, such as United States, the United King, Sweden and Germany, it seems economic growth and law ethic has close relationship. However, labour economy includes how to measure labour's emotion to raise productivity, as well as how technological change, education, employment and wages which can assist labour to raise productivity. Due to good labour emotion and labour ethic can raise productivity, then raising productivity can also raise economic growth finally. So, I believe which have close cause and effect relationship.

However, many economists have long been pessimistic that an experimental approach could offer such illustrations of labour ethic and economic growth of cause and effect relationship in their field. Who feel labour bad emotion or bad labour ethic has no any influence to economic growth. In fact, the economic world is extremely complicated, so human needs to have economic laws is set by controlled experiment to measure or judge whether labour ethic and economic growth which has or has no any close relationship. If economists have no such test, economic laws, who can't perform such as the controlled experiments of chemists or biologists very well because who can't easily control other important factors to observe why labour emotion or ethic has reason to influence overall economic growth to any country if they neglect to carry on researching experiment between the relationship of ethic and productivity and economic growth. So I recommend economists need have participants in the natural field experiment to carry on researching to any labour emotion or ethic issue to gather statistic information of population to get prediction more accurately if who want to measure whether labour emotion or ethic and productivity which has close relationship to any country's economic growth for long term.

CHAPTER VIII

Outsource strategy

Entrepreneurs need to concern whether outsourcing is suitable to whose entrepreneur culture. Generally, outsourcing can be defined as an organization is entering into a contract with another organization to operate and manage one or more of its business processes. Due to employers face increasing competitive pressure to remain focused, flexible, cost competitive and competent, so outsourcing can access to low cost specialized talent. However, outsourcing means the contracting out of a employer's non core, non efficient, non revenue producing activities to specialists.

It is a strategic management tool, such as restructure or contracting out to third party to carry out certain functions efficiently. The most common types of outsourcing are manufacturing outsourcing, information technology outsourcing and business process outsourcing (including processes related to accounting, human resources, benefits, payroll and finance etc. aspects). In fact, employers decide outsourcing reasons which include such as: market pressure to be price competitive, availability of cheap labour elsewhere, abundance of highly talented skilled labour in themselves country, pressure is from investing to cut cost, increase profit and show growth, focusing on core business operations and expanding global presence etc. factors. Many employers begin to concern the ethical and moral implication of outsourcing issue to cause the political and business discussion nowadays. Also, many economists have for-or-against social debates for outsourcing ethic issue. However, outsourcing can bring these benefits to some businesses. For example, if a car can be made more cheaper in China, it should be; if a telephone enquiry can be processed more cheaper in any Asia country, it should be. All such transactions raise real incomes on both sides as resources are advantageously redeployed, with added investment and growth in the exporting country, and lower prices in the importing country.

However, conservative economists argue that the sole mission of a corporation is to maximize profit for the benefits of shareholders. They also contend that in a global economy, outsourcing does not mean net job loss. They argue that more jobs will be created global since the cost labour lowered. The term "global" comes to mind when discussing today's large Corporations. It is hard to say which locally a company belongs to. In fact, outsourcing can also cause disadvantages. Sudden loss of jobs and loss of income can lead to economic depression in smaller regions. As the biggest employer in a those towns/cities closes down factories and start manufacturing in Asia or outsource the manufacturing altogether to a foreign this party. So, the country will raise unemployment rate suddenly when local jobs are outsourced to overseas.

Morality of local employees in favor of outsourcing hiring low wage employees elsewhere is another point of contention of this debate. The (capitalist) economy based on the law of supply and demand. In such economy, allocation or resources, including capital and labour is generally determined by market forces. Therefore, it is reasonable and expectable that companies would seek the best option available to employ their capital and recruit in a global economy. Due to it is assumed that local responsibility has less meaning when the economy and company operate globally. So, it causes any country employers don't concern labour ethic issue after outsourcing influences to its local labour.

Nowadays, many employers would agree that the acts of downsizing/outsourcing for pure financial reasons (i.e. choosing short-term investor gain over employee welfare) are very often morally wrong. However, without clear morally relevant distinction (either in academia or business press) between a company's priority to the shareholder and that to its workers, it is very hard defend that position. This is justified because shareholders have taken a risk in placing their money in the hands of the corporation, and are thereby due compensation. Shareholders can potentially lose something who have placed into the corporation. However, workers have placed something at risk when accepting a job, they lose future potential earnings due to corporate outsourcing. At the very least, the worker has foregone other possible job opportunities. Even more importantly, many workers have invested in their houses, their local communities and in their lifestyle with the expectation of a steady income. When the worker's investment in a corporation is not of the same sort as the shareholder's, it constitutes a risk nevertheless, and so the worker's position is not different to that of the shareholder.

However, I believe that evaluating the differences of that risk will depend upon of each individual's relationship with the company and their personal values. For example, CEO pay is a completely separate issue on its own. It is a very popular subject in current academic and business press. Even if it is different subject, it has moral implications in regards to outsourcing. In general, CEO can earn a more percent raise to compare to regular worker's percent raise. In common, companies show the reason of CEO percent raise more is that there is enough causation to conclude that outsourcing contributes to profitability / stock price increase of a company, this the rise in CEO compensation. The ethic issue here is that, if the market rewards a company for improving it is bottom line or for cutting costs why is it ethically wrong for a company to outsource at the expense of local labour force. After all, the reason for an existence of company is to provide value to its shareholders. However, I think CEOs aims to achieve themselves benefits, who may improve their bottom line when hurting workers and communities. The morality of further rewarding CEO's who knowingly undertook layoffs of his employees in favor of outsourcing their work to a third party or move those jobs to a low wage country is very troubling.

In fact, outsourcing raises many concerns for working professional for and communities. It has long held personal and community values, such as , loyalty and commitment to employees. However, as much as economic prosperity global trade can bring, if does bring devastation as well. Availability of cheap products is appreciable, but you need to have a job and a income to consume those products. For many, outsourcing hurts at the heart of their livelihoods. Also, I argue to against outsourcing is that growing concern of issues of privacy related to outsourcing information creates an ethical and legal issue. The concern is against outsourcing (in specific cases of Accounting, Human Resource and Medical outsourcing) because of the fear of sensitive information's safety and confidentiality. So, employers ought check references and transcripts and perform background checks to minimize the risk of hiring someone who lacks ethic or morality to do whose outsourcing job duties. Moreover, outsourcing firms may indicate that all of their employees are highly educated, trained professionals of the highest honesty. Finally, I recommend employers ought to consider these questions before who decide to outsource, such as: does stockholders welfare out weight that of a company's employees? Is profit maximization ethical? Is it ethical to reward the upper management for cutting cost by eliminating jobs? Should the compensation for upper management with held if the profit is achieved by outsourcing? Is it ethical to reward a management that repeatedly shown disregard to its employees? (increasing workload, constant layoff, choosing the cheapest labour over quality). Is it right for the public to expect a company to keep all its employment locally, (at a higher cost) but at the same time sell products at comparable rate with foreign companies who use cheap labour? Does a company ethically bound a provide maximum occupation in its home country? Does it have a duty to its local community? In case of outsourcing is the employer ethically bound to retrain the employees? So, all these questions are very important concerning outsourcing influence, if every employer can concern these questions, then who can decide whose outsourcing reason is right or wrong more clearly. To conclude, any employer ought need to decide whether outsourcing is the best of one method to raise productivity for long term strategic plan.

CHAPTER IX

Labor morality strategy

Entrepreneur needs to understand why labor morality concept can reduce poverty to influence positive productivity to raise performance. I shall use labour morality concept can assist society to reduce poverty to influence positive productivity to raise performance. In labour economy view, a livelihood comprises the capabilities of assets (including both material and social resources) and activities required for a means of living. A livelihood is sustainable when it can cope with and recover from shocks, maintain or enhance its capabilities and asset, when not undermining the natural resource base.

It has three elements: livelihood resources, livelihood strategies and institutional processes and organizational structures. So, I think that when productivity will raise, even poverty and crime will be also reduced, due to the low income level householder family which can be upgraded to increase whose income level and quality of living standard to the middle income level householder family. When governments can promote the labour morality to which employers to let them to know labour morality and productivity has close relationship.

How to understand the complex and differentiated process through which livelihoods are constructed, governments need to analyse which countries themselves local citizen to let their knowledge, perceptions and interests be heard. There are three insights into poverty as below:

The first is the realization that when economic growth may be essential for poverty reduction, there is not an automatic an automatic relationship between the two since if all depends on the capabilities of the poor to take advantage of expanding economic opportunities.

Secondly, there is the realization that poverty as conceived by the poor themselves. It is not just a question of low income, but also includes other factors, such as bad health, illiteracy, lack of social services etc.

Finally, it is now often know their situation and need best and must therefore be involved in the design of policies and project intended to better their lot. So, governments and employers need to identify those issues of subjects areas for effective poverty reduction, either at the local level or at the policy level. This is in principle on open-ended process, certain emphasis is given to the introduction of improved technologies as well as social and economic investments to every country's government.

The three fundamental attributes to any developing countries or developed countries themselves countries if which plan to raise economic growth and to reduce poverty to upgrade or low income level householders to rise to the middle income level householder family. The three attributes include the possession of human capabilities, such as education, skills, health, psychological orientation; access to tangible and intangible assets and the existence of economic activities.

However, a livelihood comprises the capabilities, assets, including both material and social resources and activities required for a means of living. A livelihood is sustainable when it can cope with and recover from stresses and shocks and maintain or enhance its capabilities and assets both now and in the future. To solve poverty problem, it includes not only physical and natural resources, but also every country's social and human capital issues. Every country's government also needs to facilitate an understanding of the causes of poverty by focusing on the variety of factors at different levels that directly or indirectly determine or constrain low income level householder's access to and assets of different kinds. Also every country's government needs to assess the direct and indirect effects on low income level householder's living conditions then, for example one dimensional productivity or income criteria.

Over the various components of a livelihood, the most complex is the portfolio of assets out of which people construct their living. This portfolio includes tangible assets, such as stores, e.g. food stocks, stores of value, such as gold, jewelry, cash saving and resources, e.g. land, water, trees, live stocks farm, equipment as well as intangible assets, such as claims, for example, demands and appeals which can be made be material, moral or other practical support and access, which is the opportunity to practice to use a resource, store or service or to obtain information, material, technology, employment, food or income.

Hence, if employers can provide enough capital input to make whose labours feel fairness, satisfactory and reasonable working environment and compensation. I believe that these satisfactory demand of labours who can raise productivity to their employers more easily. In labour economic view, any employers, governments or companies organizational resources inputs can divide four kinds of capital nature.

Firstly, the natural capital is natural resources stocks, e.g. soil, water, air, genetic resources etc. and environmental services, e.g. hydrological cycle, pollution sinks, etc. from which resources flows and services useful for livelihoods are derived . Secondly, economic or financial capital is the capital base, e.g. cash , credit/debt, savings and other economic assets, including basic infrastructure and production equipment and technologies which are essential for the pursuit of and livelihood strategy. Thirdly, human capital is the skill, knowledge, ability to labour and good health and physical capability important for the successful pursuit of different livelihood strategies and finally, social capital is the social resources, e.g. networks, social claims, social relations, which people draw when pursuit different livelihood strategies, requiring co-ordinated action. So, any country or employee which has a plan to know how to allocate which resources efficiently, it will raise productivity and economic growth and poverty reducing more easily. So, it seems labour morality can raise productivity which has close relationship to any employer, even labour morality and economic growth which has close relationship to any country. So, any country and any employer which ought not neglect labour morality for long term if who hope labor's producivity will raise and performance will raise efficiency.

CHAPTER X

The historical development of behavioral economics to entrepreneur's advantage

Entrepreneur needs to know whose employees' behavior and job attitude will be influenced by working environment. At the core of behavioral economics is used psychology of economics analysis to improve economics on its own terms generating theoretical insights, making better prediction of field phenomena, and suggesting better policy. It rejects economic theories based on utility maximization, equilibrium and efficiency. It is useful because it provides economists with a theoretical framework that can be applied to almost any form of economic (and even non-economic) behavior.

Simplifying much assumption that are not central to the economic theory. For example, there is nothing in core theory that specifies that people should not care about fairness, that they should weight risky outcomes in a linear fashion, or that they must discount the future at a constant rate. Other assumption simply acknowledge human limits on computational power and self-interest. These assumptions can be considered procedurally rational because human needs to solve problems that are often so complex that who can't be solved exactly by even modern computer technology.

Theories in behavioral economics should be judged by reality, generality and tractability concepts. We share the positivist view that the ultimate test of a theory is the accuracy of its predictions. But we also believe that better predictions are likely to result from theories with more realistic assumptions. In psychology, such as connectionist models that capture some of the essential features of neural functioning, which are based on utility maximization, yet are reaching the point where they are able to predict many judgement and behavioral phenomena. Contrary to the positivistic view, however, we believe that predictions of feelings (e.g., of subjective well-being) should be an important goal.

Most of the ideas in working behavioral economics environment are not new. When economics first became identified as a distinct field of study, psychology didn't exist as a discipline. For example, "invisible hand" and "the wealth of Nations" which belong to theory to moral sentiments, which laid out psychological principles of individual behavior that are arguably as profound as whose economic observations. Another example, such as a simple model of social utility means that one worker person's utility was affected by another person's payoff. However, the rejection of academic psychology by economists, which constructed an account of economic behavior built up from assumptions about the nature-that is, the psychology of homo-economics.

Nowadays, economists hoped their discipline could be like a natural science. But employee psychology was not very scientific. The economists thought it provided too unsteady a foundation for economics, who make assumption to utility led to a movement to the psychology from economics. In the early part of the 20th century, economists still included rich speculations about how employee behavior feel and think about economic choices generally. However, later economists are very much appealed to psychological insights, but by the middle of the century discussions of psychology had largely disappeared. Throughout the second half of the century, many criticisms of the positivistic perspective took place in both economics and psychology. The economists of the time had less disagreement with psychology with psychology than they realized. They assume without foundation that employee behavior always aims at the goal of maximum pleasure and minimum pain; but employee behavior is not goal-oriented. Also the economists of the time believed false conclusions are drawn from false psychological assumptions. The importance of psychological measures and bounds on rationality. These commentators attracted attention, but did not alter the fundamental direction of economics. One development was the rapid acceptance by economists of the expected utility and discounted utility models which are making decision under uncertainty and choice for organizations respectively. Whereas the assumptions and implications of utility analysis are rather flexible, and the expected utility and discounted utility models have numerous precise and testable implications. As a result, they provided some of the first "hand targets" for critics of the standard theory.

As economists began to accept counterexamples that could be not be permanently ignored, developments in psychology identified promising directions for new theory. Beginning around 1960 year, psychology became dominated by the brain as an information-processing device replacing the behaviorist conception of the brain as a stimulus-response machine. The information-processing permitted a fresh study of neglected topics like memory, problem solving and decision making. These new topics were more obviously relevant to the conception of utility maximization than behaviorism had appeared to be. However, employee psychologists began to use economic models as a benchmark against which their psychological models. Early research in employee behavioral have followed. First, identify assumption or models that are used by economists, who expected utility and discounted utility. Second, the assumption or model is a rule out alternative explanations (such as subjects' confusion or transactions costs). And third, the assumption or model creates alternative theories that generalize existing models. The fourth step is to construct economic models of behavior using the behavioral assumptions to test them from the third step. This final step of economic models of employee behavior has only been taken more recently to apply. Thus, it seems employee behaviors or performance will be influenced by organization environment.

CHAPTER XI

Experimental control method measures consumption behavior

Entrepreneur needs to understand consumer individual consumption behavior will be influenced by organizational behvioral change environment. The methods in behavioral economics are the same as those in other areas of economies. In fact, behavioral economics relied heavily on evidence generated by experiments. More recently, however, behavioral economists have moved beyond experimentation and the full range of methods are employed by economists. The experiments played a large role in the initial phase of behavioral economics because experimental control is exceptionally helpful for distinguishing behavioral explanations from standard ones. I shall indicate the reasons why consumer consumption behavior will be influenced by organizational behavioral change environment as below:

Suppose we observed this phenomenon in these any one of cares, in the form of failures of legal cases to settle before trial, costly divorce proceedings, and labor strikes. They are phenomenon of human' behaviors are caused by costs and benefits measurement of result. Also, behavioral economy would be difficult to tell whether rejection of offers was the result of reputation-building in repeated games, agency problems (between clients and lawyers), confusion, or an expression of distaste for being treated unfairly. However, in these game experiments of failures of legal cases to settle before trial, costly divorce proceedings, and labor strikes.

The first three of these explanations are ruled out because the experiments are played once, have no agents, and are simple enough to rule out confusion. Thus, the experimental data clearly establish that subjects are expressing concern for fairness. Other experiments have been useful for testing whether judgment errors which individuals commonly make in psychology experiments also affect prices and quantities in markets. The lab is especially useful for these studies because individual and market-level data can be observed.

Although behavioral economists relied on experimental data, however, behavioral economics subject is seen as a very different method from experimental economics. As noted, behavioral economists are methodological profession. They define themselves, not on the basis of the research methods that who employ, but rather their application of psychological insights to economics. Experimental economists, on the other hand, define themselves on the basis of use of experimentation which is as a research tool. Also, economists have made a major investment in developing experimental methods that are suitable for addressing economic issues, and have achieving among themselves on a number of important issues. For example, experimental economists often make instructions and software available for precise replication, and raw data are typically shared for reanalysis.

Experimental economists also insist on paying performance-based. However, experimental economists have also developed rules that many behavioral economists are likely to find excessively . For example, experimental economists rarely collect data like demographics, self-reports, response times and other cognitive measure which behavioral economists have found useful. Descriptions of the experimental environment are usually abstract rather than which are carried on experiment in the outside world because economic theory rarely makes a prediction about how a happen would matter, and experimenters are concerned about losing control over incentives if choosing strategies with certain labels is appealing.

Finally, economic experiments also typically use "stationary replication", in which the same task is repeated over and over in each period. Data from the last few periods of the experiment are typically used to draw conclusions about equilibrium behavior outside the lab. When economists believe that examining consumption behavior after it is of great interest, it is also obvious that many important aspects of economic life are like the first few periods of an experiment rather than the last. Supposing if we need to make decision of marriage, educational decisions, and saving for retirement, or the purchase of large durables like houses, sailboats, can cars, which happen just a few times in a person's life, a focus on behavior is clearly not warranted. All said, the focus on psychological realism and economic applicability of research promoted by the behavioral-economics perspective suggests the usefulness research outside the lab and of a broader range of approaches to laboratory research. So, economists realize that who have ideal opportunity to learn by trial-and-error, in a stationary environment, and uses the opportunity to learn how to carry on experimenting any psychology and behavioral researches. Thus, consumption behavior will be influenced by external variable economy environment influences.

CHAPTER XII

Judgement and choice influences behavioral consumption

Entrepreneur needs to understand consumer individual judgement and choice will influence behavioral consumption. The field of behavioral decision research, on which behavioral economics has drawn more than any other subfield of psychology, typically classifies research into two categories: judgement and choice. Judgement research deals with the processes people use to estimate probabilities. Choice deals with the processes people use to select among actions, considering of any relevant judgements who may have made. Everyday, we need to make probable judgements. Due to judging the likelihood of events is central to economic life. For example: Will you lose your job in a poor economic environment? Will you be able to find another house you like as much as the one you must bid for right away? Will the government raise interest rates? Will a merger strategy increase profits?

These questions are answered by some process of judging likelihood. The standard principles used in economic to model probability judgement in economic are concepts of statistical sampling, which are concerned probabilities in the face of new evidence. However, it requires a separation between previously judged probabilities and evaluations of new evidence. However, people often overestimate the probability who previously attached to events which later happened. This leads to "second guessing". For example, Monday morning quarterbacking and may be partly responsible for lawsuits against stockbrokers who lost money for their clients. (The clients think the brokers should have known). For example, anybody has tried to learn from a computer manual has seen the curse of knowledge in action. Another example for making probability judgements is called "representativeness": People judge conditional probabilities like P(hypothesis /data) or P(example/class) by how well the data represents the hypothesis or the example represents the class. Representativeness is an economical shortcut that delivers reasonable judgements with minimal effort in many cases. For example, in judging whether a certain student described in a profile is, say, a psychology major or computer science major, the student decides how well the profile matches the psychology or computer science .

For example, judgements of the fairness or non misleading or reasonable of clients‘ financial report to accounting auditors, consumers buying products and classroom negotiation. It is important to judge whether it is both a good attitude and bad attitude. A good attitude provides fast, close to optimal, answers when time or capabilities are limited, but it also needs logical principles and leads to situations. So, optimal is largely a critique (a reasonable one) of the later applied research. Assume that people specify a set of hypotheses, or encode new evidence incorrectly. For example, assuming that people believe hypothesis A is more likely than B will never encode pro-A evidence mistakenly, but will sometimes encode pro-B evidence as being supportive. For another example, investors will think there is wide variation in skill of, say, mutual-fund managers, even if there is no variation at all. (A manager who does well several years is a surprise if performance is mistakenly thought due to non replacement, so concluding that the manager must be really good.)

A question concerns stock market, such as: Overreacts in the long term. In their model, earnings follow a random walk but investors believe, mistakenly, that earnings have positive attitude. After one or two periods of good earnings, the stock market can not be confident that exists and hence expects, but since earnings are really a random walk, the stock market is too pessimistic and is underreacting to good earnings news. After a good earnings, however, the stock market believes many investors are increasing. Since, it is not the stock market is too optimistic and overreact. For another example, valuable consumer products (A $100 wireless keyboard, a fancy computer mouse, bottles of wine, and a box of chocolate) are sold to postgraduate (MBA) business students. The students were presented with a product and asked whether who would buy it for a price equal to the last two digits of their own social security number (a roughly random identification number required to obtain work in the United States) converted into a dollar figure, e.g. , if the last digits were 99, then the postgraduate business students will accept the hypothetical price was $99 to buy any of it for a price to the last two digits of their own social security number . After giving a yes/no response to the question. Would you pay $99? subjects were asked to state the most who would pay (using a procedure that gives people an incentive to say what who really would pay). Although subjects were reminded that the social security number is essentially random, those with high numbers were willing to pay more for the products. However, many studies have also shown that the method used to elicit preferences can have dramatic consequences. Nevertheless, when required to make an economic decisions-to-choose a brand of toothpaste, a car, a job, or how to invest, people do make some kind of decision. Behavioral economists refer to the process by which people make choices with ill defined preferences as "constructing preferences".

However, in classical consumer theory, preferences among different commodities are assumed to be invariant with respect to an individual's current consumption. Specifically, people seem to dislike losing commodities from their consumption much more than they like gaining other commodities. For example, the research of "contingent valuation" studies that attempt to establish the dollar value of products which are not routinely trades. Contingent valuation is often used to do government cost-benefit analysis or establish legal penalties from environment damage. These surveys typically show very large differences between buying prices (e.g. paying to clean up oil of beaches) and selling prices (e.g. having to be paid to allow beaches to be ruined). Thus, consumer judgement and choice will be influenced by external seller business behaviors and variable economy environment factors.

Nowadays, a quarter of the wealth in the USA has more interesting opportunities to do behavioral economies in consumption research. They find that motivated sellers should regard the price who paid as a sunk cost and choose at a nominal loss from the purchase price. Sellers' listing prices and subsequent selling behavior reflects to nominal losses. There are some cases in which no effect would be expected, such as when products are purchased for resale rather than for utilization. For example, do art or antique dealers like with pieces who buy to resell? What about surrogate mothers who agree to bear a child for a price paid in advance? However, evidence on the degree of commercial attachment is mixed. Reference points can also serve as social focal points for judging performance. For an interesting example from corporate finance. In general, when managers whose firms face possible losses (or declines from a previous year's earnings) are very reluctant to report small losses. As a result, the distribution of actual losses and gains show a very large at zero, and hardly any small reported losses (compared to the number of small gains). A manager who does not have the skill to shift accounting profits to erase a potential loss (i.e. has some earnings in his pocket.) is considered a poor manager. It seems that the bad performance manager whose behavior is bad to mislead public to believe his firm have better performance in this year.

Hence, in the mental accounting view, people set up mental accounts for outcomes which are psychologically separate, much as financial accountants lump expenses and revenues into separated accounts to guide managerial attention. Otherwise, mental accounting stands in opposition to the standard view in economics that it predicts, accurately , that people will spend money coming from different sources in different ways. So, a generalization of the notion of mental accounting is the concept of "choice bracket" , which refers to the fashion in which people make decisions narrowly, in either a piece meal fashion, or board, i.e. taking account of interdependencies between decisions. For example, when making many separate choices between products, consumers tend to choose more diversity when the choices are bracketed broadly than when they are bracketed narrowly

CHAPTER XIII

Expected utility theory estimates behavioral consumption

Entrepreneur can apply expected utility theory to estimate consumer consumption behavior. The expected utility (EU) hypothesis explains that the utility of a risky distribution of outcomes (says, monetary payoffs) is a probability weighted average of the outcome utilities. It follows logically from apparently reasons. Most notably the independence (or " cancellation") choice. The independent choice says that if you are comparing two gambles, you should cancel events which lead to the same consequence with the same probability, your choice should be independent of those utility also simplifies matters because a person's taste for risky money distributions can be fully captured by the share of the utility function for money.

However, many studies document predictive failures of expected utility in simple situations in which subjects can earn substantial sums of money from their choices. Some of these new theories alter the way in which probabilities are weighted, but preserve a "between ness" property which says that if A is preferred to B, then any probabilistic gamble between them must be preferred to B, but dis preferred to A (i.e. the gambles like "between" A and B in preference). Other new theories suggest that probability weights are "rank-dependent", outcomes are first ranked, then their probabilities are weighted in a way which is sensitive to how who rank within the gamble that is being considered. For example, if a person is attitude towards gambles really came from the utility of wealth function, even large gains in wealth would not tempt who to risk $50 or $100 losses, if who really dislikes losing $10 more than who likes gaining $11 at every level of wealth. For example, linear probability weighting in expected utility (EU) works reasonably well except when outcome probabilities are very low or high. But low-probability events are important in the economy in the form of "gambles" with positive (lottery tickets and also risky business ventures in biotechnology and pharmaceuticals) and high risk compensation events which required large insurance industries. Another theory example, such as prospect theory is experimental choices more accurately than (EU) because it gets the psychological of judgement and choice right. It consists of two main components, a probability weighting function, and a "value function" which replaces the utility function of (EU). The weighting function P(P) combines two elements: (1) The level of probability weight is a way of expressing risk tastes (if you hate to gamble, you will place low weight on any chance of winning anything) and (2) P(P) captures how sensitive people are to differences in probabilities. If (a group consumers) people are move sensitive in the neigh hoods of possibility and certainty. i.e. changes in probability near zero and 1, then their P(P) curve will overweight low probabilities and underweight high ones. For another theory example, such as technical motivation for "rank dependent" theories, ranking outcomes, than weighting their probabilities is that when separate probabilities are weighted, it is easy to construct examples in which people will be dominance by choosing a "dominated" gamble A which has a lower chance of winning at each possible outcome amount, compared to the higher chance of winning the same outcome amount for a dominant gamble B.

If (consumers) people rarely choose such dominated gambles or the unique brands of products, who are acting as if who are weighting the differences in probabilities which is the essence of the rank dependent approaches. So, new information can help any decision maker to feel better to make better decisions. These theories effect may explain demand for information in settings like medicine or personal finance, where new information usually does not change choice, but relieves anxiety people have from knowing there is something who could know but don't. However, the planning problem for economic agents who would like to behave in fashion and discussed the important time discounting for choice. Most big decisions, e.g. savings, educational investments, labor supply, health and diet, crime and drug etc. decisions use have costs and benefits which occur at different point in time. Thus, time discounting is basically standard time discounting plus an immediacy effect, a decision discounts delays in equally at all moments except the current one, caring differently about well being. This functional form provides one sample and powerful model of the taste to individual to make right or reasonable behavior economic decision. However, most analyses of choice assume that people integrate new consumption with planned consumption. It is infeasible and perhaps for this reason, descriptively inaccurate. When people make decisions about new sequences of payments or consumption, they tend to evaluate them in isolation, e.g. treating negative outcomes as losses, rather than as reductions to their existing money flows or consumption plans.

How to decide fairness and social preferences. The assumption that people maximize their own wealth and other personal material goals just self-interest is a correct simplification that is often useful in economics. However, people may sometimes choose to spend their wealth to punish others who have harmed them, reward whose, so who have helped, or to make outcomes more fair. Just as understanding demand for products requires specific utility function, the key to understanding this sort of social preferences is a specification of social utility which can explain many types of date with a single function.

Behavioral economy can also use to assist firms to choose right behavior to decide to do any matters. I show hypothesis to establish any reference level of consumer surplus and product profit. Both sides are entitled to any firm's levels of profit, so price changes which threaten any matter are considered unfair. So raising any product price, it will reduce consumer surplus and is considered unfair. But the cost of a firm's inputs rises, subjects said it was fair to raise prices. Because not raising prices would reduce the firm's profit (compared to the reference profit). Everyday observation that firms don't change prices and wages as frequently commonly. For example, when the fourth Hary potter story book was released in summer 2000 year, most stores were allocated a small number of books that were pre-sold in advance. Why not raise prices or auction the books off? It is possible that it concerned about customer goodwill and excess demand to cause book stores limit such book price increases. Offended consumers are often able to affect firm behavior by media attention or provoking legislation. For example, scalping tickets for popular sports and entertainment events (resulting them at a large premium over the printed ticket price) is constrained by law in most countries. For example, some countries have "anti-laws" penalizing sellers who take advantage of shortages of water, fuel and other necessities by raising prices after natural disasters. So, the countries' governments can protect which citizen benefits to balance the natural resource supply and demand to sell in the reasonable price fairly after the natural disaster occurrence.

A few years ago, responding to public anger at rising CEO salaries when the economy was being restructured through downsizing and many workers lost their jobs. Otherwise, some countries passed a law prohibiting firms from deducting CEO salaries for tax purposes beyond $1 million a year. because the countries need to earn much tax income from these high salary CEO income every year. So, explaining why these laws and regulations come from is one example of now economics might be used to expand the scope of law and behavioral economic relationship.

CHAPTER XIV

How behavioral game theory influences shareholder's individual investment behavior

Entrepreneur needs to understand who can apply behavioral game theory to influence shareholder's individual investment behaviors. Game theory has rapidly become an important foundation for many areas of economic theory, such as bargaining in decentralized markets, contracting and organizational structure. The descriptive accuracy of game theory in these application can be questioned because equilibrium predictions often assume strategic reasoning and direct field tests are difficult. In fact, behavioral game theory uses any experimental evidence and psychological research to generalize the standard assumptions of game theory.

One component of behavioral game theory is a theory of social preferences for allocations of money to oneself and others. Another component is a theory of how people choose in one shot games or in the first period of a repeated game. For example, in share buying and selling market, shareholders shall buy or sell shares from their judgement in the economic cycle market everyday. So share investment is seemed as allocation of game to these shareholders. Also, shareholders whose mind can influence whose psychological behavior to decide how to invest whose shares in their share investment economic activities. The component of behavioral game theory can include a model of learning to either individual or a population. Also, game theory is one area of economy in which serious attention has been paid to the process by which can equilibrium comes about.

Many learning theories have been proposed and carefully tested with experimental data. Theories about population never predict as well as theories of individual learning through who are useful for other purposes. So, behavioral game theory can be applied to these complex environments. e.g. consumer supermarket purchase, share market etc. How to apply behavioral game theory to macroeconomics and saving aspect? Many concepts in macroeconomic probably have a behavioral style that could be influenced by research in psychology. For example, it is common to assume that prices and wages are in nominal terms, which has important implications for macroeconomic behavior. Behavioral economics suggests some ideas for among consumers and workers, perhaps it is influenced by workers' concern for fairness. An important model in macroeconomics is the life cycle model of savings or permanent income hypothesis. This theory assumes that people make a guess about their lifetime earnings profile, and plan their lifetime earnings profile, and plan their savings and consumption in each period has diminishing marginal utility; and preferences for consumptions streams are time-separable (i.e. overall utility is the sum of the discounted utility of consumption in each separate period). The theory also assumes people lump together different types income when they guess how much money who will have (i.e. different sources of wealth are different). So, why many young people won't spend too much money for unnecessary expenditure, e.g. entertainment easily. Because who plan to save for their old age to use in their long time life time.

In consumer personal consumption and shopping choice decision view point, a behavioral life cycle theory of savings in which different sources of income are kept track of in different mental accounts. Mental accounts can reflect natural perceptual or divisions. For example, it is possible to add up the travelers' pay check and dollar value of whose frequent flyer miles, but it is simply unnatural to do so. It is important to note that many key implications of the life-cycle hypothesis have never been well supported (e.g. consumption is far more closely related to current income than it should be according to theory. However, predictions can be improved by introducing utility functions with habit formation in which utility in a current depends on the reference point of previous consumption, and by more carefully accounting for uncertain about future income.

So, mental accounting is only one of several behavioral approaches that may prove useful. Economics is money illusion, it is the tendency to make decisions based on nominal quantities rather than converting those figures into real terms by adjusting for inflation. Money illusion seems to be pervasive in some domains. So, it appears that employees don't seem to mind if their real wage falls as long as their nominal wages doesn't fall. Labor macroeconomics is involuntary unemployment. Why can some people not find work beyond of switching jobs, or a natural rate of unemployment? A popular account of unemployment push that wages are deliberately paid above the market clearly level, which creates an excess supply of workers and hence unemployment. But why are wages too high ? As efficiency wage theory shows that paying workers more than who deserve is necessary to ensure that who have something to lose if they are unemployed, which motivates them to work hand and economizes on monitoring.

Another viewpoint indicates that employer and worker is such as into a gift exchange relationship. Employers pay more than who have to as a gift and workers repay the gift by working harder than necessary. They show how gift exchange can be an equilibrium and show some of its macroeconomic implications. In labor economics, gift exchange is clearly evident of experimental labor markets. In practical working environment, firms offer wages; workers who take the jobs than choose a level of effort, which is costly to the workers and valuable to the firms. For example, firms and workers can enforce wages, but not effort levels. Since workers and firms are matched for just one period, and do not learn each other's identities, there is no way for either side to build reputations or for firms to punish workers who chose low effort. However, self-interested workers should shirk, and firms should anticipate that and pay a low wage. In fact, firms deliberately pay high wages as gifts and workers choose higher effort levels when they take higher wage jobs. It seems that it has strong relationship between wages and effort is stable over time. For example, standard life-cycle theory assumes that if people can borrow they should prefer wage profiles which maximize the present value of lifetime wages. Holding total wage payments constant, and assuming a positive real rate of interest, present value maximization implies that workers should prefer declining wage profiles over increasing ones. However, in fact, most wages profiles are clearly rising over time which is such as a phenomenon. Rather, workers derive utility from positive changes in consumption, but have self-control problems. That would prevent them from positive changes in consumption, but have self-control problems that would prevent them from saving for later consumption of wages were more front-loaded in the life cycle. In addition, workers seem to derive positive utility from increasing wage profiles, it is perhaps because rising wages are a source of self-esteem and the desire for increasing payments is much weaker for non wage income.

The standard life-cycle of labor supply also implies that workers should substitute labor and leisure based on the wage rate who face and the value who place on leisure at different points in time. If wage fluctuations are temporary workers should work long hours when wages are high and short hours when wages are low. However, because changes in wages are often persisting and because work hours are generally fixed in the short-run. So, it is difficult to tell whether workers are substituting. For example, taxi drivers who target daily will drive longer hours on low income days and guilty early on high income days. This behavior is exactly the opposite of substitution. Also inexperienced taxi drivers support the daily targeting prediction. But experienced taxi drivers don't have negative elastic, either because target minded drivers earn less and self select or taxi drivers learn over time to substitute rather than target. Perhaps the simplest prediction of labor economics is that the supply of labor should be upward sloping in response to a increase in wage.

In finance, standard equilibrium models of asset pricing assume that investors only care about asset risks if who affect marginal publicly available information to forecast stock returns as accurately as possible the efficient markets hypothesis. When those hypotheses do make some accurate predictions and some investors in assets have limited rationality of behavioral finance. Also, in share stock market, it is common, shareholders should not want to trade with them, but the volume of stock market transaction is large. So, it presents data on individual trading behavior which suggests that the extremely high volume may be driven, in part, by overconfidence on the part of investors. For example, property agent's individual behavior is similar to share agent's individual behavior. In the economy view, property agent bases a list price for a house on the selling prices of nearly houses that is similar ("comparable"). Every nearest neigh our techniques bases on similarity is also used in credit scoring and other kinds of evaluations. Also, one firm whose every share sale on the selling price is comparable to its similar firms whose every share price in its same business industry. The shareholder will evaluate whose every share issued sale price in the stock (share) market. Otherwise, in behavioral economy view, for example, property or share buyer who has risky choice to decide to buy in the property or share market. It is a process of comparing the similarity of the probabilities and outcomes in two gambles and choosing on dimensions which are dissimilar.

As we mentioned above, behavioral economics simply includes an interest in psychology. In fact, we believe that many familiar economic distinctions do have a lot of behavioral content, they are implicitly behavioral, and could surely benefit from more explicit ties to psychological ideas and data. However, some people do not feel psychology and economy which have close relationship. Such as, substantial debate is ongoing in psychology about whether knowing the precise details of how the brain carries out computations is necessary to understand functions and mechanisms of driving car skill at higher levels, (knowing the mechanical details of how a car works may not be necessary to turn the key and drive it). Most psychology experiments use indirect measures like response times, error self reports and natural experiments, due to brain has been fairly successful in codifying what we know about thinking, but pessimists think brain scan studies won't add much. The optimists think the new tools will lead to some discoveries. Another couple is the distinction between short run and long run price elasticity which concerns behavioral economy. In fact, economy needs have theories concepts to support any evidence to prove any matter has happened. Concerning short run and long run price elasticity cause and effort issue, with a casual suggestion that the run is the time it takes for markets to adjust, or for consumers to learn new prices, after a demand or supply stock. Adjustment costs undoubtedly have technical and social component, but probably also have some behavioral factors influence in the form of gradual adaption to loss and learning.

Another macroeconomic model which can be interpreted as implicitly behavioral is that business cycles can emerge if it is not general price inflation, so why the consumers shall not decide to buy this kind of product in the competitive market. For example, risky choice is as a process of comparing the similarity of the probabilities and outcomes in two gambles, and choosing on dimensions which are dissimilar. Behavioral economic simply includes an interest in psychology. In fact, we believe that many familiar economic distinctions do have a lot of behavioral content, they are implicitly behavioral and could surely benefit from more explicit ties to psychological ideas and data. However, some people do not feel psychology and economy which have close relationship. Such as psychology is about whether knowing the precise details of how the brain carries out computations is necessary to understand functions and mechanisms at higher levels. (knowing the mechanical details of how a car works may not necessary to turn the key and drive it.) Most psychology experiments use indirect measures like response times, error rates, self reports and natural experiments due to brain has been fairly successful in codifying what we know about thinking. However, pessimists think brain scan studies won't add much. The optimists think the new tools will lead to some discoveries and the potential is great that they cannot be ignored. However, economy needs have theories or concepts to support evidence to prove why any matters had happened. An example, is the distinction between short term and long term price elasticity. This distinction, mentions between of them, with a casual suggestion that long run is the time it takes for markets to adjust, or for consumers to learn new prices, after a demand or supply shock. Adjustment costs undoubtedly have technical and social components, but probably also have some behavioral factors influence in the form of gradual adaption to loss and learning.

However, organizational behavioral theory concerns that organizational contracting are shot through with implicitly behavioral economics. Some economists motivate the incompleteness of contracts as a consequence of rationality in foreseeing the future, but do not tie the research directly to work on memory and imagination. For example, agency theory begins with the presumption that there is some activity the agent doesn't like to do. Why markets are better at making dramatic changes than managers influence cost. So, influence costs are the costs managers preform for projects who like or personally benefit from like promotion or raises. A lot of influence costs are undoubtedly inflated by optimistic, each division manager really does think their division desperately needs funds and social comparison of pay and benefits. Otherwise, why are salaries kept so secret? In all these cases, conventional economic behavior has deeper psychological questions of where adjustment costs, effort and influence costs come from. So, it beings these questions: Could these phenomena surely produce surprising testable prediction?

Is psychology regularity an assumption or a conclusion?

Behavioral economics generally begins with assumption rooted in consumer psychological regularity and asks what follows from those assumptions. An alternative approach is to work backward, regarding a psychological regularity as a conclusion that must be proved an explanation that must be derived from deeper assumption before we fully understand and accept it. The alternative approach is caused by a fashionable new direction in economic theory and consumer psychology too, which is to explain human behavior as the product of evolution. However, we may not believe that behavior of intelligent, modern people lived in socialization and cultural influence can only be understood by guessing what their lives were like and how their brains might have adapted generally.

There are other models that treat psychological regularity as a conclusion to be proved rather than an assumption to be used. Such models usually begin with an observed regularity. Economists have for deriving behavior from first principles and rationalizing apparent irrationality. Theories of this sort are useful behavioral economics and what fresh predictions do they make. However, critics have pointed out that behavioral economics is not a unified theory, but is instead a collection of tools and ideas. This is true. However, some economists believe that economic models do not derive much predictive power from the single tool of utility maximization. The goal of behavioral economic is to develop better tools that, in some cases, can do both jobs at once. Economists like to point out the natural division of labor between scientific disciplines: Psychologists should concern to individual minds, and economists to behavior in games, markets, and economies. But the division of labor is only efficient if there is effective coordination, and all too often economists fail to conduct intellectual trade with those who have a comparative advantage in understanding individual human behavior. The only question is whether the implicit psychology in economics is good psychology or bad psychology. We think it is simply unwise, and inefficient to do economics without paying some attention to good psychology.

CHAPTER XV

How to apply behavioral economic principles to make any business strategy

Entrepreneur needs to understand behavioral economy principles can be applied to himself/herself to judge to do the right decision more accurate. Behavioral economics theories can also apply to assist any policy makers to make right and reasonable decision in right time. I shall indicate new principles to recommend and I also shall give any psychological cases to explain how policy makers can apply behavioural economic theories to judge how to make their any decision is the most right and the most reasonable.

Behavioural economy is an independent and demonstrates real economic well-being. It aims to improve quality of life by promoting innovative solutions that challenge mainstream thinking on economic, environment and social issues. Also, behavioural economy is different branches of more alternative economies into a form that is useful primarily for policy-makers. I think behavioural economy can be given an aid to policy makers how who use economic tools to the broader policy making community by providing a theoretical behaviour for many policy approaches to be used. The standard economic analysis assumes that humans are rational and behave in a way to maximize their individual self-interest. This rational man assumption indicates a powerful tool for analysis. However, it has many shortfalls that can lead to unrealistic economic analysis and policy-making. Also, I think behavioural economics and psychology has these principles to influence human behaviour. These principles include, such as below:

In common, people do many things by observing others and copying; people are encouraged to continue to do things when they feel other people approve of their behaviour. People do many things without consciously thinking about time. These habits are hard to change. There are cases where money is de-motivating as it undermines people's intrinsic motivation. People want their actions and commitments to be values usually. People put undue weight on recent events and who can't calculate probabilities well and worry too much about unlikely events and who are strongly influences by how the problem/information is presented to them. People need to feel effective to make a change, even just giving who the incentives and information is not necessarily enough in any environment usually. So policy makers ought concern about these human behaviour principles to judge whose behaviours are right or wrong, then who can decide to do any economic activities more reasonable, e.g. decisions of consumption, policies making, investment etc.

In fact, much of our behaviour is strongly influenced by other people's behaviour. Social learning is a process by which we take in the behaviour of others to learn how to behave. In more complex situations with which we are unfamiliar, we consciously watch and learn from the behaviour of others. For example, when use a new library for the first time. When we make a conscious decision on how to behave, our sense of social identity is important, we think: how would other from my group behave in this situation? In situations where there is high social capital. i.e. where there are strong networks between people and a high level of mutual trust, so its seems other people's behaviour and our sense of social identity may be extremely important in influencing our own behaviour and policy makers ought need to know how to judge their behaviour whether their behaviour is either right and reasonable or wrong and unreasonable in any learning process of environment. The standard economic theory is tried to explain where people's preferences come from, so it does not take account of the direct influence of the people's behaviour and social norms on our behaviour. The theory assumes we independently know what we want and that our preferences are fixed. This standard theory is very good at explaining short-term decision making. For example, I want green vegetables and choose fruits as they are on special offer, but it cannot explain longer term changes in preferences. I now only choose organic food. Along the same lines the importance of institutions, such as regulations, for example, how people organize markets and the evolution of the whole economic system are not subjects of general economic analysis. This has significant implications for policy design.

In fact, the standard economic theory also assumes that people carry out a full rational analysis of all consumers' available options. This is not what we do; we often just copy the actions of other people. For example, it would require too much effort to look up all the rules when driving in a new country, to find out all the fines/punishments for failing to meet the rules, to work out the probability of being caught and the possible costs, before deciding how to drive there. Instead we just copy other people, and perhaps adjust our behaviour according to the feedback we receive. However, some psychologists indicate to see people how to behave, in especial in crises situations and when others are experts. These psychologists have identified that we are open to influence from people in authority or people we like. When we are influenced by authority, an expert, someone with legitimate power to direct our actions, someone who can either reward or punish us. The effects are less likely to be lasting than we are influenced by someone we like.

However, some people's psychological behaviour is similar to economic behaviour to judge to make any decision. For example, why do you wear a seatbelt in your car? Most of us wear seatbelts as it has became normal behaviour, everyone does it. We neither evaluate the likelihood of having an accident, nor the chance of getting caught without our seatbelt on and incurring a fine. The enforcement of seatbelt wearing is now hardly necessary, as it has become a social norm. What does this mean for policy makers? Policy makers focusing only on economic analysis may often devise a system that has an immediate effect. In psychologists view this issue point, knowing that there is a fine for speeding and a high likelihood of getting caught, the driver will probably drive more slowly, but who will drive just as fast one who realize the chance of being caught is low. However, of policy makers can change the social norm, perhaps in this case by encouraging us to frown on others who drive dangerously fast with campaigns against dangerous driving, then less enforcement will be needed after the change. In other words policy makers might want to take preferences as fixed in the short term, but they should consider shifting preferences in the medium term.

An example where policy appears to have successfully changes people's preferences in the US and Singapore and Hong Kong is banning smoking in public places. This change appears to reduce the social proof of the amount people smoke in private places and public places both also. It seems that government policies can influence the decreasing numbers of consumers require to buy cigarette to smoke habitually, due to fine and punishment is regulated to be ban effectively. Such daily routines quickly became habits. Even when we consciously think about what we do, it can be difficult to change our behaviour. Perhaps I think it is a good idea for people to use public transport, but I do not know where the bus stop is or when the bus runs. I think to use private car to drive to work place is more preference choice. The reward feeling , my journey by car was easy and free to reinforce my old bad habit. Psychologists theories on changing habits generally involve raising it to a conscious level where we can consider the merits of alternative behaviour. This is followed by adopting the new behaviour, which, with time, becomes frozen as a new habit. Thus, I think that we need have regulation to control my behaviour, then we can change my behaviour to be new habit from old habit of behaviour easily. For example, human blood sale is an economic product, due to paying donors for blood would increase supply. Supplies would be provided at a cost advantage in the future, if demand continued to rise. Such as supplies to hospitals for blood will has cost from donors when there are many patients need much blood to use to treat any diseases in any hospitals. Otherwise, if there are not many patients need much blood to use, but there are many donors have effort to provide blood to any hospitals, then it will be economic inefficiency and it is highly wasteful of blood. Thus, the blood donors whose blood supplies of behaviour and the cost of blood which will concern to the hospitals patients' numbers of demand, so their behaviour and economy has close relationship in the hospital blood demand market.

For shareholder behaviour example, if you hold some shares in a firm that has gone down in value. What do you do? Many people hold on to their shares in this situation, in the hope that they will recoup their losses. Conversely, when shares have gone up in share, people are happy to sell them to realize their gain, A similar behaviour is also observed for professional traders who tend to hold on to shares with a loss for longer than those with a gain. The traders who exhibit this type of loss to a lesser degree tend to be the more successful ones. For another example, this is a case where the theory is directly applicable within economic cost-benefit-type analyses that include valuations of no-market products, such as valuations of pollution damage. Policy makers have a choice as to whether-to-accept, and as these may vary by up to a factor, the outcome of such an analysis many well depend on which value is chosen. When a policy maker reasonably has a right to something that might be taken away from them, the willing-to-accept value would be used. On the other hand, when the policy maker only reasonable has a right to the status quo and an improvement is proposed, then the willingness-to-pay is the correct value to use.

What behavioral economic preferences regarding time discounting theory would pay and the conclude that the discounted psychologists have long established utility model, which continues to be that people don't make decisions in widely used by economists, has little the way assumed. In generally, people are expected to rationally make the best choices given their preferences, independent of how these choices are presented. Therefor more information and choice is always considered good. Using this theory, policy makers should ensure that people always have as much information and as many things to choose between as possible, the process of introducing policy is irrelevant. Ideas from behavioral economic indicate, however that this is not the right approach.

However, we know from experimental economics that more choice and more information can lead to a feeling of helplessness or reduced self-efficiency. Hence, if people hope have better solutions to a problem. Instead, providing people with opportunities for understanding, exploration and participation engages powerful motivations for competence, being needed. In summary, people 's self-efficacy increases and they are motivated toward implementing the solutions. i.e. changing their behaviour in a desired way. So, a participatory approach not only improves policy, it also makes to any policy makers more happier. In most cases these principles cannot be used directly as part of any mathematical economics analysis, but highlight situations where this standard analysis will not accurately describe human behaviour and therefore might have unintended consequences when implemented in policy. However, that the policy implications could be quite powerful as the behavioural approach provides quite different lines of analysis to the standard economic model. It is heartening to see policy makers focusing more on the psychology of behaviour when devising policy. So behavioural economics is a relatively new field of economics that attempts to incorporate insights from psychology into economic models and analyses. As above cases seem any policy maker's economic activities which are relative to whose psychology's decision. However, psychologists are often interest in understanding at the level of individual or social group of behaviour, the primary interest in economic is usually in understanding how behaviour and interactions play out in a system to shape economic outcomes. Economists are interested in system-level outcomes, such as the level and path of wages, the effect of taxes on economic output, how rates of savings respond to interest rates etc. However, those economic outcomes depend on complex interactions of individuals. So, behavioural economy concerns to how to judge individual to do the reasonable or right behaviour to hope to get the reasonable economic result as well as it's goal rather to help improve any policy makers to understand their behaviour in ways that allow economists to make better predictions and suggest better economic policies. However, new elements about information processing or individual preferences might impact economic models and analyses.

Is psychology influencing all field of economics? It is possible that behavioural economy needs theoretical contributions and laboratory evidence to support to make any reasonable or right decision to any policy makers. This type of work generally uses existing observational data and estimates relationships between variables of interest by either using naturally occurring variation in the data i.e. natural experiment. Perhaps more than any other field, behavioural economics has had a large impact on finance to the point that behaviour finance is often considered a separate field as opposed to being of behavioural economics. Also, public economic is the study of how government policies influence economic markets. A primary emphasis of public economic involves the topic of taxation. Otherwise, the biggest impact that the behavioural approach has had in economic is the analysis of retirement saving to influence any employees' decisions about their retirement savings. However, when employees can do make any active savings choices to prepare their retirement. If employers can assist whose employees to design any methods to allocate fund, then accumulates interest and is tax free until the retirement funds are withdrawn to every retirement employee. The tax advantage make effort to save for retirement.

Behavioural economic is in understanding how individuals do or do not smooth consumption over time. Smoothing consumption is a standard economic models. It suggests that individuals should borrow or save in order to consume a similar amount throughout one's lifetime. For example, a teacher who is paid a salary 12 months a year, who should not spend all whose salary within one year. Rather, the teacher should smooth whose consumption over the 12 month period. How to allocate to spend pay checks, food and social security payments which concerns the teacher decide to spend whose salary efficiently. Hence, who needs to plan how he shall spend whose one year salary to be reasonable use in the future. Public economic is to understand how people respond to taxation and social benefit programs. This has been an area that has seen an explosion of behavioural work in recent year. i.e. how taxpayers can experience over-withholding and receive tax refunds from tax department.

Policymakers and insurers are also increasingly turning to psychology for approaches to improve health behaviour. Traditionally health-policy focused largely on information provision, assuming that as long as individuals were well informed, their decisions would maximize their health choices. Influential work on the effects of smoking taxes, however, well being of smokers appears to increase with higher taxes to influence health behaviours are not completely rational.

Behavioural economic has also had a small impact on the study of criminal behaviour. For example, individuals are not less likely to commit a crime when who are 18 age and of doing so increases dramatically. However, some economists explain the motivations people have for giving to charity and who understand the psychological motivations for charitable giving. So, it seems that charity award giving has probable to reduce 18 age people who choose to do crime behaviour easily because who feel who have effort to assist charity in their life time.

Industrial organization economists study why firms exist and how which function and compete with each other. Insights and psychology and behavioural economics have made a significant contribution to develop that model the interactions of profit maximizing firms with their customers. In fact, firms often need to evaluate whether their products if prices are needed to set what of price of level is the most reasonable and attractive to customers to choose to buy their products. For example, individuals choose cell phone plans with fixed minute allotments and steep charges for going over the minute limits, but frequently exceed their plan limits. This behaviour is the best explained by a model in which people overestimate the precision of their demand forecasts. So, cell phone firms need to research how cell phone plans with fixed minute allotments and steep charges of cell phone call fee charge plan is the most acceptance method to cell phone clients generally. However, cell phone call charge plan and various cell phone product features and the way cell phone clients allocate their limited attention affects cell phone products markets which are external important factors can influence any cell phone clients why who will choose to use the cell phone call plan because any cell phone will be very large durable product to any cell phone consumer after who choose to buy the cell phone product. Hence, who will not often choose to use the old cell phone firm call charge plan if who feel it provides the excellent cell phone call service and reasonable phone call plan to use to compare other cell phone call plans in the cell phone call market. Hence, the cell phone call firm needs to research why consumers need to choose to use which cell phone call plan among of other cell phone call plans in the cell phone call market. Also, researching the cell phone buyers' choice behaviour why who choose to buy the cell phone to use issue, which will have influence to the cell phone buyer why who choose to use the cell phone call charge plan because expensive cell phone is needed to use excellent quality of cell phone call service usually. Otherwise, cheap cell phone is needed to use poor quality of cell phone call service usually. So, cell phone call plan is needed to follow the cell phone quality and price to be used and they ought have direct relationship to influence why the cell phone buyer who chooses to use the cell phone call plan.

Finally, behavioural economic can also apply to be used to labour supply as a motivating in negative or positive labour supply elasticities example. For example, it is possible that taxi drivers work fewer hours when wages are high-consistent with a model of daily income targeting. This finding is that when wages are high (perhaps it is raining and thus it is easy to find people who want a taxi ride), taxi drivers are able to hit their daily target quickly and then go home. However, when wages are low, taxi drivers are not able to hit their target quickly and thus work additional hours in order to hit their target. It means taxi driver's behaviour produce the effect that taxi driver works more when wages are low than when wagers are high. This work has resulted to analyse taxi driver of labour supply decisions with daily reference points in non taxi domains. So, instead of the weather and client numbers and taxi charge factors, the factors of taxi drivers' hours worked and the quality of service is produced is another important factor to influence any taxi drivers' numbers to supply to the taxi market.

Behavioural economic has also influenced the understanding of how staffs can impact worker productivity and job satisfaction. For example, it is possible that poor cooperation can cause worker productivity decreases and it can also cause poor job satisfaction to the worker. So, when working environment can impact productivity, social comparisons can have an impact on job satisfaction as well as the worker's job satisfaction and search intentions are affected by knowing about the salaries of their peers in whose firm. Hence, the worker's positive or negative psychological feeling to whose employers which will have effort to influence whose working performance and productivity to whose firm in possible.

Behavioural economic is increasingly being used in the field of development economics or low income countries. Such as, how Philippines can offer commitment to individuals who wanted to save money in whose country or how Philippines can change to smoking behaviour when commitment devices were offered to Philippine smokers. So, Philippines policy makers need to concern resource scarcity and resource allocation issue to solve how to let its low income level householders can raise to the middle income level to achieve the high income level householders and the low income level householders whose income level is not distant very much.

CHAPTER XVI

Behavioural economy and business strategy relationship

Why behavioural economy and business strategy which has cause and effect relationship. This is any entrepreneur's psychological issue. I shall analyze whether the relationship between the discipline of behavioural economy and psychology which two branches are totally opposite or if the behavioural theories only extend and complement that mainstream economics. I think study of economics is the behaviour of the complex human beings; this science examines how people choose to act and allocate resources in different market situations. So the economic analysis, is based on the implications that arise from a series of simple assumptions (which are sometimes cited as unrealistic) regarding the human nature. However, in psychological view, the individual is characterized by unlimited rationality and by the ability to follow time consistent, in every situation, his self-interest.

In these conditions, behavioural economic attempts to consider a field of analysis in the study of economic phenomena. Because economics deals with the study of human behaviour on the market, it highlights the human character of the science and the fact that, besides of all the patterns and models, the analysis refers to the real individual. It is also behavioural because it attempts to combine approaches from several sciences mainly from economics and psychology, and also from sociology, philosophy, anthropology or biology. This is not an easy mission, in the conditions in which these various disciplines have adopted in time different approaches that became, in many ways, contradictory. So, behavioural economics is that a multidisciplinary approach will increase the explanatory power of economics.

On one hand, there are specialists two argue that behavioural economic is a field of economics that continues the hand, there are others who see it as a distinctive school of thought, which proposes a new paradigm. However, behavioural economists propose a multidisciplinary study, criticize certain assumptions on which the traditional model is built (such as rationality and self-interest, in their unlimited form), resource to experiments (the classical method of psychology) to validate some assumptions, propose new theories (such as the prospect theory) and advance different interpretations of the economic behaviour, e.g. how to maximize consumers satisfy their needs. This issue is concerned to concern consumption of psychology and social economic situation research aspect. Also, I think that behavioural economics can help the economic science by describing more realistically the utility functions of the individuals.

This field of study is based rather it is a natural extension of the basic approach. However, it is can be claimed that behavioural economics is also built on the premise that psychology methods and assumptions are equally important. Also, models of behavioural economics, allow the utility to depend on the differences between one's own level and a reference level. People are sensitive to changes and preferences are not stable in time. The vision of behavioural economics concerning the inter-temporal choice (which assumes that individuals prefer immediate gains and delay unpleasant activities) seems to be more appropriate to the human behaviour that the one of the traditional model (which assumes that utility is updated over time).

In conclusion, I shall indicate two theories to explain why economy and psychology has close relationship to influence human do any behavioural economic activities daily. For example, through the prospect theory, behavioural economics adds new parameters to improve the mathematical modelling method, which was advanced by economists for decisions taken under uncertainty. However, the theory also proposes a slightly different interpretation. The results are interpreted by the individual as positive or negative deviations from a reference point, which has a neutral psychological value. Last but not least, in addressing social preferences, behavioural economics adds parameters that increase the concern of decision-makers to also assess their utility function in relation to others. For another example, the choice theory; secondly there is not a common consensus between the specialists of behavioural economics regarding the variables that should be included; and finally, many variables that affect the behaviour are not quantitative, but qualitative, and cannot be precisely measured. The findings of behavioural economic are relevant and can help the mainstream theory by providing a more realistically base of study.

However, this argument has contributed to the development of behavioural economics, because there are a large number of phenomena that cannot be entirely explained by the mainstream economics. So, why in the beginning, I indicated why behavioural economics does not imply the totally exclusion of the neoclassical approach and the most studies in this area try to provide a more realistic base of the standard theory. In the concluding, I believe that in time, behavioural economic models will replace the simplified ones, based on unlimited rationality. Also, economists have provided a great importance to the quantitative structures, departing from the human nature. However, behavioural economics can become truly revolutionary only it will always be receptive and will provide a critical insight to their own theories and perspectives, and especially the ones regarding the aspects that they reproach to the traditional economic theory. However, I also feel that the individual's behaviour on the market is determined only be economic factors. In brief, individual choices and, by this, the demand variation are explained only and the variations in the prices of products/services and the available personal income. Am important discussion in the field of determine directly the economic behaviour of an individual (like the sociological and psychological of factors) are actually active elements in the process the reshaping of the utility functions. Finally, in my view, I believe that the conduct of the market phenomena, as it occurs in reality. In this sense, the research of behavioural economics aims to see how the neoclassical model could be improved, using mainly psychology concepts. Although, there are some specialists who argue that behavioural economics can be an alternative to the neoclassical theory.

Most findings of my study conducted in this research, modify some of standard economical assumptions, in order to provide a greater psychological realism. However, the additions proposed by behavioural economists simply recognize the human limitations on (mentally) calculations, will and self-interest. So, I think psychology and economy has close relationship to influence any policy makers or decision makers to do any economic psychology daily. Because the purpose of economics is to better understand and explain the conduct of the economic activities as which occur in reality. Otherwise, human being is complex and its behaviour and constitution is studied by all the social sciences. Consequently, multi and interdisciplinary approaches can bring real benefits to the economic science, by providing a more realist foundation to cause any policy makers or decision makers how to decide to make any behaviours or economic activities by behavioural economic activities support daily.

CHAPTER XVII

How labour behavior influences efficiency

Why labour behavior can influence efficieny?Economics of risky health behaviours can include these personal behaviour, such as smoking, drinking alcohol, drug use, unprotected sex and poor diets is a major source of preventable death. How traditional economics approaches emphasize utility maximization, under certain assumptions which is result of a limited role for policy interventions. Also, non traditional models, e.g. hyperbolic time discounting or bonded rationality how government intervention has greater potential to increase social welfare.

The consequences of risky health behaviours for economic outcomes, such as medical care cost, educational cost, employment wages and crime. Also how policies and strategies modify risky health behaviours, such as taxes or subsidies, cash incentives, restrictions on purchase and use, providing information and restricting advertisement etc. government intervention behaviour. Why health behaviours are important. Because health market includes market products and services, such as medical care, investments of time, environmental conditions, such as air pollution, sanitation and water purity. In special, industrial countries need to concern morality more than infections diseases, health behaviours are particularly important. However, alcohol consumption is also serious in developed countries, e.g. United States, England.

Why is health behaviour important? Because tobacco smoking, diet, physical activity and alcohol and drug consumption and useful sexual behaviours, driving and illicit drug use etc. unhealthy behaviour or consumption is increasing to cause many people to be dead easily in developing countries and developed countries both. As a result, many of the risk factors may reflect a combination of health behaviours and medical treatments. For example, high blood pressure has risk factor to be affected by health behaviour, such as smoking, physical in activity and diet. In fact, the risks of death included child underweight, unsafe water sanitation and indoor smoke for solid fuels which are a direct consequence of poverty. However, poverty could affect unhealthy behaviours. So, low income household families play roles of high risk factors to cause who choose to do unhealthy behavior to cause death easily.

Health behaviours, such as physical in activity (no leisure-time physical activity), medical screening tests. Overall, changes in health behaviours since the 1970 year, particularly the rapid decline in smoking have mostly operated in the direction of improving overall health. However, the race/ethnicity, age, education and annual family income factors can influence health behaviours. Usually, high income and education and Western or Asia race people who are more concerning about their health. So, the countries‘ governments can spend less expenditure on medical welfare assistance to prepare to them to use when who are old age to reach retirement time. Although, these countries' governments can expand less medical expenditure to give welfare to these kind of people, but their hospitals income will be also decreasing, due to these high income and educational people who are concerning their health to avoid to eat bad foods and eat the health foods, so their sick will be also increasing in their life time, it means that who will not often see doctors, so hospitals‘ income will also decrease because which will decrease these patient numbers often.

However, differences in health behaviours are one possible explanation for why socio-economic status is positively related to health status and life expectancy. So, it can explain that behaviour is only a small fraction of the better health and longer life expectancy experienced by high individuals with high socio-economic status. It seems behavioural choices increase the estimated effect of behaviours on health outcomes and reduce the death or illness causes. For example, high educated people began to concern to eat health foods, e.g. fruits and vegetables between 1988 year to 1994 year and 1999 year to 2002 year. Hence, it can cause the fresh foods, e.g. vegetables and fruits markets consumption increased, due to the high educational consumers of numbers are increasing because who began to change diet behaviours to choose to buy much fruits or vegetables to eat daily. It is possible that who began to believe those are health foods. Also, some liking driving consumers who liked to drive cars to be relax in their entertainment time. However, due to many doctors promote health message from televisions or radios or newspapers or sport magazines etc. media, such as often walking, running, riding bicycles sports are more health to any people to cause long time life easily. So, these often driving consumers will reduce much time to drive their cars in their leisure or rest time on Sunday or Saturday or holidays. However, who will choose to carry on walking or running or riding bicycles in their leisure or rest time often. So, their physical activities are changed to do sport behaviour from driving their cars of behaviour because who feel sport can be health to them. Otherwise, driving is not health to them. It will cause the oil, gas, electric battery car energy supplied companies income will be decreased because who will not spend much expenditure to buy these energy power to drive their cars often. So, these driving householder families consumer numbers will be decreasing when who choose to spend their rest or relax time to change their driving behaviour to do health physical activities often. It seems consumers who change their behaviours can influence the product or service suppliers' income in possible. So, it seems that consumer health behaviours can caused some businessmen income will be increased, such as vegetables or fruits foods. Otherwise, the beefs foods businessman income will be decreased. When the many consumers change their diet behaviours immediately. For another example, the smoke companies income will be decreased, when many smokers choose to reduce their smoking of numbers every day. Also, the hospitals income will be decreased if many people are health and who have no any diseases, e.g. cancer. So, hospital cancer patients of numbers will reduce. Also, it is possible that hospitals will not employ many cancer doctors because cancer patients of numbers decrease immediately. But in the long term, these countries‘ governments will avoid to spend much medical welfare allowance to assist many poor householder or low income householder families in the future because it is possible that these are many cancer patients of numbers will decrease. Also, the countries' air pollution will be reduced due to less people have smoke habit. For another example, when many liking driving people who reduce time to drive cars in their relax or rest time when who do not need to drive to work. So, their cars won't need much oil or gas or electric battery power to consume, it means that these power suppliers will decrease to sell private car oil or gas or electronic battery products to these liking driving householder families. So, it seems consumers‘ health behaviour can influence the economic income to some businessmen.

The importance of health behaviour in explaining morality in economically developed countries. Smoking, alcohol consumption, drug use consumption behaviours are economic concepts that relate to all behaviours and the important differences across the various health behaviours. The traditional economic approach to studying health behaviours. Basic aspects of the model are that people receive health capital at birth, which depreciates with age, but can be raised through investment, death occurs when the health stock falls below a minimum level. Health has both consumption and investment aspects, as life time is available for market and non market activities. People produce health by combining market products and services with time. For example, on individual might choose to buy sport running shoes and spending time to run on their rest time for relax on Sunday, Saturday or holiday. Individual can allocate time and money to maximize the present discounted value of lifetime utility. Indirectly, length of life is a choice in the original model.

Specially, the timing of death results from conscious decisions regarding health investments made with full knowledge of health education. Assuming that health has only investment aspects, i.e. it doesn't enter the utility function directly and is only valuable for producing healthy days. Health capital is characterized by an equality of the supply of health capital, i.e. the opportunity cost of health capital and the demand for health capital, i.e. the marginal monetary return on health investment. Usually, people invest in such behaviours until the margin, the return on investments in health equals the opportunity cost of health capital.

The model also applies to unhealthy behaviours, as negative investments in health. The marginal costs of the unhealthy behaviour, including both the monetary cost of purchasing market products, such as cigarettes and alcohol and cost of reduced health and shorter life time and the marginal benefits, such as the pleasure derived from consumption of these unhealthy market products, such etc. However, schooling may improve health by enhancing allocative efficiency (participation in healthier behaviours) or productive efficiency (obtaining more health from the same set of inputs). Economists have used a variety of identification strategies to measure the causal effect of education on health behaviours. In the past, schooling concentrated on measure the causal unhealthy behaviours on smoking, but it neglected to measure the causal unhealthy behaviours on drinking alcohol, unhealthy diet and drug mislead. The habit and addition can cause unhealthy behaviour to anyone daily.

The marginal utility of current consumption rises with the stock of past consumption to cause habit consumption. So, why the smokers who can not choose to buy any cigarettes to smoke or alcohol to drink easily because whose past buying behaviours are caused to habitual consumption. For example, the first time, an individual consumes the addictive substance, who has a stock of past consumption of zero, but after the individual has been heavy user for sufficiently long to have the maximum stock of past consumption when whose consumption is not only for below the utility who enjoyed during whose first use of additive substance. Hence, this past consumption behaviour has become habitual over longer periods of time.

However, concerning responsiveness of consumption to price, consumption at a point in time is related not only to current prices, but also to past prices. So if permanent price changes can affect demand more than temporary ones because forward-looking persons anticipate and make decisions based on future dynamics in prices. Moreover, the price elasticity of demand for the additive product will be greater in the long run than in the short run and that difference will rise with the level of addictiveness. Specifically, if a rise in price of unhealthy products, such as cigarettes and alcohol that which is expected to cause less consumption in the future. So it becomes optimal to hold a lower quantity of addictive stock, which is achieved by reducing consumption to habitual behaviours.

Rational choice theory assumes that consumers make choices, such that their utility is maximised, subjects to budget constraints. Under rational choice theory, regulation which relaxes budget constraints, increases income, alters relative prices or changes consumer preferences will be effective in changing behaviour. Hence, behavioural economics draws on psychology and behavioural sciences in assessing consumer behaviour. So, social and emotional variables can impact on choice. For example, including simple message which reinforce social norms was found to influence electricity consumption. Such as bad health to smoking or often sit down driving private cars on rest time habits is also good message to reduce consumers who spend too much time to carry on bad health behaving. Under these conditions, some evidence suggests that interventions can be: cost-effective relative to more direct or traditional government intervention, used existing regulatory approaches, targeted in influence and easy to implement. When behavioural economics and rational choice theory provide a useful foundation for policy makers, however both theories also face challenges in their application to regulatory design. So, policy makers ought consider to the specific of markets and market participants when applying any form of consumer theory for purposes of designing and predicting the effects of regulatory policy.

Rational choice theory means consumers rank preferences over all products, makes consumption choices based on these ranking, such their utility is maximized. It is further assumed that individuals rationally pursue their self-interest subject to all economics constraints, such as time, income and capital. Rational choice theory is both positive or negative attitude to any consumer. it seeks to describe how people do behaviour and also how who ought to behave. It will impact on consumer behaviour when it relaxes the consumer's budget constraint, alters prices of products and/or services, e.g. mobile gas price or private car price, smoking price and/or influences a consumer's preferences, such as through information disclosure. Examples of those type of regulation include: financial (dis)incentives, banning or limiting choices, and/or requiring the disclosure of certain information. So, behavioural economics is essentially a series of observations about how people do behaviour in certain situations. It is therefore purely positive. For example, why consumers like to choose to smoke, although who know smoking has bad influence to whose health or why consumers like often drive private cars on rest or relax time on Sunday or Saturday or holiday, although who know who need to pay much gas, even who will lose time to do sport and it is tired to them to drive their private cars often.

Rational choice theory indicates any consumer needs to understand all prices, including opportunity costs, preferences and constraints to make comparison to decide whether who will choose to buy the product or enjoy the service. Could behavioural economics help improve diet quality for nutrition to raise any consumer health? Recognizing that consumption choices are determined by factors other than prices, income and information for consumers' food choices. How to make food choices that promote health and prevent disease. Food manufacturers and marketers have discovered that certain psychological cues, such as packaging and presentation are efficient ways to increase consumption of their products. Could similar marketing approaches be used in public health efforts to improve diet quality and reduce body weight. So, improving diet quality among any nutrition program has the potential to guide food choices at a critical time, when a child's dietary preferences are being defined. For example, letting students preselect menu options to school lunch or school breakfast programs or giving food stamp participants the options to pre order groceries by telephone or online may improve the healthfulness of their food students with parents or guardians could specify purchased with prepaid cards. So, students will consume to select using prepayment (fixed costs), those school nutrition dietary preference often then choice that can be purchased only with cash (variable costs). Hence, this consumption behaviour will influence any student to choose to consume to buy any school breakfast or lunch to eat from dietary preference program by using prepayment prepaid cost purchase method more easily. Because this prepaid card method will cause these students choose to consume school breakfast or lunch habitually more than every time cash payment method in school.

However, the most successful public health programs are based on an understanding of health behaviour and how which can occur. Therefore, interventions to improve health behaviour can be best designed with an understanding of relevant theories of behaviour change and the ability to use than skill. So, development and implementation and evaluation of public health and health behaviour promotion needs to follow theories and key concepts and summarize the evidence about who use of theory in health behaviour research. A theory is a set of interrelated concepts, definitions that explains or predicts events or situations by specifying relations among variables. Theories can guide the health behaviour research to understand why people do or do not practize health promoting behaviours, helping identify what information is need to design and effective intervention strategy and providing insight into how to design a health behaviour program. It has two types of theory, explanatory theory and change theory. For example, understanding why employee smokes is one step toward a successful effort, but even the least explanations won't e enough by themselves to fully guide change to improve health. Both explanatory and change theories can understand the social determinants of health behaviour. Many social cultural and economic factors contribute to the development, maintenance and change of health behaviour patterns. For another example, employees may bring food with the from home or buy food form workplace, cafeterias and vending machines. Their consumption choices are influenced by personal preferences, habits, nutrition information, availability, cost and placement among other things. The choice process is complex and determined not only by multiple factors, but by factors at multiple. Today, no single theory or conceptual framework dominates research or practice in health promotion and education. For example, lifestyle behaviours, such as sexual risk behaviours and injury prevention, the sexual behavioural players who believe about whether or not who are not at risk for a disease or health problem and their perceptions of the benefits of taking action to avoid it, influence their readiness to take action. So predicting health behaviour changing is needed readiness to change or stage of change has been examined in health behaviour research and found useful in explaining and predicting changes for a variety of behaviours, including smoking, physical activity, e.g. householder families often spend time to drive private car to relax and reduce time to do health sport activities.

Labor economy indicates factors of production uses to create products or services, which are not themselves significantly consumed in the production process. The method to create human capital can be categorized into two types. The first is to utilize human as labor force in the classical economic perspective. It means input of labor force is as other production factors, such as financial capital, land machinery and labor hours. Labor capital includes the reading of human as creator who frames knowledge skills, competency and experience originated by continuously connecting between self and environment. Microeconomic model shows that education investment for workers significantly affects whose productivity in the workplace.

Education can raise to improve workers productivity. Because it is difficult that human capital itself independently contributes to individual development and national economy growth. In fact, it is necessary to link between human capital and economic preference should be considered within a social and political context to precisely measure the human capital. So human capital is one of important factors for a national economic growth. The production oriented perspective of human capital shows to human capital is as a fundamental source of economic productivity.

Many employers prefer to high productive individuals to improve productivity in the internal labor market by the increasing of productivity in the workplace from internal training to raise old or current workers' skill and knowledge in companies. What is labor surplus mean? Labor surplus exists in the sense that a substantial portion of labor force contributes less to output than it requires, i.e. its marginal product falls below surplus designation than arises from the fact that if such workers were reallocated to enhance the total output of the system. For example, agricultural sectors concentrated especially in subsistence agriculture, characterized by family farm, i.e. excluding planation agricultural which consists of profit maximizing, able to hire or fire workers easily. Surplus labor makes its appearance in the owner-operated extended family networks. The company income or output shares are determined via bargaining in relative to through not necessarily equal to the average rather than the marginal product of labor. Large determination is thus based on a sharing principle, a function of the fact that when high man/land rates are part of the initial conditions low marginal productivity workers can't dismissed or otherwise eliminated. Hence, labor surplus phenomenon will raise unemployed and unfair and unreasonable treatment to the job seekers in labor market because employers only concern family relationship business culture and who only feel the old or current workers who have much effort productivity to compare to other job seekers from labor market. I think who are doing unethical behavior not to give chance to employ any other job seekers to fill their internal job positions, due to they only believe their old or current workers working experience and skills must have more effort to be promoted to higher positions in their companies. So, labor surplus economy will raise unemployment ratio and many labor market of proficient and skillful and knowledgeable owned job seekers who can not get more job opportunities if employers only like to do family relationship workplace culture to protect whose current or old labors benefits only. So, these family relationship employers can not raise productivity and also increasing employment ratio in society if who still do not give chance to accept to employ outside job seeker to assist whose business development for long term.

However, labor market policies succeed or fail at least concerning for behavioral response. Insight from behavioral economics, hence consequences for the design and function of labor market policies. For example, the human costs of labor market have rarely been clearer at the value of public policies, such as unemployment insurance and job training programs that assist workers in managing, gaining new skills and navigating the labor of joblessness have been apparent in most major economics in recent years. For the design of unemployment insurance with job search requirements intended to minimize worry to incentives to return to work. I think behavioral economy can apply to labor market finds in these areas to solve labor challenges: unemployment insurance, job search assistance and job training. Hence solving labor moral hazard problems in unemployment compensation schemes of unemployed workers not putting in adequate search efforts and setting inefficiently high reservation wages in response to more generous benefits when unemployed. However, economists have noted several advantages to wage loss insurance, such as the ability to better target benefits to those workers who face the most severe consequence of job loss. Although, behavioral economists doesn't change that logic, it does identify additional advantages to wage loss insurance. There behavioral concerns are consistence with the limited impacts on reemployment rates and job search efforts for encourage the unemployed people have more effort to find new jobs during this period of unemployment period if governments can provide temporary wage loss insurance to them. In any country's labor market, it has supply two sides, the factors affect the decision of an individual. On the supply side, factors include working nature, career path top choose a particular job, requiring education and on the job training, providing effort in particular job. Also, on the demand side, factors that affect the decision of an individual firm factors include: how the firm hires and fires workers, how it offer jobs with different characteristics, how it discriminate among different workers and how it chooses particular compensation policies and to offer different career paths to workers. So, behavioral economist is the combination of psychology and economic that investigates what happens in markets in which some of the agents display human limitations. Does some combination of market formed, learning and evolution these human qualities irrelevant? Because of limits of perfect agents (human) survive and influence what outcomes. Surely, all of economic is meant to be about the behavior of economic agents be whose firms or consumers, suppliers or demanders, bankers or farmers. So what is behavioral economic and how does it differ from other economic? Do only the rational agents survive? Do the workings of markets at least render the actions of rational irrelevant? So, what the decision if it was a mistake to do any rational calculation before the consumer does any decision. So, it seems behavioral economy and psychology has close relationship. It means that human psychology will influence whose decision how to do any economic activities. For example, public economic is the study of how government economic is the study of how government policies influence economic market. Hence, economic analysis is part of the decision making process in any organizations or individuals.

To conclude labor behaviors or performance and consumption behaviors and entrepreneurs environment have different functions to influence any enterprise development to be success . Behavioural economy has close relationship to consumer and employee psychology research. Behavioural economists need to find what causes the consumer why who choose to do whose behaviour or how to predict the consumer avoids to do whose behaviour. Otherwise, labour economists need to concern how to assist the employer to avoid whose employees who feel unfair or unreasonable moral behaviour from whose employer to reduce low productivity caused. Hence, labour economy concerns on individual benefit more than public benefit. Otherwise, behavioural economy concerns on public benefit more than individual benefit. Labour economy concerns on raising individual productivity. Otherwise, behavioural economy concerns on change individual or public habit of behaviour to raise sale.

Bibliography

Roberston, R. (1992), Globalization, Social Theory and

CHAPTER XVIII

How utility maximization, equilibrium and efficiency concepts influence employee's individual behavior

At the core of behavioral economics is used psychology of economics analysis to improve economics on its own terms generating theoretical insights, making better prediction of field phenomena, and suggesting better policy. It rejects economic theories based on utility maximization, equilibrium and efficiency. It is useful because it provides economists with a theoretical framework that can be applied to almost any form of economic (and even non-economic) behavior.

Simpifying much assumption that are not central to the economic theory. For example, there is nothing in core theory that specifies that people should not care about fairness, that they should weight risky outcomes in a linear fashion, or that they must discount the future at a constant rate. Other assumption simply acknowledge human limits on computational power and self-interest. These assumptions can be considered procedurally rational because human needs to solve problems that are often so complex that who can't be solved exactly by even modern computer technology.

Theories in behavioral economics should be judged by reality, generality and tractability concepts. We share the positivist view that the ultimate test of a theory is the accuracy of its predictions. But we also believe that better predictions are likely to result from theories with more realistic assumptions. In psychology, such as connectionist models that capture some of the essential features of neural functioning, which are based on utility maximization, yet are reaching the point where they are able to predict many judgement and behavioral phenomena. Contrary to the positivistic view, however,
we believe that predictions of feelings.

Most of the ideas in behavioral economics are not new. When economics first became identified as a distinct field of study, psychology didn't exist as a discipline. For example, "invisible hand" and "the wealth of Nations" which belong to theory to moral sentiments, which laid out psychological principles of individual behavior that are arguably as profound as whose economic observations. Another example, such as a simple model of social utility means that one person's utility was affected by another person's payoff. However, the rejection of academic psychology by economists, which constructed an account of economic behavior built up from assumptions about the nature-that is, the psychology of homo-economicus. Nowadays, economists hoped their discipline could be like a natural science. But psychology was not very scientific. The economists thought it provided too unsteady a foundation for economics, who make assumption to utility led to a movement to the psychology from economics. In the early part of the 20th century, economists still included rich speculations about how people feel and think about economic choices generally. However, later economists are very much appealed to psychological insights, but by the middle of the century discussions of psychology had largely disappeared. Throughout the second half of the century, many criticisms of the positivistic perspective took place in both economics and psychology. The economists of the time had less disagreement with psychology with psychology than they realized. They assume without foundation that behavior always aims at the goal of maximum pleasure and minimum pain; but behavior is not goal-oriented. Also the economists of the time believed false conclusions are drawn from false psychological assumptions. The importance of psychological measures and bounds on rationality. These commentators attracted attention, but did not alter the fundamental direction of economics. One development was the rapid acceptance by economists of the expected utility and discounted utility models which are making decision under uncertainty and choice, respectively. Whereas the assumptions and implications of utility analysis are rather flexible, and the expected utility and discounted utility models have numerous precise and testable implications. As a result, they provided some of the first "hand targets" for critics of the standard theory.

As economists began to accept counterexamples that could be not be permanently ignored, developments in psychology identified promising directions for new theory. Beginning around 1960 year, psychology became dominated by the brain as an information-processing device replacing the behaviorist conception of the brain as a stimulus-response machine. The information-processing permitted a fresh study of neglected topics like memory, problem solving and decision making. These new topics were more obviously relevant to the conception of utility maximization than behaviorism had appeared to be. However, psychologists began to use economic models as a benchmark against which to their psychological models. Early research in behavioral have followed. First, identify assumption or models that are used by economists, who expected utility and discounted utility. Second, the assumption or model is a rule out alternative explanations (such as subjects' confusion or transactions costs). And third, the assumption or model creates alternative theories that generalize existing models. The fourth step is to construct economic models of behavior using the behavioral assumptions to test them from the third step. This final step of economic models of behavior has only been taken more recently to apply.

CHAPTER XIX

Costs and benefits analysis concept measures consumer's individual or employee's individual behavior

Entrepreneur needs to know costs and benefits analysis can be applied to predict when consumption behavior will be caused. The methods in behavioral economics are the same as those in other areas of economies. In fact, behavioral economics relied heavily on evidence generated by experiments. More recently, however, behavioral economists have moved beyond experimentation and the full range of methods are employed by economists. The experiment played a large role in the initial phase of behavioral economics because experimental control is exceptionally helpful for distinguishing behavioral explanations from standard ones.

Suppose we observed this phenomenon in these any one of cares, in the form of failures of legal cases to settle before trial, costly divorce proceedings, and labor strikes. They are phenomenons of human‘ behaviours are caused by costs and benefits measurement of result. Also, behavioural economy would be difficult to tell whether rejection of offers was the result of reputation-building in repeated games, agency problems (between clients and lawyers), confusion, or an expression of distaste for being treated unfairly. However, in these game experiments of failures of legal cases to settle before trial, costly divorce proceedings, and labor strikes. The first three of these explanations are ruled out because the experiments are played once, have no agents, and are simple enough to rule out confusion. Thus, the experimental data clearly establish that subjects are expressing concern for fairness. Other experiments have been useful for testing whether judgment errors which individuals commonly make in psychology experiments also affect prices and quantities in markets. The lab is especially useful for these studies because individual and market-level data can be observed. Although behavioral economists relied on experimental data, however, behavioral economics subject is seen as a very different method from experimental economics. As noted, behavioral economists are methodological profession. They define themselves, not on the basis of the research methods that who employ, but rather their application of psychological insights to economics. Experimental economists, on the other hand, define themselves on the basis of use of experimentation which is as a research tool.

Also, economists have made a major investment in developing experimental methods that are suitable for addressing economic issues, and have achieving among themselves on a number of important issues. For example, experimental economists often make instructions and software available for precise replication, and raw data are typically shared for reanalysis. Experimental economists also insist on paying performance-based. However, experimental economists have also developed rules that many behavioral economists are likely to find excessively . For example, experimental economists rarely collect data like demographics, self-reports, response times and other cognitive measure which behavioral economists have found useful. Descriptions of the experimental environment are usually abstract rather than which are carried on experiment in the outside world because economic theory rarely makes a prediction about how a happen would matter, and experimenters are concerned about losing control over incentives if choosing strategies with certain labels is appealing because of the labels themselves.

Finally, economic experiments also typically use "stationary replication", in which the same task is repeated over and over in each period. Data from the last few periods of the experiment are typically used to draw conclusions about equilibrium behavior outside the lab. When economists believe that examining behavior after it is of great interest, it is also obvious that many important aspects of economic life are like the first few periods of an experiment rather than the last. Supposing if we need to make decision of marriage, educational decisions, and saving for retirement, or the purchase of large durables like houses, sailboats, can cars, which happen just a few times in a person's life, a focus on behavior is clearly not warranted. All said, the focus on psychological realism and economic applicability of research promoted by the behavioral-economics perspective suggests the usefullness research outside the lab and of a broader range of approaches to laboratory research. So, economists realize that who have ideal opportunity to learn by trial-and-error, in a stationary environment, and uses the opportunity to learn how to carry on experimenting any psychology and behavioral researches.

The field of behavioral decision research, on which behavioral economics has drawn more than any other subfield of psychology, typically classifies research into two categories: judgement and choice. Judgement research deals with the processes people use to estimate probabilities. Choice deals with the processes people use to select among actions, considering of any relevant judgements who may have made. Everyday, we need to make probable judgement. Due to judging the likelihood of events is central to economic life. For example: Will you lose your job in a poor economic environment? Will you be able to find another house you like as much as the one you must bid for right away? Will the government raise interest rates? Will a merger strategy increase profits? These questions are answered by some process of judging likelihood. The standard principles used in economic to model probability judgement in economic are concepts of statistical sampling, which are concerned probabilities in the face of new evidence. However, it requires a separation between previously judged probabilities and evaluations of new evidence. However, people often overestimate the probability who previously attached to events which later happened. This leads to "second guessing". For example, Monday morning quarterbacking and may be partly responsible for lawsuits against stockbrokers who lost money for their clients. (The clients think the brokers should have known). For example, anybody has tried to learn from a computer manual has seen the curse of knowledge in action. Another example for making probability judgements is called "representativeness": People judge conditional probabilities like P(hypothesis /data) or P(example/class) by how well the data represents the hypothesis or the example represents the class. Representativeness is an economical shortcut that delivers reasonable judgements with minimal effort in many cases. For example, in judging whether a certain student described in a profile is, say, a psychology major or computer science major, the student decides how well the profile matches the psychology or computer science career to the student generally.

Many studies show how this sort of feature-matching can lead people to under weigh the "base rate", in this example, the overall frequency of the two majors. Another byproduct of representativeness is the "law of small numbers": Small samples are though to represent the properties of the statistical process that generated them (as if the law of large numbers, which guarantees that a large sample of independent draws does represent the process, is in a hurry to work). If a baseball player get hits 30% of his times at bat, but is 0 for 4 , so far in a particular game, then he is "due" for a hit in his next at bat in this game, so that this game's hitting profile will more closely represent his overall ability. Field and experimental studies with basketball shooting and betting on games that people believe that there is positive attitude that players experience the "hot hand", when there is no evidence that such an effect exists. For example, judgements of the fairness or non misleading or reasonable of clients' financial report to accounting auditors, consumers buying products and classroom negotiation. It is important to judge whether it is both a good attitude and bad attitude. A good attitude provides fast, close to optimal, answers when time or capabilities are limited, but it also needs logical principles and leads to situations. So, optimal is largely a critique (a reasonable one) of the later applied research. Assume that people misspecify a set of hypotheses, or encode new evidence incorrectly. For example, assuming that people believe hypothesis A is more likely than B will never encode pro-A evidence mistakenly, but will sometimes encode pro-B evidence as being supportive. For another example, investors will think there is wide variation in skill of, say, mutual-fund managers, even if there is no variation at all. (A manager who does well several years is a surprise if performance is mistakenly thought due to non replacement, so concluding that the manager must be really good.)

A question concerns stock market, such as: Overreacts in the long term. In their model, earnings follow a random walk but investors believe, mistakenly, that earnings have positive attitude. After one or two periods of good earnings, the stock market can not be confident that exists and hence expects, but since earnings are really a random walk, the stock market is too pessimistic and is underreacting to good earnings news. After a good earnings, however, the stock market believes many investors are increasing. Since, it is not the stock market is too optimistic and overreact. For another example, valuable consumer products (A $100 wireless keyboard, a fancy computer mouse, bottles of wine, and a box of chocolate) are sold to postgraduate (MBA) business students. The students were presented with a product and asked whether who would buy it for a price equal to the last two digits of their own social security number (a roughly random identification number required to obtain work in the United States) converted into a dollar figure, e.g. , if the last digits were 99, then the postgraduate business students will accept the hypothetical price was $99 to buy any of it for a price to the last two digits of their own social security number . After giving a yes/no response to the question. Would you pay $99? subjects were asked to state the most who would pay (using a procedure that gives people an incentive to say what who really would pay). Although subjects were reminded that the social security number is essentially random, those with high numbers were willing to pay more for the products. However, many studies have also shown that the method used to elicit preferences can have dramatic consequences. Nevertheless, when required to make an economic decisions-to-choose a brand of toothpaste, a car, a job, or how to invest, people do make some kind of decision. Behavioral economists refer to the process by which people make choices with ill defined preferences as "constructing preferences".

However, in classical consumer theory, preferences among different commodities are assumed to be invariant with respect to an individual's current consumption. Specifically, people seem to dislike losing commodities from their consumption much more than they like gaining other commodities. For example, the research of "contingent valuation" studies that attempt to establish the dollar value of products which are not routinely trades. Contingent valuation is often used to do government cost-benefit analysis or establish legal penalties from environment damage. These surveys typically show very large differences between buying prices (e.g. paying to clean up oil of beaches) and selling prices (e.g. having to be paid to allow beaches to be ruined).

Nowadays, a quarter of the wealth in the USA has more interesting opportunities to do behavioral economies. They find that motivated sellers should regard the price who paid as a sunk cost and choose at a nominal loss from the purchase price. Sellers' listing prices and subsequent selling behavior reflects to nominal losses. There are some cases in which no effect would be expected, such as when products are purchased for resale rather than for utilization. For example, Do art or antique dealers like with pieces who buy to resell? What about surrogate mothers who agree to bear a child for a price paid in advance? However, evidence on the degree of commercial attachment is mixed. Reference points can also serve as social focal points for judging performance. For an interesting example from corporate finance. In general, when managers whose firms face possible losses (or declines from a previous year's earnings) are very reluctant to report small losses. As a result, the distribution of actual losses and gains show a very large at zero, and hardly any small reported losses (compared to the number of small gains). A manager who does not have the skill to shift accounting profits to erase a potential loss (i.e. has some earnings in his pocket.) is considered a poor manager. It seems that the bad performance manager whose behavior is bad to mislead public to believe his firm have better performance in this year. Hence, in the mental accounting view, people set up mental accounts for outcomes which are psychologically separate, much as financial accountants lump expenses and revenues into separated accounts to guide managerial attention. Otherwise, mental accounting stands in opposition to the standard view in economics that it predicts, accurately , that people will spend money coming from different sources in different ways. So, a generalization of the notion of mental accounting is the concept of "choice bracket" , which refers to the fashion in which people make decisions narrowly, in either a piece meal fashion, or boardly, i.e. taking account of interdependencies between decisions. For example, when making many separate choices between products, consumers tend to choose more diversity when the choices are bracketed broadly than when they are bracketed narrowly.

CHAPTER XX

Preferences over risky and uncertain outcomes of individual behavior economic theories

The expected utility (EU) hypothesis explains that the utility of a risky distribution of outcomes (says, monetary payoffs) is a probability weighted average of the outcome utilities. It follows logically from apparently reasons. Most notably the independence (or " cancellation") choice. The indepence choice says that if you are comparing two gambles, you should cancel events which lead to the same consequence with the same probability, your choice should be independent of those utility also simplifies matters because a person's taste for risky money distributions can be fully captured by the share of the utility function for money.

However, many studies document predictive failures of expected utility in simple situations in which subjects can earn substantial sums of money from their choices. Some of these new theories alter the way in which probabilities are weighted, but preserve a "between" property which says that if A is preferred to B, then any probabilistic gamble between them must be preferred to B, but dispreferred to A (i.e. the gambles like "between" A and B in preference). Other new theories suggest that probability weights are "rank-dependent", outcomes are first ranked, then their probabilities are weighted in a way which is sensitive to how who rank within the gamble that is being considered. For example, if a person is attitude towards gambles really came from the utility of wealth function, even large gains in wealth would not tempt who to risk \$50 or \$100 losses, if who really dislikes losing \$10 more than who likes gaining \$11 at every level of wealth. For example, linear probability weighting in expected utility (EU) works reasonably well except when outcome probabilities are very low or high. But low-probability events are important in the economy in the form of "gambles" with positive (lottery tickets and also risky business ventures in biotechnology and pharmaceuticals) and high risk compensation events which required large insurance industries. Another theory example, such as prospect theory is experimental choices more accurately than (EU) because it gets the psychological of judgement and choice right. It consists of two main components, a probability weighting function, and a "value function" which replaces the utility function of (EU). The weighting function P(P) combines two elements: (1) The level of probability weight is a way of expressing risk tastes (if you hate to gamble, you will place low weight on any chance of winning anything) and (2) P(P) captures how sensitive people are to differences in probabilities.

If people are move sensitive in the neighborhoods of possibility and certainty. i.e. changes in probability near zero and 1, then their P(P) curve will overweight low probabilities and underweight high ones. For another theory example, such as technical motivation for "rank dependent" theories, ranking outcomes, than weighting their probabilities is that when separate probabilities are weighted, it is easy to construct examples in which people will be dominance by choosing a "dominated" gamble A which has a lower chance of winning at each possible outcome amount, compared to the higher chance of winning the same outcome amount for a dominant gamble B. If people rarely choose such dominated gambles, who are acting as if who are weighting the differences in probabilities which is the essence of the rank dependent approaches. So, new information can help any decision maker to feel better to make better decisions. These theories effect may explain demand for information in settings like medicine or personal finance, where new information usually does not change choice, but relieves anxiety people have from knowing there is something who could know but don't. However, the planning problem for economic agents who would like to behave in fashion and discussed the important time discounting for choice. Most big decisions, e.g. savings, educational investments, labor supply, health and diet, crime and drug etc. decisions use have costs and benefits which occur at different point in time. Thus, time discounting is basically standard time discounting plus an immediacy effect, a decision discounts delays in equally at all moments except the current one, caring differently about well being. This functional form provides one sample and powerful model of the taste to individual to make right or reasonable behavior economic decision. However, most analyses of choice assume that people integrate new consumption with planned consumption. It is infeasible and perhaps for this reason, descriptively inaccurate. When people make decisions about new sequences of payments or consumption, they tend to evaluate them in isolation, e.g. treating negative outcomes as losses, rather than as reductions to their existing money flows or consumption plans.

How to decide fairness and social preferences. The assumption that people maximize their own wealth and other personal material goals just self-interest is a correct simplification that is often useful in economics. However, people may sometimes choose to spend their wealth to punish others who have harmed them, reward whose, so who have helped, or to make outcomes more fair. Just as understanding demand for products requires specific utility function, the key to understanding this sort of social preferences is a specification of social utility which can explain many types of date with a single function.

Behavioral economy can also use to assist firms to choose right behavior to decide to do any matters. I show hypothesis to establish any reference level of consumer surplus and product profit. Both sides are entitled to any firm's levels of profit, so price changes which threaten any matter are considered unfair. So raising any product price, it will reduce consumer surplus and is considered unfair. But the cost of a firm's inputs rises, subjects said it was fair to raise prices. Because not raising prices would reduce the firm's profit (compared to the reference profit). Everyday observation that firms don't change prices and wages as frequently commonly. For example, when the fourth Hary Potter story book was released in summer 2000 year, most stores were allocated a small number of books that were pre-sold in advance. Why not raise prices or auction the books off? It is possible that it concerned about customer goodwill and excess demand to cause book stores limit such book price increases. Offended consumers are often able to affect firm behavior by media attention or provoking legislation. For example, scalping tickets for popular sports and entertainment events (resulting them at a large premium over the printed ticket price) is constrained by law in most countries. For example, some countries have "anti-laws" penalizing sellers who take advantage of shortages of water, fuel and other necessities by raising prices after natural disasters. So, the countries' governments can protect which citizen benefits to balance the natural resource supply and demand to sell in the reasonable price fairly after the natural disaster occurrence.

A few years ago, responding to public anger at rising CEO salaries when the economy was being restructured through downsizing and many workers lost their jobs. Otherwise, some countries passed a law prohibiting firms from deducting CEO salaries for tax purposes beyond $1 million a year. because the countries need to earn much tax income from these high salary CEO income every year. So, explaining why these laws and regulations come from is one example of now economics might be used to expand the scope of law and behavioral economic relationship.

CHAPTER XXI

What is behavioral game theory

Game theory has rapidly become an important foundation for many areas of economic theory, such as bargaining in decentralized markets, contracting and organizational structure. The descriptive accuracy of game theory in these application can be questioned because equilibrium predictions often assume strategic reasoning and direct field tests are difficult. In fact, behavioral game theory uses any experimental evidence and psychological research to generalize the standard assumptions of game theory. One component of behavioral game theory is a theory of social preferences for allocations of money to oneself and others. Another component is a theory of how people choose in one shot games or in the first period of a repeated game. For example, in share buying and selling market, shareholders shall buy or sell shares from their judgement in the economic cycle market everyday. So share investment is seemed as allocation of game to these shareholders. Also, shareholders whose mind can influence whose psychological behavior to decide how to invest whose shares in their share investment economic activities. The component of behavioral game theory can include a model of learning to either individual or a population. Also, game theory is one area of economy in which serious attention has been paid to the process by which can equilibrium comes about. Many learning theories have been proposed and carefully tested with experimental data. Theories about population never predict as well as theories of individual learning through who are useful for other purposes. So, behavioral game theory can be applied to these complex environments. e.g. consumer supermarket purchase, share market etc. How to apply behavioral game theory to macroeconomics and saving aspect?

Many concepts in macroeconomic probably have a behavioral style that could be influenced by research in psychology. For example, it is common to assume that prices and wages are in nominal terms, which has important implications for macroeconomic behavoir. Behavioral economics suggests some ideas for among consumers and workers, perhaps it is influenced by workers' concern for fairness. An important model in macroeconomics is the life cycle model of savings or permanent income hypothesis. This theory assumes that people make a guess about their lifetime earnings profile, and plan their lifetime earnings profile, and plan their savings and consumption in each period has diminishing marginal utility; and preferences for consumptions streams are time-separable (i.e. overall utility is the sum of the discounted utility of consumption in each separate period). The theory also assumes people lump together different types income when they guess how much money who will have (i.e. different sources of wealth are different). So, why many young people won't spend too much money for unnecessary expenditure, e.g. entertainment easily. Because who plan to save for their retirement in the future.

A behavioral life cycle theory of savings in which different sources of income are kept track of in different mental accounts. Mental accounts can reflect natural perceptual or cogitive divisions. For example, it is possible to add up the travelever paycheck and dollar value of whose frequent flyer miles, but it is simply unnatural to do so. It is important to note that many key implications of the life-cycle hypothesis have never been well supported (e.g. consumption is far more closely related to current income than it should be according to theory. However, predictions can be improved by introducing utility functions with habit formation in which utility in a current depends on the reference point of previous consumption, and by more carefully accounting for uncertain about future income. So, mental accounting is only one of several behavioral approaches that may prove useful. Economics is money illusion, it is the tendency to make decisions based on nominal quantities rather than converting those figures into real terms by adjusting for inflation. Money illusion seems to be pervasive in some domains. So, it appears that employees don't seem to mind if their real wage falls as long as their nominal wages doesn't fall. Labor macroeconomics is involuntary unemployment. Why can some people not find work beyond of switching jobs, or a natural rate of unemployment? A popular account of unemployment pushs that wages are deliberately paid above the market clearly level, which creates an excess supply of workers and hence unemployment. But why are wages too high ? As efficiency wage theory shows that paying workers more than who deserve is necessary to ensure that who have something to lose if they are unemployed, which motivates them to work hand and economizes on monitoring. Another viewpoint indicates that employer and worker is such as into a gift exchange relationship. Employers pay more than who have to as a gift and workers repay the gift by working harder than necessary. They show how gift exchange can be an equilibrium and show some of its macroeconomic implications. In labor economics, gift exchange is clearly evident of experimental labor markets. In practical working environment, firms offer wages; workers who take the jobs than choose a level of effort, which is costly to the workers and valuable to the firms. For example, firms and workers can enforce wages, but not effort levels. Since workers and firms are matched for just one period, and do not learn each other's identities, there is no way for either side to build reputations or for firms to punish workers who chose low effort. However, self interested workers should shirk, and firms should anticipate that and pay a low wage.

In fact, firms deliberately pay high wages as gifts and workers choose higher effort levels when they take higher wage jobs. It seems that it has strong relationship between wages and effort is stable over time. For example, standard life-cycle theory assumes that if people can borrow they should prefer wage profiles which maximize the present value of lifetime wages. Holding total wage payments constant, and assuming a positive real rate of interest, present value maximization implies that workers should prefer declining wage profiles over increasing ones. However, in fact, most wages profiles are clearly rising over time which is such as a phenomenon. Rather, workers derive utility from positive changes in consumption, but have self-control problems. That would prevent them from positive changes in consumption, but have self-control problems that would prevent them from saving for later consumption of wages were more front-loaded in the life cycle. In addition, workers seem to derive positive utility from increasing wage profiles, it is perhaps because rising wages are a source of self-esteem and the desire for increasing payments is much weaker for non wage income. The standard life-cycle of labor supply also implies that workers should substitute labor and leisure based on the wage rate who face and the value who place on leisure at different points in time. If wage fluctuations are temporary workers should work long hours when wages are high and short hours when wages are low. However, because changes in wages are often persisting and because work hours are generally fixed in the short-run. So, it is difficult to tell whether workers are substituting. For example, taxi drivers who target daily will drive longer hours on low income days early on high income days. This behavior is exactly the opposite of substitution. Also inexperienced taxi drivers support the daily targeting prediction. But experienced taxi drivers don't have negative elastic, either because target minded drivers earn less and self select or taxi drivers learn over time to substitute rather than target. Perhaps the simplest prediction of labor economics is that the supply of labor should be upward sloping in response to a increase in wage.

In finance, standard equilibrium models of asset pricing assume that investors only care about asset risks if who affect marginal publicly available information to forecast stock returns as accurately as possible the efficient markets hypothesis. When those hypotheses do make some accurate predictions and some investors in assets have limited rationality of behavioral finance. Also, in share stock market, it is common, shareholders should not want to trade with them, but the volume of stock market transaction is large. So, it presents data on individual trading behavior which suggests that the extremely high volume may be driven, in part, by overconfidence on the part of investors. For example, property agent's individual behavior is similar to share agent's individual behavior. In the economy view, property agent bases a list price for a house on the selling prices of nearly houses that is similar ("comparables"). Every nearest neighbour techniques bases on similarity is also used in credit scoring and other kinds of evaluations. Also, one firm whose every share sale on the selling price is comparable to its similar firms whose every share price in its same business industry. The shareholder will evaluate whose every share issued sale price in the stock (share) market. Otherwise, in behavioral economy view, for example, property or share buyer who has risky choice to decide to buy in the property or share market. It is a process of comparing the similarity of the probabilities and outcomes in two gambles and choosing on dimensions which are dissimilar.

As we mentioned above, behavioral economics simply includes an interest in psychology. In fact, we believe that many familiar economic distinctions do have a lot of behavioral content, they are implicitly behavioral, and could surely benefit from more explicit ties to psychological ideas and data. However, some people do not feel psychology and economy which have close relationship. Such as, substantial debate is ongoing in psychology about whether knowing the precise details of how the brain carries out computations is necessary to understand functions and mechanisms of driving car skill at higher levels, (knowing the mechanical details of how a car works may not be necessary to turn the key and drive it). Most psychology experiments use indirect measures like response times, error self reports and natural experiments, due to brain has been fairly successful in codifying what we know about thinking, but pressimists think brain scan studies won't add much. The optimists think the new tools will lead to some discoveries. Another couple is the distinction between short run and long run price elasticity which concerns behavioral economy. In fact, economy needs have theories concepts to support any evidence to prove any matter has happened. Concerning short run and long run price elasticity cause and effort issue, with a casual suggestion that the run is the time it takes for markets to adjust, or for consumers to learn new prices, after a demand or supply stock. Adjustment costs undoubtedly have technical and social component, but probably also have some behavioral factors influence in the form of gradual adaption to loss and learning.

Another macroeconomic model which can be interpreted as implicitly behavioral is that business cycles can emerge if it is not general price inflation, so why the consumers shall not decide to buy this kind of product in the competitive market. For example, risky choice is as a process of comparing the similarity of the probabilities and outcomes in two gambles, and choosing on dimensions which are dissimilar. Behavioral economic simply includes an interest in psychology. In fact, we believe that many familiar economic distinctions do have a lot of behavioral content, they are implicitly behavioral and could surely benefit from more explicit ties to psychological ideas and data. However, some people do not feel psychology and economy which have close relationship. Such as psychology is about whether knowing the precise details of how the brain carries out computations is necessary to understand functions and mechanisms at higher levels. (knowing the mechanical details of how a car works may not necessary to turn the key and drive it.) Most psychology experiments use indirect measures like response times, error rates, self reports and natural experiments due to brain has been fairly successful in codifying what we know about thinking. However, pessimists think brain scan studies won't add much. The optimists think the new tools will lead to some discoveries and the potential is great that they cannot be ignored. However, economy needs have theories or concepts to support evidence to prove why any matters had happened. An example, is the distinction between short term and long term price elasticity. This distinction, mentions between of them, with a casual suggestion that long run is the time it takes for markets to adjust, or for consumers to learn new prices, after a demand or supply shock. Adjustment costs undoubtedly have technical and social components, but probably also have some behavioral factors influence in the form of gradual adaption to loss and learning.

However, organizational behavioral theory concerns that organizatonal contracting are shot through with implicitly behavioral economics. Some economists motivate the incompleteness of contracts as a consequence of rationality in foreseeing the future, but do not tie the research directly to work on memory and imagination. For example, agency theory begins with the presumption that there is some activity the agent doesn't like to do. Why markets are better at making dramatic changes than managers influence cost. So, influence costs are the costs managers preform for projects who like or personally benefit from like promotion or raises. A lot of influence costs are undoubtedly inflated by optimistic, each division manager really does think their division desperately needs funds and social comparison of pay and benefits. Otherwise, why are salaries kept so secret? In all these cases, conventional economic behavior has deeper psychological questions of where adjustment costs, effort and influence costs come from. So, it beings these questions: Could these phenomena surely produce surprising testable prediction? Is psychology regularity an assumption or a conclusion?

Behavioral economics generally begins with assumption rooted in psychological regularity and asks what follows from those assumptions. An alternative approach is to work backward, regarding a psychological regularity as a conclusion that must be proved an explanation that must be derived from deeper assumption before we fully understand and accept it. The alternative approach is caused by a fashionable new direction in economic theory and psychology too, which is to explain human behavior as the product of evolution. However, we may not believe that behavior of intelligent, modern people lived in socialization and cultural influence can only be understood by guessing what their lives were like and how their brains might have adapted generally. There are other models that treat psychological regularity as a conclusion to be proved rather than an assumption to be used. Such models usually begin with an observed regularity. Economists have for deriving behavior from first principles and rationalizing apparent irrationality. Theories of this sort are useful behavioral economics and what fresh predictions do they make. However, critics have pointed out that behavioral economics is not a unified theory, but is instead a collection of tools and ideas.

This is true. However, some economists believe that economic models do not derive much predictive power from the single tool of utility maximization. The goal of behavioral economic is to develop better tools that, in some cases, can do both jobs at once. Economists like to point out the natural division of labor between scientific disciplines: Psychologists should concern to individual minds, and economists to behavior in games, markets, and economies. But the division of labor is only efficient if there is effective coordination, and all too often economists fail to conduct intellectual trade with those who have a comparative advantage in understanding individual human behavior. The only question is whether the implicit psychology in economics is good psychology or bad psychology. We think it is simply unwise, and inefficient to do economics without paying some attention to good psychology.

CHAPTER XXII

How entrepreneur applies behavioral economic strategy to do decision

Behavioral economics theories can also apply to assist any policy makers to make right and reasonable decision in right time. I shall indicate new principles to recommend and I also shall give any psychological cases to explain how policy makers can apply behavioral economic theories to judge how to make their any decision is the most right and the most reasonable.

Behavioral economy is an independent and demonstrates real economic well-being. It aims to improve quality of life by promoting innovative solutions that challenge mainstream thinking on economic, environment and social issues. Also, behavioral economy is different branches of more alternative economies into a form that is useful primarily for policy-makers. I think behavioral economy can be given an aid to policy makers how who use economic tools to the broader policy making community by providing a theoretical behaviour for many policy approaches to be used. The standard economic analysis assumes that humans are rational and behave in a way to maximize their individual self-interest. This rational man assumption indicates a powerful tool for analysis. However, it has many shortfalls that can lead to unrealistic economic analysis and policy-making. Also, I think behavioral economics and psychology has these principles to influence human behaviour. These principles include, such as below:

In common, people do many things by observing others and copying; people are encouraged to continue to do things when they feel other people approve of their behaviour. People do many things without consciously thinking about time. These habits are hard to change. There are cases where money is de-motivating as it undermines people's intrinsic motivation. People want their actions and commitments to be values usually. People put undue weight on recent events and who cann't calculate probabilities well and worry too much about unlikely events and who are strongly influences by how the problem/information is presented to them. People need to feel effective to make a change, even just giving who the incentives and information is not necessarily enough in any environment usually. So policy makers ought concern about these human behavior principles to judge whose behaviors are right or wrong, then who can decide to do any economic activities more reasonable, e.g. decisions of consumption, policies making, investment etc.

In fact, much of our behaviour is strongly influenced by other people's behaviour. Social learning is a process by which we take in the behavior of others to learn how to behave. In more complex situations with which we are unfamiliar, we consciously watch and learn from the behavior of others. For example, when use a new library for the first time. When we mist make a conscious decision on how to behave, our sense of social identity is important, we think: how would other from my group behave in this situation? In situations where there is high social capital. i.e. where there are strong networks between people and a high level of mutual trust, so its seems other people's behaviour and our sense of social identity may be extremely important in influencing our own behavior and policy makers ought need to know how to judge their behaviour whether their behavior is either right and reasonable or wrong and unreasonabe in any learning process of environment. The standard economic theory is tried to explain where people's preferences come from, so it does not take account of the direct influence of the people's behaviour and social norms on our behaviour. The theory assumes we independently know what we want and that our preferences are fixed. This standard theory is very good at explaining short-term decision making. For example, I want green vegetables and choose fruits as they are on special offer, but it cannot explain longer term changes in preferences. I now only choose organic food. Along the same lines the importance of institutions, such as regulations, for example, how people organise markets and the evolution of the whole economi system are not subjects of general economic analysis. This has significant implications for policy design.

In fact, the standard economic theory also assumes that people carry out a full rational analysis of all consumers' available options. This is not what we do; we often just copy the actions of other people. For example, it would require too much effort to look up all the rules when driving in a new country, to find out all the fines/punishments for failing to meet the rules, to work out the probability of being caught and the possible costs, before deciding how to drive there. Instead we just copy other people, and perhaps adjust our behaviour according to the feedback we receive. However, some psychologists indicate to see people how to behave, especically in crises situations and when others are experts. These psychologists have identified that we are open to influence from people in authority or people we like. When we are influenced by authority, an expert, someone with legitimate power to direct our actions, someone who can either reward or punish us. The effects are less likely to be lasting than we are influenced by someone we like.

However, some people's psychological behaviour is similar to economic behaviour to judge to make any decision. For example, why do you wear a seatbelt in your car? Most of us wear seatbelts as it has become normal behaviour, everyone does it. We neither evaluate the likelihood of having an accident, nor the chance of getting caught without our seatbelt on and incurring a fine. The enforcement of seatbelt wearing is now hardly necessary, as it has become a social norm. What does this mean for policy makers? Policy makers focusing only on economic analysis may often devise a system that has an immediate effect. In psychologists view this issue point, knowing that there is a fine for speeding and a high likelihood of getting caught, the driver will probably drive more slowly, but who will drive just as fast one who realise the chance of being caught is low. However, of policy makers can change the social norm, perhaps in this case by encouraging us to frown on others who drive dangerously fast with campaigns against dangerous driving, then less enforcement will be needed after the change. In other words policy makers might want to take preferences as fixed in the short term, but they should consider shifting preferences in the medium term. An example where policy appears to have successfully changes people's preferences in the US and Singapre and Hong Kong is banning smoking in public places. This change appears to reduce the social proof of the amount people smoke in private places and public places both also. It seems that government policies can influence the decreasing numbers of consumers require to buy cigeratte to smoke habitually, due to fine and punishment is regulated to be ban effectively. Such daily routines quickly became habits. Even when we consciously think about what we do, it can be difficult to change our behaviour. Perhaps I think it is a good idea for people to use public transport, but I do not know where the bus stop is or when the bus runs. I think to use private car to drive to work place is more preference choice. The reward feeling , my journey by car was easy and free to reinforce my old bad habit. Psychologists theories on changing habits generally involve raising it to a conscious level where we can consider the merits of alternative behaviour. This is followed by adopting the new behaviour, which, with time, becomes frozen as a new habit. Thus, I think that we need have regulation to control my behaviour, then we can change my behaviour to be new habit from old habit of behaviour easily. For example, human blood sale is an economic product, due to paying donors for blood would increase supply. Supplies would be provided at a cost advantage in the future, if demand continued to rise. Such as supplies to hospitals for blood will has cost from donors when there are many patients need much blood to use to treat any diseases in any hospitals. Otherwise, if there are not many patients need much blood to use, but there are many donors have effort to provide blood to any hospitals, then it will be economic inefficiency and it is highly wasteful of blood. Thus, the blood donors whose blood supplies of behavior and the cost of blood which will concern to the hospitals patients' numbers of demand, so their behavior and economy has close relationship in the hospital blood demand market.

For shareholder behaviour example, if you hold some shares in a firm that has gone down in value. What do you do? Many people hold on to their shares in this situation, in the hope that they will recoup their losses. Conversely, when shares have gone up in share, people are happy to sell them to realise their gain, A similiar behaviour is also observed for professional traders who tend to hold on to shares with a loss for longer than those with a gain. The traders who exhibit this type of loss to a lesser degree tend to be the more successful ones.

For another example, this is a case where the theory is directly applicable within economic cost-benefit-type analyses that include valuations of no-market products, such as valuations of pollution damage. Policy makers have a choice as to whether-to-accept, and as these may vary by up to a factor, the outcome of such an analysis many well depend on which value is chosen. When a policy maker reasonably has a right to something that might be taken away from them, the willing-to-accept value would be used. On the other hand, when the policy maker only reasonable has a right to the status quo and an improvement is proposed, then the willingness-to-pay is the correct value to use.

What behavioral economic preferences regarding time discounting theory would pay and the conclude that the discounted psychologists have long established utility model, which continues to be that people don't make decisions in widely used by economists, has little the way assumed. In generaly, people are expected to rationally make the best choices given their preferences, independent of how these choices are presented. Therefor more information and choice is always considered good. Using this theory, policy makers should ensure that people always have as much information and as many things to choose between as possible, the process of introducing policy is irrelevant. Ideas from behavioural economic indicate, however that this is not the right approach.

However, we know from experimental economics that more choice and more information can lead to a feeling of helplessness or reduced self-efficiency. Hence, if people hope have better solutions to a probem. Instead, providing people with opportunities for inderstanding, exploration and participation engages powerful motivations for competence, being needed. In summary, people 's self-efficacy increases and they are motivated toward implementing the solutions. i.e. changing their behaviour in a desired way. So, a participatory approach not only improves policy, it also makes to any policy makers more happier. In most cases these principles cannot be used directly as part of any mathematical economics analysis, but highlight situations where this standard analysis will not accurately describe human behaviour and therefore might have unintended consequences when implemented in policy. However, that the policy implications could be quite powerful as the behavioural approach provides quite different lines of analysis to the standard economic model. It is heartening to see policy makers focusing more on the psychology of behaviour when devising policy. So behavioral economics is a relatively new field of economics that attempts to incorporate insights from psychology into economic models and analyses. As above cases seem any policy maker's economic activites which are relative to whose psychology's decision. However, psychologists are often interest in understanding at the level of individual or social group of behaviour, the primary interest in economic is usually in understanding how behaviour and interactions play out in a system to shape economic outcomes. Economists are interested in system-level outcomes, such as the level and path of wages, the effect of taxes on economic output, how rates of savings respond to interest rates etc. However, those economic outcomes depend on complex interactions of individuals. So, behavioural economy concerns to how to judge individual to do the reasonable or right behaviour to hope to get the reasonable economic result as well as it's goal rather to help improve any policy makers to understand their behaviour in ways that allow economists to make better predictions and suggest better economic policies. However, new elements about information processing or individual preferences might impact economic models and analyses.

Is psychology influencing all field of economics? It is possible that behavioral economy needs theoretical contributions and laboratory evidence to support to make any reasonable or right decision to any policy makers. This type of work generally uses existing observational data and estimates relationships between variables of interest by either using naturally occurring variation in the data i.e. natural experiment.

Perhaps more than any other field, behavioral economics has had a large impact on finance to the point that behavior finance is often considered a separate field as opposed to being of behavioral economics. Also, public economic is the study of how government policies in fluence economic markets. A primary emphasis of public economic involves the topic of taxation. Otherwise, the biggest impact that the behavioral approach has had in economic is the analysis of retirement saving to influence any employees‘ decisions about their retirement savings. However, when employees can do make any active savings choices to prepare their retirement. If employers can assist whose employees to design any methods to allocate fund, then accumuates interest and is tax free until the retirement funds are withdrawn to every retirement employee. The tax advantage make effort to save for retirement.

Behavioral economic is in understanding how individuals do or do not smooth consumption over time. Smoothing consumption is a standard economic models. It suggests that individuals should borrow or save in order to consume a similar amount throughout one's lifetime. For example, a teacher who is paid a salary 12 months a year, who should not spend all whose salary within one year. Rather, the teacher should smooth whose consumption over the 12 month period. How to allocate to spend paychecks, food and social security payments which concerns the teacher decide to spend whose salary efficiently. Hence, who needs to plan how he shall spend whose one year salary to be reasonable use in the future. Public economic is to understand how people respond to taxation and social benefit programs. This has been an area that has seen an explosion of behavioral work in recent year. i.e. how taxpayers can experience over-withholding and receive tax refunds from tax department.

Policymakers and insurers are also increasingly turning to psychology for approaches to improve health behavior. Traditionally health-policy focused largely on information provision, assuming that as long as individuals were well informed, their decisions would maximize their health choices. Influential work on the effects of smoking taxes, however, well being of smokers appears to increase with higher taxes to influence health behaviours are not completely rational.

Behavioral economic has also had a small impact on the study of criminal behaviour. For example, individuals are not less likely to commit a crime when who are 18 age and the pubishment of doing so increases dramatically. However, some economists explain the motivations people have for giving to charity and who understand the psychological motivations for charitable giving. So, it seems that charity award giving has probable to reduce 18 age people who choose to do crime behaviour easily because who feel who have effort to assist charity in their life time.

Industrial organization economists study why firms exist and how which function and compete with each other. Insights and psychology and behavioral economics have made a significant contribution to develop that model the interactions of profit maximizing firms with their customers. In fact, firms often need to evaluate whether their products if prices are needed to set what of price of level is the most reasonable and attractive to customers to choose to buy their products. For example, individuals choose cell phone plans with fixed minute allotments and steep charges for going over the minute limits, but frequently exceed their plan limits. This behavior is the best explained by a model in which people overestimate the precision of their demand forecasts. So, cell phone firms need to research how cell phone plans with fixed minute allotments ans steep charges of cell phone call fee charge plan is the most acceptance method to cell phone clients generally. However, cell phone call charge plan and various cell phone product features and the way cell phone clients allocate their limited attention affects cell phone products markets which are external important factors can influence any cell phone clients why who will choose to use the cell phone call plan because any cell phone will be very large durable product to any cell phone consumer after who choose to buy the cell phone product. Hence, who will not often choose to use the old cell phone firm call charge plan if who feel it provides the excellent cell phone call service and reasonable phone call plan to use to compare other cell phone call plans in the cell phone call market. Hence, the cell phone call firm needs to research why consumers need to choose to use which cell phone call plan among of other cell phone call plans in the cell phone call market. Also, researching the cell phone buyers' choice behaviour why who choose to buy the cell phone to use issue, which will have influence to the cell phone buyer why who choose to use the cell phone call charge plan because expensive cell phone is needed to use excellent quality of cell phone call service usually. Otherwise, cheap cell phone is needed to use poor quality of cell phone call service usually. So, cell phone call plan is needed to follow the cell phone quality and price to be used and they ought have direct relationship to influence why the cell phone buyer who chooses to use the cell phone call plan.

Finally, behavioral economic can also apply to be used to labor supply as a motivating in negative or positive labor supply elasticities example. For example, it is possible that taxi drivers work fewer hours when wages are high-consistent with a model of daily income targeting. This finding is that when wages are high (perhaps it is raining and thus it is easy to find people who want a taxi ride), taxi drivers are able to hit their daily target quickly and then go home. However, when wages are low, taxi drivers are not able to hit their target quickly and thus work additional hours in order to hit their target. It means taxi driver's behaviour produce the effect that taxi driver works more when wages are low than when wagers are high. This work has resulted to analyze taxi driver of labor supply decisions with daily reference points in non taxi domains. So, instead of the weather and client numbers and taxi charge factors, the factors of taxi drivers‘ hours worked and the quality of service is produced is another important factor to influence any taxi drivers' numbers to supply to the taxi market.

Behavioral economic has also influenced the understanding of how staffs can impact worker productivity and job satisfaction. For example, it is possible that poor cooperation can cause worker productivity decreases and it can also cause poor job satisfaction to the worker. So, when working environment can impact productivity, social comparisons can have an impact on job satisfaction as well as the worker's job satisfaction and search intentions are affected by knowing about the salaries of their peers in whose firm. Hence, the worker's positive or negative psychological feeling to whose employers which will have effort to influence whose working performance and productivity to whose firm in possible.

Behavioral economic is increasingly being used in the field of development economics or low income countries. Such as, how Philippines can offer commitment to individuals who wanted to save money in whose country or how Philippines can change to smoking behaviour when commitment devices were offered to Philippine smokers. So, Philippines policy makers need to concern resource scarcity and resource allocation issue to solve how to let its low income level householders can raise to the middle income level to achieve the high income level householders and the low income level householders whose income level is not distant very much.

CHAPTER XXIII

Consumer psychology and economy environment close relationship

Entrepreneurs need to understand consumer psychology and economy environment has close relationship. Finally, I shall analyze whether the relationship between the discipline of behavioral economy and psychology which two branches are totally opposite or if the behavioral theories are only complement that mainstream economics.

I think study of economics is the behavior of the complex human beings; this science examines how people choose to act and allocate resources in different market situations. So the economic analysis, is based on the implications that arise from a series of simple assumptions (which are sometimes cited as unrealistic) regarding the human nature. However, in psychological view, the individual is characterized by unlimited rationality and by the ability to follow time consistent, in every situation, his self-interest. In these conditions, behavioral economic attempts to consider a field of analysis in the study of economic phenomena. Because economics deals with the study of human behaviour on the market, it highlights the human character of the science and the fact that, besides of all the patterns and models, the analysis refers to the real individual. It is also behavioural because it attempts to combine approaches from several sciences mainly from economics and psychology, and also from sociology, philosophy, anthropology or biology. This is not an easy mission, in the conditions in which these various disciplines have adopted in time different approaches that became, in many ways, contradictory. So, behavioural economics is that a multidisciplinary appraoch will increase the explanatory power of economics.

On one hand, there are specialists two argue that behavioural economic is a field of economics that continues the hand, there are others who see it as a distinctive school of thought, which proposes a new paradigm. However, behavioural economists propose a multidisciplinary study, criticize certain assumptions on which the traditional model is built (such as rationality and self-interest, in their unlimited form), resource to experiments (the classical method of psychology) to validate some assumptions, propose new theories (such as the prospect theory) and advance different interpretations of the economic behaviour, e.g. how to maximize consumers satisfy their needs. This issue is concerned to concern consumption of pshchology and social economic situation research aspect.

Also, I think that behavioural economics can help the economic science by describing more realistically the utility functions of the individuals. This field of study is based rather it is a natural extension of the basic approach. However, it is can be claimed that behavioural economics is also built on the premise that psychology methods and assumptions are equally important. Also, models of behavioural economics, allow the utility to depend on the differences between one's own level and a reference level. People are sensitive to changes and preferences are not stable in time. The vision of behavioural economics concerning the inter-temporal choice (which assumes that individuals prefer immediate gains and delay unpleasant activities) seems to be more appropriate to the human behaviour that the one of the traditional model (which assumes that utility is updated over time).

In conclusion, I shall indicate two theories to explain why economy and psychology has close relationship to influence human do any behavioural economic activities daily. For example, through the prospect theory, behavioural economics adds new parameters to improve the mathematical modelling method, which was advanced by economists for decisions taken under uncertainty. However, the theory also proposes a slightly different interpretation. The results are interpreted by the individual as positive or negative deviations from a reference point, which has a neutral psychological value.

Last but not least, in addressing social preferences, behavioural economics adds parameters that increase the concern of decision-makers to also assess their utility function in relation to others. For another example, the choice theory; secondly there is not a common consensus between the specialists of behavioural economics regarding the variables that should be included; and finally, many variables that affect the behaviour are not quantitative, but qualitative, and cannot be precisely measured. The findings of behavioural economic are relevant and can help the mainstream theory by providing a more realistically base of study. However, this argument has contributed to the development of behavioural economics, because there are a large number of phenomena that cannot be entirely emplained by the mainstream economics. So, why in the beginning, I indicated why behavioural economics does not imply the totally exclusion of the neoclassical approach and the most studies in this area try to provide a more realistic base of the standard theory.

In the concluding, I believe that in time, behavioural economic models will replace the simplified ones, based on unlimited rationality. Also, economists have provided a great importance to the quantitative structures, departing from the human nature. However, behavioural economics can become truly revolutionary only it it will always be receptive and will provide a critical insight to their own theories and perspectives, and especially the ones regarding the aspects that they reproach to the traditional economic theory. However, I also feel that the individual's behaviour on the market is determined only be economic factors. In brief, individual choices and, by this, the demand variation are explained only and the variations in the prices of products/services and the available personal income. Am inportant discussion in the field of determine directly the economic behaviour of an individual (like the sociological and psychological of factors) are actually active elements in the process the reshaping of the utility functions. Finally, in my view, I believe that the conduct of the market phenomena, as it occurs in reality. In this sense, the research of behavioural economics aims to see how the neoclassical model could be improved, using mainly psychology concepts. Although, there are some specialists who argue that behavioural economics can be an alternative to the neoclassical theory.

Most findings, of my study conducted in this book, modify some of standard economical assumptions, in order to provide a greater psychological realism. However, the additions proposed by behavioural economists simply recognize the human limitations on (mentally) calculations, will and self-interest. So, I think psychology and economy has close relationship to influence any policy makers or decision makers to do any economic psychology daily. Because the purpose of economics is to better understand and explain the conduct of the economic activities as which occur in reality. Otherwise, human being is complex and its behaviour and constitution is studied by all the social sciences. Consequently, multi and interdisciplinary approaches can bring real benefits to the economic science, by providing a more realist foundation to cause any policy makers or decision makers how to decide to make any behaviours or economic activities by behavioural economic activities support daily.

CHAPTER XXIV

Body Shop case study

Critically assess the extent to which whether Body Shop to be a truly marketing oriented organization throughout its 30 years history.

- Body Shop Background

The body shop international power line carrier (the body shop) was founded by Dame Anita Roddick in the England in 1976. It sold personal beauty care products, such as baby and child specific products, bath and shower and colour cosmetics, deodorants, skin care, hair care, fragrances, sun care etc skin health products to provide human body benefits. Nowadays, the body shop was skin and body care manufacturer and retailer operating in 55 countries with over 2,100 stores. It had 42 exclusive outlets in Hong Kong. It's missions were to dedicate to pursuit of social and environment change to meaningfully contribute to local, national and international communities in which trade to passionately campaign for the protection of the environment, human and civil rights and against animal testing and to make fun, passion and care part of our daily lives (Adrian, P. 2012).

- What is the difference between production orientation and societal marketing orientation and sales orientation

There are five main marketing orientations of which a company will adopt one. This will determine the way it interacts with the customer. Such as product orientation suggests that a company focuses inwards looking at what it is capable of, rather than the needs and wants of the client; sales orientation is based upon selling existing products with a turnover sale numbers relationship marketing orientation recognizes the value of repeat business over, not only with customers but suppliers as well; societal marketing orientation is relatively new in the scheme of things but suggests on top of meeting the needs and wants of the customer and the organization there is the societies interests to be looked and marketing orientation is based around the needs and wants of a customer to meet business objectives and it assumes that a sale depends on a customer's decision to purchase a product or provide a service.

- What is marketing two levels meaning ?

Marketing can be seen at two levels, the first level is such as a business philosophy, marketing puts customers at the center of an organization's consideration and which is reflected in basic values , such as the requirement to understand and respond to customers' needs and the necessary to search constantly for new market opportunity. In a truly marketing oriented organization, these values are instilled in all employees and should influence their behavior without any need for prompting. The personnel manager would have a selection policy that recruited staff who could fulfil the needs of customers rather than simply minimizing the wage bill in any marketing oriented organization. The other level is techniques of marketing also include pricing, the design of channels of distribution and new product development.

- What are the three components of market orientation ?

The assessing the nature and importance of market orientation for large firms, such as body shop. The three components of market orientation could be analytically separated. The components of market orientation organization include the first component is the customer orientation, it means an organization must have a thorough understanding of its target buyers, so that it can create a product of superior value to give client benefits ; the second component is the competitor orientation, it means any firm should look at how well its competitors are able to satisfy buyers' needs. It should understand the short term strengths and weaknesses and long term capabilities and strategies of current and potential competitors as well as the third component is to develop marketing plans that are not acted upon by people who are capable of delivering promises made to customers and a marketing orientation organization requires that the organization draws upon and integrates its human and physical resources effectively and adapts them to meet client's needs. Otherwise, a production and sales orientation may be appropriate to firms at certain stages in the evolution of markets. Where the dominant business environment is based on the need for good production planning above all, the company that does this best will achieve the greatest overall business success. It is either production orientation, it means organizations that produce what they imagined consumers wanted, rather than what they actually wanted. Planning for full utilization of capital equipment are often seen as more important than ensuring that equipment is used to provide goods and services that people actually wants. Production-oriented firms generally aim for efficiency in production rather than effectiveness in meeting customer's needs . It is either or selling orientation, it means advertising, sales promotion and personal selling techniques are used to emphasize product differentiation and brands and it does not focus on satisfying client needs or desire new product offerings and production led. Hence, one market orientation organization needs to focus on satisfying clients' needs profitably by these marketing mix, such as product, price, place, physical evidence, processed, people and promotion. Anyway ,Market orientation implied that body shop , which ought seek information about clients, such as current and future needs and took action based this information (client orientation); it ought seek information about competitors' current strengths and weaknesses and their long term strategies and took actions based on these information (competitor orientation) ; it ought coordinate the actions taken by sharing clients and competitors information internally (intra-firm communication).

- What is the three components of market orientation ?

The three components of market orientation meant social marketing and understanding boarder concerns and ethical environmental, legal and social context of marketing activities and programs. The cause and effects of marketing clearly beyond the company and the consumer to society as whole. New terms humanistic marketing and ecological marketing were suggested to societal marketing concept.

- What is the social marketing concept ?

The social marketing concept holds that the organization's task is to determine the needs, wants and interests of target markets and to deliver the desired satisfactions more effectively and
efficiently than competitors and the society's welling being, such as body shop had achieved sales and profit gains by

adopting and practicing a form of the societal marketing concept called cause related marketing.

● DISCUSSION

Body Shop is marketing orientation organization in 30 years.

Critically assess the extent to which I consider Body Shop to be a truly marketing oriented organization throughout its 30 years history . It seemed body shop had achieved cause-related marketing as an opportunity to enhance their corporate reputation, raised brand awareness, increased customer loyalty and built sales.

It's corporate values were composed of five core values. The first one was to oppose animal testing. The opposing animal testing for both cosmetic products and ingredients began in 1976 years.

In the 1980 year and 1990 year, who successfully campaigned with animal protection groups to change the UK and European laws to support the development products were tried on human

volunteers. Along with the development of technology testing had played a leading role to protect the rights of both human and animals . The second one was to support community trade, it initiated the trade not aid objective of creating trade to help people in the third world utilizing their resources to their own needs. This reflects communities needed a fair price for natural ingredients who purchased from these often marginalized countries. The third one was to activate self esteem. Women were the main customers and employees in the body shop. The fourth one was to defend human rights. The body shop had long campaign on human rights, highlighting abuses and increasing the global awareness of issues by making full use of the geographic advantages of their shops and supporting other human rights organizations. The last one was protect our plant. In 2001 year, huge campaign against global warming was hosted by the body shop and green peace, who advocated the use of recyclable source and materials (Adrian, P. 2012). Although profits were an essential element of long run survival in body shop and it was likely to be overall corporate and marketing objectives, but body shop seemed more to be required level of profits rather than profit that there were many other objectives, which might pursue through its pricing strategies . For example, if body shop wanted to maximize market share or simply survive, a different set of prices would be delivered than if the objectives were to maximize profits. Hence, body shop ought to see viewpoint the marketing side of pricing and it ought not to see viewpoint the production / supply side of pricing if it was a truly marketing oriented organization. The key inputs for body shop to make pricing decision whether it was marketing oriented or productive / supply oriented included production objectives or marketing objectives, demand or supply numbers were considered cost or sale price and competitors or clients consideration factors, such as beauty skin care products in competitive markets demand, i.e. To decide the price whether customers are willing and able to pay is a major consideration in the selection of pricing strategies and levels of demands . Hence, body shop ought to consider demand numbers , it ought not consider production / supply numbers if it was a truly marketing oriented organization. For example, since most of the body shop's factories were still located in the UK, where wages and salaries were much higher than in Asia, so UK itself sale product prices were higher than that from Asia itself sale product prices.

I think Body Shop was a truly marketing oriented organization more than production/supply oriented organization throughout its 30 years history. In fact, Body Shop was experiencing market level growth. It could expand its sales market in Europe, America, Middle East, Asia and Africa etc different countries. It seemed that it had attempted to carry on marketing research to decide to choose which countries would have more client numbers to demand to buy its personal care products, then it would follow the countries' estimated client numbers to produce its products to sell to the countries. So, it was why some Asia countries sold its bath and shower and skin and hair care and colour cosmetics products more than its fragrances products, such as Hong Kong young people were more acceptable to use bath and show and color cosmetic and skin and hair care products more than fragrances products . It seemed that Hong Kong Body Shop sold fragrance products numbers were less than bath and shower and color cosmetics etc. products. Nowadays, I think the personal beauty care products new businesses which planned to entry this market was more difficult. It was possible than Body Shop was a famous personal beauty care products sale company, it had owned many clients too many years. So , it caused barriers to any new personal beauty care product competitors felt difficult to entry this market .Furthermore, Body Shop had build strong buyer and seller power to increase clients had more confident to use its products, it was possible that who felt its different kind of products could give more health to their skin or body more than other similar personal beauty care products. Moreover, I believe Body Shop had attempted to carry on technological experimenting to aim to build different countries' clients had more confident to use its products forever.

In conclusion, it seemed that Body Shop was truly marketing oriented organization more than productive/ supply oriented organization oriented organization throughout its 30 years history.

2. To what extent are the pursuits of profit and meeting the needs of wider groups of stakeholders incompatible? Whether Body shop pursuits social responsibility aim or profit aim more.

Any companies need to consider the social responsibility during which are the pursuits of profit and meeting the needs of wider group of stakeholders incompatible. Without this self interest, there will be little motivation for firms to provide better services, workers couldn't earn better salaries and clients couldn't aspire for a high level of consumption. Hence, self interest which helps markets work more effectively for the benefits of all. Hence, companies should adopt a code of behavior and conduct and ethical behavior which would not influence any stakeholders groups' benefits to pursuit their profit honestly. Corporate social responsibility is a form of corporate self regulation integrated into a business model. It aims to give responsibility for corporate actions and to encourage a positive impact on the environment and stakeholders including consumers, employees, investors, communities and others and it is titled to aid an organization's mission as well as guide to what the company can give the best benefits to serve its customers. I shall use body shop company as one example to judge whether what extent are the pursuits of profit and meeting the needs of wider groups of stakeholders will be incompatible. Factually, body shop could adopt a code of behavior and conduct and ethical behavior which would not influence any stakeholders groups' benefits to pursuit their profit honestly. Such as, one of the major and most successful initiatives which body shop used an effective supply chain for their products and body shop made use of their sustainable chain supply strategy to ensure that there was the promotion and the maintenance of the social ethical behavior in its business.

Hence, it seemed that body shop could be compatible to achieve an effective supply chain to deliver to different countries' stores to meet clients who had more need to buy different kinds of skin care products to provide them to choose to buy in the reasonable price choices in the short time. It is therefore in the best practices and interests for body shop to reach out to the communities in their businesses to provide raw materials to help the manufacturers of the beauty products. It also partook in the development of the market for such small scale suppliers. In many cases the body shop tried to outsource its raw materials to its customers. This had ensured the sustainability of its customer base this included it's sensitivity to its environment and the required standards of the labor practices of its partners. Hence, it seemed that body shop could be compatible to help its partners to earn profits and any countries' partners could provide more job chances to unemployed people to work from body shop's outsourcing strategy. Hence, this had been developed by the body shop by including strategies, such as third party logistic providers and intermediaries in which who had no ownership. The body shop was a multinational company also adopted trading to purchasing approach where it shifted from short term where focus of buying articles to long term focus of fewer suppliers. This was an attempt of it to develop quality products where prices were also fair and affordable to sell to different countries' clients. It seemed that body shop could be compatible to sell reasonable prices of products to it's clients. Moreover, it had included in its strategies the aspect of business promotion using catalogues. For the same reason, it had been involved in printing of catalogues which were given out to the clients with their purchases. It was important to note that it' catalogues always contained all it's information descriptions and any person who purchased it's products was bound to receive the explanation of all it's product. This was an attempt of it to develop quality products where prices were also fair and affordable to sell to different countries' clients. It seemed that body shop could be compatible to provide clear information description in catalogues to let whose clients to know what it's different kinds of style body skin care products ingredients and benefits were , then who could compare it's products to other competitors to decide to buy or not buy fairly.

In Oct. 2007 the campaign for safe cosmetic products, in which 25 multinational companies participated, tested 33 brand name lipsticks and found one-third of the sampled exceeded the limit of lead allowed in confectionery. The affected brands included L'Oreal and Christian Dior. A definite effect would be that consumers would be more concerned regarded the ingredients of products who used, which was likely to have an effect on cosmetics and skin care products were released to capture share. It seemed body shop needed to consider its beauty personal care products were the most ensure to own organic ingredients to let any countries clients (stakeholder) to meet their body health care needs (Adrian, P. 2012).

On the health and natural aspect, body shop had health and safe responsibility to consumers. Although, I felt who had considered this issue because it had 30 years history to operate this business and it had not received any serious negative complaints damage its health product image from clients before. However, with consumers were increasingly informed and were educated, who were now more demanding for more information regarding products and were becoming more aware of health issue. Products with organic ingredients and natural ingredients, such as tea and plants were gaining popular. Furthermore, consumers were looking for healthier substitutes to seemingly unhealthy products, such as color cosmetics. Hence, body shop began to sell the reducing numbers, it was possible due to clients compared it's body care products quality to the other competitors and who felt it's product's ingredients existed some poor ingredients to cause every one's body to be unhealthy. Hence, it's productive processing was very important. It seeméd that body shop could be compatible to consider its individual client body skin health issue whether after who had used it's body skin care products to have skin hurt or skin pain feeling. In conclusion, to judge what extent are the pursuits of profit and meeting the needs of wider groups of stakeholders incompatible for any individual business, it is depended on whether the company's any stakeholders, such as employees, clients, suppliers, partners, society (communities) etc. who will have positive or negative influence from it. I feel that it will be incompatible if the company give negative influence to any one of its stakeholder. Hence, if any one company's at least one stakeholder who felt who had negative influence due to it did business to relate to whom unwillingly, then it's pursuit of profits aim would be incompatible to meet it's needs of its any one of stakeholder. Such as body shop will give positive influence to its all stakeholders. Hence, I feel it is compatible extent to pursuit of profit and meeting the needs of its wider groups of stakeholders definitely.

3. What companies, if any have managed to sustainable reconcile these two aims?

I feel that Nestle company has managed to sustainable reconcile to pursuit profits and meeting the needs of its wider groups of stakeholders two aims compatibly. Nestle was the world's largest food and beverage company. Nestle in the United States, which represented seven operating across the USA country and it was the first expanded effort in USA and achievement tied to Nestle 's global sustainability principle and commitment. Nowadays, It served 97% of American householders and Nestle 's mission was to lead the industry in nutrition, health and wellness and to create a more sustainable future. Instead of it's mission was to pursuit of profits aim, it had also achieved specific sustainability commitment and progress in the categories of nutrition, environmental impact and water use, social impact, rural development and responsible sourcing to meet the needs of it's wider of groups of stakeholders' aim. On the nutrition, health and wellness aspect, Nestle met the needs to its stakeholder (clients), such as, Nestle rolled out new portion guidance tools and launched an educational campaign and balance your plate to help consumers build nutritious and delicious and convenient meals that met the dietary guidelines for Americans; Nestle also reduced sodium content in many of its most popular brands, such as Stouffer's and DiGiorno and committed to further reduce sodium content by 10 percent in products that did not meet the Nestle; Nestle also reduced sugar content, such as ninety six percent of Nestle 's children's products met the Nestle criteria for low sugar and by the end of 2014 year, 100 percent of children's products would meet these criteria as well as Nestle also removed trans-fat content, such as Nestle committed to reach zero food and beverage products with trans-fat originating to use as functional ingredients by 2016 year. It seemed that Nestle had considered its food and beverage production content whether these content would have negative influence to its stakeholder (clients) nowadays (Adrian, P. 2012). On the environmental impact aspect, Nestle reduced waste during it's food and beverage products were producing. As part of its commitment to eliminate all forms of waste, Nestle reduced 44 percent of waste per ton of product since 2010 year in the USA five factory locations reached zero waste to landfill status by the end of 2013 year; Nestle also considered responsible packaging responsibility, such as Nestle Waters North America led the USA bottled water industry in light weighting packaging, in part by reducing the plastic content of its 1/2 liter bottles by 60 percent since 1994 year. Since 2003 year alone, more than 3.3 billion pounds of plastic had been saved by Nestle as well as Nestle also adopted responsible sourcing, such as Nestle Purina Pet Care implemented responsible sourcing guidelines for seafood that align with Nestle 's global responsible sourcing guidelines, working with experts to track suppliers and contribute to healthier ecosystem. In 2013 year, Nestle also reached an important target for palm oil, with 100 percent of palm oil now Round table on sustainable palm oil certified. It seemed that Nestle also considerate whether environment would have negative influence occurrence during it's production (Adrian, P. 2012). On social impact aspect, Nestle supported local communities, such as Nestle in USA donated more than $2.3 million dollars to support local United Way organizations; It also provided disaster relief, such as Nestle waters donated more than 685,000 bottled of water and Nestle Purina contributed more than 60,000 pounds of pet food and 41,000 pounds of cat little to local shelters across the USA for disaster relief as well as it grew supplier diversity, such as Nestle works with over 4,100 small, minority, women and veteran owned businesses to help to spur local economies. It seemed that Nestle also considerate social needs. Thus, it is seemed Nestle company have managed to sustainable reconcile these two aims to pursuit profit as well as it also could gave positive influence to its stakeholders. Such as consumer could feel safe to enjoy to eat Nestle company's health foods; societies could be reduced unemployment from its outsourced assistance job to partners; natural environment could be reduced pollution from its productive protection. Hence, it was not actually neglect its shareholders' benefits during it was doing business as the same time (Adrian, P. 2012).

4. What are basic lessons in marketing that the Body Shop might have taken on board in its early years in order to improve its chances of long term success?

The body shop is a global manufacturer and retailer of naturally inspired , ethically produced beauty and cosmetics products. Founded in the UK in 1976 year by Dame Anita Roddick, who now have 2,133 stores in 55 countries with a range of over 1,200 products in Europe, America, Middle East, Asia and Africa. However, the body shop has not entered the China market. It takes a strong position on activism, ethical business, human rights and environmentalism in a global perspective. The body shop is banned in China because cosmetics sold there have to be tested on animals, according to Roddick. In, 2006 when it was bought by the French cosmetics company L'Oreal which is a big player in China. China has launched scientific developing strategy for future the current policies of advocating. Hence, it is the perfect time for the body shop to enter China market. However, prior to that, as an independent member of the L'Oreal family, the body shop has to make decisions on differentiation marketing strategies, market segmentation and marketing position (Adrian, P. 2012). It might have taken two purposes to body shop marketing in its early years in order to improve its chances from short term to long term success. The short term objective was to generate more sales for the body shop. Through, the introduction of a new service, the market up class, it was hoped that clients could try and experience the body shop cosmetic products. Positive experience of using its products could then be developed through their trial using the market up class. It was estimated that this positive experience could push up the sales.

The long term objective was to educate the belief of the body shop to the young potential clients, so that who would become those who preferred natural cosmetic products and were loyal to the body shop in the future. Objectives could provide the starting point for marketing plans and strategies and should be specific targets that are obtained but also challenging. Specific, measurable, agreed, realistic and time related objectives might be taken to body shop to improve early years in chances in long term success. It seemed that Hong Kong was one good market for body shop to satisfy an unfulfilled customers needs to pursue body shop investment chance. Therefore, the objective were to push up sales and built a loyal customer basis for the future. For example, Hong Kong was one young student clients growth market to body shop. In the past, one cosmetic products market statistic was indicated that the colour cosmetic retail value had been increasing from 2002 year, HK$938.3 million dollars to 2007 year, HK$1,132,3 million dollars, so percentage was increased to 5.12% . (Adrian, P. 2012). It seemed Hong Kong might be one good skin cosmetic care products developed market to this body shop in early years. The another factor might improve body shop long term success factor was whether body shop had attempted to analyze direct competition. The body shop's direct competition was not from the name brand like Dior, Chanel or Olay, but rather the less well known brands, from Japan or Korea. Along with the great impact of Korean fashion, many Korean cosmetics brands like Missha and the Face shop had already established shops in China. These two brands also promoted their natural ingredients and target the young customer segment as what the body shop products competition concept could be offered to a market to satisfy a want or need and offered five levels, which were the core benefits, basic product, expected product, augmented product and potential product. Each level added more customer value and the five constitute client value hierarchy products of these three brands were all using natural ingredients and simple and natural in packaging. The body shop , however, differentiated itself at the top levels of the five product and transformations the products might undergo in the future.

Marketing management and planning was essential to body shop, it was the implementation of strategies to achieve long run profitability to body shop and growth. When body shop was looking at how it would achieve this in early years in order to improve the chances long term success, its two keys points to consider are: What was body shop man activity at a particular time? And how it would reach its goals? It might design a strategy that insured a consistent approach to offer its skin care products to raise competition in mind the skin care products changing market. These included product line, distribution methods, marketing communication and pricing. For example, achieving marketing research to Hong Kong and China skin care products market to analyze what were these factors to influence these country people who felt needs to buy its skin care products: Such as internal factors include personality, motivation, learning, perception and attitude; external factors included culture, social class, reference groups , family and personal influences and situational factors included time, income, mobility and availability. The reason was because due to consumers bought skin care products to protect whose skin (core benefits) and their expectations if who were willing to pay more basic product. To enhance the product level, body shop skin health product needed emphasize that skin products were natural. Products of the body shop offered the same effective and natural and flavor and unique corporate values. Body shop was mostly natural (augmented level). Far more than the visible products, the shop shop's unique corporate values create the potential value to fulfil customer's desire of making a better health world. It's good corporate desire citizenship went beyond supplying rational and emotional benefits. Body shop might enter China market to improve long term success. The body shop divided its markets to include overseas Pacific Europe, America , Australia and New Zealand, Middle East, Africa and local UK countries. Adrian, P.(2012) indicated that a sampling questionnaire survey was conducted among 200 consumers, ranging from 18 to 50 ages in May 2006, a total of 170 valid responses that were used for analysis. Among the 170 responses, 66% were females. The findings were:

(1) About 60 % hoped that cosmetics could be a symbol of being environmental friendly.
(2) 90% would choose products made of natural ingredients.
(3) 90% spent less than 300 RMB on cosmetics and skin care products quarterly.
(4) 83% Chinese youth (age range from 18 to 25 ages) were innovators and conscious of environment.

Hence, the body shop might take a share of potential market in China. It should launch its products among younger cosmetic industry were young females who chased beauty and were willing to spend money on it. So, packaging was one of the vital factors in attracting client. The body shop took a unique approach by choosing simple packaging. The package was not made for mature women. It was made for young female students, who could enjoy on international brand at an inexpensive cost. The body shop was not only to meet young people's demand for beauty , but the demand of being responsible to environment and human rights. Hence, the target market of the body shop should focus on young people ageing from 15 ages to 30 ages. Hence, body shop might take marketing research in Hong Kong and China market to have more confident to invest in these market to improve more success. Next, Whether body shop might achieve price strategy to improve to raise success chance. An assumption is when the individual client is considering the price of any a body shop's beauty skin health product. Economic theory suggests that the customer will act in a totally rational economic manner, such that body shop's every client total utility (or satisfaction) is maximized. In deciding whether try or not try body shop's product, which totally rational consumer will carefully equate whether ought to buy or ought not buy body shop's product at the asking price set will maximizing whose utility. In making judgment, the economist assumes that the consumer has perfect information about both the prices and utility of all the other competitive products in the market and that price is the only consideration in choice. Clearly there are unrealistic assumptions. Price could be determined easily when a target market was identified. (Adrian, P. 2012) From survey indicated 64% of the 170 responses spent less than 1000 RMB on cosmetics and skin care every quarter and 24% of their expenditure was between 100 RMB and 300 RMB on cosmetics an skin care. This number could not be ignored if a cosmetics company wanted to enter this large market and be a leader. For the younger generation, the prices of the products could not be high. The price of these main competitors ranges from 10RMB to 200 RMB. The prices in Hong Kong have higher than that in the USA or the UK. And the consumer's purchasing power in mainland China is much lower than that of Hong Kong . Hence, body shop should adopt a price range in China which was similar to that of the USA or the UK rather than of Hong Kong. Once the body shop established greatly reduced and the capability of price adjustment would be achieved accordingly. Further, body shop might have chain stores selling channel strategy to attempt to achieve long term success. Sample survey revealed that supermarket was for Chinese to purchase skin care and cosmetics. 120 out of the 170 responses hoped that who could choose products from the chain stores in the future, which suggested that the body shop should build up its own stores was regarded as cares about corporate culture and corporate image. It insisted on selling in its own stores rather than setting up counters in a shopping mall. The stores of body shop could be found easily worldwide because of stores were importance in this competitive buyer. Hence, in China, its appearance should be same as worldwide. Some housewives joined the body shop as sales agent and hold sales parties for other housewives. The sales channel allowed the body shop to reach out to more clients by bringing the store directly into client's homes. This would be a totally new method of marketing in China, but it offered a good opportunity for women to choose products and share feedback in a relaxed atmosphere. This fresh concept could attract female consumers. Nowadays, students in China could only obtain famous skin care products and cosmetics brands from campus agents, as who could not afford the products sold over the counters. It was a major problem that agents could not guarantee the ingredients and the quality of the goods. If the body shop could hold small parties to share products and opinions, that would be a good way to boost sales among students. Hence, body shop might take price strategy to Hong Kong and china market to predict whether what price who could accept to raise more confident to invest to this market to improve more success. Further, body shop might also have promotion strategy to attempt to achieve long term success. The body shop adopted environmental friendly manufacturing, opposed abuses of human rights and was accountable for its actions. The unique values attracted numbers of media groups in many countries. This results in its establishing a good reputation without any advertisements. The body shop also joined numerous social causes, which substitute advertisements. In China, however, it was totally different. In this brand new market, most people were out aware of this company. If it carried on a marketing promotion of no commercials it was impossible to reach a high market share. Hence, commercial advertisements were needed in China. The body shop could use this advertisement to give on impression that women should care about their well being both mentally and physically and it had created a sexy grand with simple packaging and without objectifying women. Many brands reach customers directly by colorful commercials and show their products in movies and TV play series. For the sakes of brand image, some movies about human rights , environmental protection and animal protection could be chosen by the body shop as carriers for particular commercial as most of the audiences were well educated, well paid and environmentally concerned. The target consumers of the body shop aged from 20 to 40 ages were energetic , knowledgeable and environmentally concerned. The body shop could give some lectures on makeup or skin care on campuses to raise feeling among students. To reach brand awareness and high brand loyalty , some samples should be given to students by experience marketing approach. Hence, body shop might take promotion to Hong Kong and China schools to let many young people to know why who needed to buy skin care products to protect their body skin to persuade who felt more needs. In conclusion, the body shop was famous for creating a niche market sector for naturally inspired skin care and cosmetic products through it's unique corporate values worldwide. The significance of the body shop's early entry into China market were strongly proposed. Once the body shop decided to enter the China market, the relevant marketing strategies and management should be implemented, such as the market segmentation and market positioning with the proper consideration of Chinese consumers should be studied in order to win the mind share of potential Chinese customers with the right marketing strategies. Overall, the findings of market survey and theoretical analysis strategy support the feasibility of the body shop's early entry into China market.

CHAPTER XXV

Case study change in the marketing environment on sales of ready meals to supermarket, such as Walt Mark

Using an appropriate framework of analysis, briefly summarize the effects of change in the marketing environment on sales of ready meals.

Although, previously dismissed and a poor substitute for real cooking and ready meal sales have grown rapidly in recent years in many western developed countries, such as UK, France or Germany. But, Ready meal manufacturers ready to respond to a changing marketing environment. Due to one big change in recent year has been growing demand for ready prepared meals bought from a supermarket. An analysis of the reasons for the growth in the ready prepared meals markets indicates the effects of boards factors in the marketing environment on the size of a particular market. In fact, this food market is changing to drive the growth in the ready meals market, but there are differences in the food market potential between countries. The effect of change in the marketing environment on sales of ready meals, such as technology has played a big role in the growing take up of ready meals and new technologies have allowed companies to develop ready meals which preserve taste and texture, which still making them easy to use by the consumer. Furthermore, great advances in distribution management, in particular the use of information technology to control inventories, has allowed fresh, chilled ready meals to be effectively and efficiently distributed without the need for freezing or added preservatives. Ready meals particularly appeal to single householders, which individual family members tend to eat at different times, so family meals together remains stronger in many continental European countries than in the UK individual ready meals. Young people have lost the ability to cook creatively, as cookery has been reduced in importance in the school, so young clients group will rise to buy ready meals from supermarket. Marketing can be seen as a system that must respond to environmental change. A food market can be defined as a meeting place for stakeholder (consumers) and sellers. Food market can be set up in a supermarket or restaurants. A food market consists of the individual's target taste, such as older group, family group, young group or business clients who are actual or potential caters of a restaurant meals or supermarket package of foods. Grocery stores (supermarkets) have an influence of meals (fast cooked food) outlets in low income urban areas, which has contributed to the income in access to healthy foods. An organization's marketing environment means the individuals, organizations, and forces external to the marketing management's ability to develop and maintain successful exchanges with its customers. The marketing environment to ready meal manufacturers had three levels.

Firstly, it includes the micro environment, it describes those elements that impinge directly on the ready meal manufacturers themselves, so the micro environment of ready meal manufacturers which include business clients who have direct contact, such as restaurants, supermarkets and individual clients who have direct contact. Otherwise, supermarket shoppers, restaurant clients and food supply competitors who have no direct contract to ready meal manufacturers, so who won't include in food market micro environment to ready meal manufacturers. Secondly, it includes the macro environment, it describes things that are beyond the immediate environment but can nevertheless affect an organization, so the macro environment of ready meal manufacturers which include the export countries' economies forces, such as unemployment ratio, GDP; technological forces, such as the export countries' factories food productive technology; social/ cultural forces, such as the export countries' people taste acceptance; political/legal forces, such as the export countries' import food quota numbers. Thirdly, it includes the internal environment, it describes ready meal manufacturers' employees and equipment and finance and functional responsibilities. Environment means everything outside influences the person, in contrast with individual or personal variables . The effects of change in the marketing environment on sales of ready meals can be analyzed by creating healthy food and eating environment changing factor and supermarket technological changing factor as below:

The ready meal manufacturers could not ignore threats to the natural ecological environment change Due to the food companies could have technology to manufacture good taste cooked ready meals to provide to supermarkets to sell. Thus, it might influence the consumers to decide whether restaurants or supermarkets or ready meals suppliers who could provide the most reasonable price and taste to satisfy whose eating needs every day. Thus, it caused the growing demand for ready prepared cooked meals bought from supermarkets. Due to it was possible that consumers felt to eat ready cooked meals in expensive restaurants or who did not like to buy foods to cook from food suppliers or who could not feel which could supply more good food taste and health food quality to compare supermarkets specially. Otherwise, although, supermarkets could provide cheaper ready cooked meals to satisfy who to feel good food taste and health food quality. Due to ready meal manufacturers had new techniques to develop ready meals which preserve taste and texture, which still making them easy to use to eat by the consumers. Furthermore, great advances in distribution management, in particular the use of information technology to control inventories, has allowed fresh , chilled ready meals to be effectively and efficiently distributed to supermarkets or restaurants without the need for freezing or added preservatives. Creating healthy food and eating environments view describes an ecological framework for conceptualizing the many food environments and conditions that influence food choices, with an emphasis on current knowledge was been regarding the home, child care, school, work site, retail store and restaurant settings. The status of measurement and evaluation of nutrition environment and the need of action to improve health are highlighted in marketing environment. More processed and convenience foods are available in large portion sizes and which were supplied at relatively low prices at supermarkets. Parents are working larger hours, there are fewer family meals and more meals are eaten away from home. The school food environment is remarkably different. It seemed that it would be changed in the marketing environment on sales of ready cooked meals to supermarket more easily. Due to supermarkets' cooked meals should focus on selling high calorie and low nutrition foods are available in multiple venues throughout the school student client group target because it was possible that supermarkets could sell ready cooked ready meals prices were more cheaper to compare to restaurants or school canters‘ cooked meals provided prices.

The effects of change in the marketing environment on sales of ready meals which indicated that consumers chose prefer to buy ready cooked meals from supermarkets. It seemed that a restaurant market failure could be caused to arise. For example, there was poor information on the part of food (ready cooked meals) to provide to the restaurant about the foods that consumers in a location(place) would demand for a given price to compare to the supermarket sale prices. The restaurant would lose clients if which cooked the kind of meals to sell higher price to compare to the supermarket sale of the kind of cooked ready meals price possibly. Large size supermarkets could sell cheaper ready cooked meals to low income group clients. It could cause competition to constitute a market failure to small size supermarkets. If the small size supermarkets lacked good information on the true food (ready cooked meals) with concentrations to sell cheaper prices, then this ready cooked meal market failure was one potential reason why small size supermarkets did not locate to close to the large supermarkets. Due to supermarkets grew in size would influence clients' choice to buy the numbers of cooked foods (ready meals) products. Moreover, The advent of computerized logistics and inventory systems were integrated with the large size supermarkets themselves occurred between the 1980 years and 1990 years .

So large size supermarkets were reliance on their own distribution and cooked food (ready meals) inventory systems along with larger supermarket sizes to allow super center to change to sell ready cooked meals at lower prices. Supermarkets marketing can promote healthful eating by increasing availability, affordability or restricting / de-marketing unhealthy foods to sell cooked Food (ready meals) marketing strategy at supermarkets, including labelling, packaging, pricing and point of sale advertising. Consumers‘ cost saving efforts and income and ready cooked meals prices increasing or decreasing factors can drive the choice of supermarkets as well as cooked meal products use of coupons and loyalty cards bargain shopping is another factor to influence their choice. Private label or store (supermarket) brands are taking an increasing share of consumers shopping dollars as the importance of brands. Supermarket shoppers stated priorities are cooked food (ready meals) quality or taste and price and healthy cooked food (ready meals) choices. However, supermarket shoppers' buying behaviors don't always reflect on favor healthful foods. Due to demand for locally grown cooked food is increasing. Anyway, restaurant meals are changed to supermarket to sell, which decide what kinds of meals to stock and how many of different kinds of meals to stock and how much variety of kinds of meals to offer to any one supermarket as well as supermarket shoppers prefer fewer options, provided that their preferred brand or cooked food (ready meals) products are available. The designs of supermarket ready cooked meal products and packaging to supermarket to sell is the focus of unusual colors or shape which can be used to increase interest and is specially pervasive among fun foods to compare to restaurant meals. Package design, including where text and images are placed, which can influences cooked foods (supermarket ready meals repurchasing again).The influence of design differs by the type of display consumer segments seek (convenience, information or images) and ready cooked meals package sizes have a relatively strong influence on consumption; larger ready cooked meals packages might increase per-use consumption ,but smaller packages might not improve self regulation and might not actually increase total consumption. In conclusion, I suggest that this ready meal manufacturers need to give more attention to be paid to food sellers, such as supermarkets' competitive differentiation and understanding the way in which customers attribute value to its ready meal products choice. Moreover, many consumers have become increasingly concerned about the health implication of the food they eat, so ready meal manufacturers will need to continue responding to such concerns. For example, who have responded with a range of low calorie meals, and addressed specific, sometimes transient, health fads, with respect to trans-fatty acids and omega 3 supplements of these cooked meal ingredients. Many consumers have also become concerned about the ecological environment and some supermarket suppliers, such as Marks and Spencer have incorporated sustainability agendas into their ready meals, for example by reducing packaging and sourcing supplies from sustainable sources. Thus, it caused ready meal manufacturers why who needed to give more attention to concern how supermarkets helped them to sell cooked ready meals in this foods market.

2. Critically discuss the link between the economic environment and sales of ready meals in supermarket

The macro environment, it describes things that are beyond the immediate environment but can nevertheless affect the organization. Such as the ready meal manufacturers in its macro environment, including the economic environment which can cause the manufacturers sell ready meal numbers whether which can sell more or less to different exported countries due to the exported countries' unemployment ratios, GDP and Government policies etc factors influence. Economic theory can help to explain why it can influence consumer behavior. In food sale market, it can include consumer behavior and demand side as well as retailer behavior and supply side two issues. Consumer behavior and demand side issue, such as the exported countries' consumer whose knowledge of the nutritional benefits of foods whether which prices were raised to choose to buy reasonably as well as retailer behavior and supply side issues, such as investing for developing a restaurant or supermarket in an underserved area whether the types of meals choices which are valued or which are not valued to buy to offer to clients from imports. On the other hand, economic environment factor, individual income can influence who chooses the type, quantity and quality of food that is purchased for a house holder and it also influenced the cooking and storage facilities available in a household to influence food choice.

On the other way, economic environment variation factor can also influence food access across areas. It is important to understand the economic conditions that may contribute to food deserts, that is the costs that food retail businesses face and the choice available to consumers who want to buy foods. Economic environment factor considers the consumer and demand factors, business and supply factors and the market conditions that interact to create differences in the food retail environment across areas and subpopulations. In general, high income meal client group can accept to choose to go to supermarkets or restaurants to spend than low income meal client group. The impact of the economic environment on sales of ready meals is such as an individual get richer, who can afford to buy ready prepared foods, rather than spend time and effort to prepare to cook them at home. It seemed that low income consumers were decreasing to eat meals at expensive restaurant to the alternative of relatively cheap ready prepared meals at home. Research could also consider how consumer knowledge and preferences and the time cost tradeoffs affect consumer decisions of which foods to eat and whether to make or to buy prepared foods from supermarkets or to eat at restaurant meals . Travel costs and time costs of acquiring foods as well as the time costs of preparing foods (meals) are also likely to affect demand for particular foods. Research on price variation at the local level and demand models could also be used to help determine which factors contribute to differences in access to food retailers. Price is also major determinant of food (meal) demand. The higher, the price of a food(meal), the lower the meal quantity demanded. On the other hand, the higher the price of a substitute food (meal), the higher demand will be for that food (meal) item. Given the budget constraints of low income consumers and the price of some specific foods (meals), low income consumers may substitute higher priced foods (meals) with lower priced foods(e.g. hamburger for steak or canned fruits for fresh fruits). Considering restaurants foods purchasing choice, such as economies of scale, which is when the costs of operating a restaurant decreases as restaurant size increases and economies of scope, which is when the costs decrease as more meals variety increases, suggests that larger restaurants that offer greater variety can offer lower meal prices. Both factors may account for the ability of larger restaurants to survive more easily than smaller restaurants. Considering supermarkets foods purchasing choice, it is possible that food retailers (supermarkets) actually have some market power, especially in setting where there are few competitors to close. It would have an incentive to increase food (ready meal) price and restrict foods(ready meals) supply quantities to increase profit. Supply side conditions, such as economies of scale, it could lead to (ready meal) food retailers (supermarkets) to have more market power, if it was not close between supermarkets. Individual behavior to make healthy choices can occur only in a supportive economic environment with accessible and affordable healthy food choices. Hence, food environment and sale strategies is needed to consider to adopt the exported countries' economic change.

Food marketing client target groups can include home parents, students and working people groups mainly and marketing and economic environment factors would cause food choices and

these factors impact health and nutrition and the focus on the connections between people and their environments. In conclusion, macro level economic environmental factors play a more indirect role but have a substantial and powerful effect on what people eat. Macro level factors operate within the larger society, include food marketing, social norms, food production and distribution systems, agriculture policies and economic price structures as well as social environmental to influence within the home, such as model of healthful dietary intake by parents feeding style, frequent family meals may promote healthful food consumption among children.

3. Discuss the factors that might affect sales of ready meals in your country over the next five years.

Hong Kong people can choose to go to restaurants to eat or go to supermarkets to buy foods to cook to eat. Although, ready meal manufacturers had increased the sale numbersof the ready prepared meals in many western countries in recent years. However, there still had any factors to limit it's sale numbers to Hong Kong market over the next five years, so it needed to aware of what was changing in Hong Kong food market environment and appreciated how change in this Hong Kong food environment to lead to change patterns of eating cooked ready meals demand to attempt to win its similar food competitors in Hong Kong market next five years. Hong Kong food environment related to Hong Kong people eating behaviors, include social environments and physical environments and macro level environment. The cooked meal quality and quantity of available can influence food numbers to produce meal to supply to Hong Kong food market. Hence, Hong Kong natural climatic change can influence the overseas food supply numbers to be imported to cause meals prices to go up or go down. If next five years, Hong Kong climate was good to grow plants and feed animals e.g. pigs and cows etc. meats. The restaurant meals or supermarket meals sale prices can be cheaper due to farmers who have much foods and vegetables to supply , so who can sell cheaper price to these restaurants or supermarkets to cause whose production cost to be decreased next five years in my country. Hence, ready meals prices could not sell more higher than Hong Kong meals prices. Hong Kong people eating behaviors are often changed over a lifetime. In general, Hong Kong people want to eat to satisfy physical hunger and psychological desires and yet want to be healthy, which may enquire adopting eating patterns that conflict with these desires. My country people make decisions about food several times a day: when to eat, what to eat, with where to eat and how much per meal prices and how much per meal numbers .

In general, Hong Kong people like to eat Chinese foods , but who also like to go to restaurants to eat or supermarkets to buy western foods, such as liking of specific tastes are important influences. However, these can be modified by experience with food from various intrapersonal and interpersonal factors to influence Hong Kong people to choose to buy uncooked or cooked meals from Hong Kong supermarkets. The next five year, food retailer behavior and supply factors of food access might affect overseas sales of ready meals numbers imported to my country. In general, supply is driven by the costs of input foods. The land, materials, machines and labor costs are needed to build and operate a restaurant or supermarkets. If these costs are increased to these food suppliers in my county next five years, overseas food demand shall be caused to be decreased if Hong Kong economy had changed to be worse and the new restaurants and supermarkets which costs were changed to be higher to much as well as Hong Kong unemployment was caused to be raised and many people lost jobs to have efforts to go to supermarkets to buy higher prices ready meals or go to restaurants to eat higher price ready meals.

My country's social environment and physical environment which also might affect sales of ready meals numbers next five years. Social environment includes interactions, with family, friends, peers and others in the community to impact food choices through mechanisms as well as physical environment includes the different places where people eat or buy food, such as whether the supermarkets or restaurants locations which are close to the buyers, e.g. schools, offices, houses. Hence, food suppliers' locations choice can influence who (target client groups) choose to buy more or less ready meals numbers. Foods prepared at home factor there may be relatively greater time costs than those to buy cooked foods(ready meals) from supermarkets or takeout foods. Hong Kong consumers may value the convenience of a fast food or takeout cooked meal more because it doesn't require spending much time to prepare to cook at home. Hence, Hong Kong people whose taste is for different kind of cooked foods (ready meals) and who feel the food suppliers' locations whether are convenient and Hong Kong economy whether is better or worse to cause unemployment numbers next five years, these factors can affect sales of imported ready cooked or uncooked meal numbers to my country Hong Kong next five year.

CHAPTER XXVI

Case study of Ryanair airline

If you are the marketing manager of an airline, such as Ryanair, how would you address the ecological concerns?

In recent years, social, economic and environment pressures have pushed airlines to accept their social responsibility. Closely tied to this acceptance is a corporate policy that aims at raising social and environmental standards on a voluntary basis and that means beyond legal and contractual requirement. It means that corporate social responsibility is not just an optional

consideration to core airline business activities, such as airlines industry fuel consumption pollutes sky air to cause global warming problem. Rather, Ryanair airline needs to concern social responsibility because it's fuel emissions would cause negative influence to stakeholders. e.g. causing bad negative climate to influence farmers to grow rice and vegetables etc foods successfully, so global warming will make farmers stakeholder can not earn more income and food buyers stakeholder won't eat rice and vegetables etc. foods easily, even global warming will damage natural environment to cause strong wind or strong raining or water natural hazard to damage any countries' houses to make house owners stakeholder who lose their houses to live. Hence, in the long term, if Ryanair airline still continue consume too much fuels to use to fly to cause emissions to pollute air to any countries as well as other airlines do not achieve any actions to reduce to consume to use more fuels together efficiently. I believe that global warming will become very serious to influence human living and eating problem occurrence in our earth as soon as possibly. Hence, such as Ryanair airline is among of global airlines, which have responsibility to consider how to reduce fuel consumption to cause too much emissions to pollute air in our earth. Such as, I was Ryanair airline marketing manager , I ought need to let Ryanair airline to measure whether it ought only concern how to sell cheaper air fares and buy many airplanes and consume much fuels to fly to raise income or it ought concern it's fuel emissions to pollute environment to cause global warming to influence global human stakeholders encounter living and eating problem to face natural foods resource shortage to supply in the future.

The ecological concerns global warming problem is serious nowadays, it brings the possible long term harmful consequences of executive emissions to the atmosphere. The developed countries, such as Northern Europe and United States people needed often to play travel entertainment by airlines transportation choice. However, scientists proved airlines used fossil fuels to harm excessive emissions to natural environment which would cause global warming problem to cause devastation of low lying areas to influence natural environment danger, even the developing countries people life and their houses would also encountered to be hazarded in the long term. If I was the marketing manager of an airline, such as Ryanair, I must concern socially responsible needs to Ryanair airline. Although, Ryanair aircraft had become more efficient in use of fuel during 1990 years, but Ryanair airline's passengers were booming demand to cause to increase aeroplane numbers to supply to satisfy passengers' travel needs and to pursue raising profit aim every year.

In fact, Ryanair airline used fuels to give energy to push aeroplanes to fly and it also polluted sky air during it's aeroplanes often were flying to cause global warming. For example, Ryanair airline marketing strategy was low fare prices to attract to increase many passengers to choose to attract to increase many passengers to choose to sit it's aeroplanes and it designed a cheap weekend break by Mediterranean travel to increase the unknown and remote possibilities of global warming. Hence, Ryanair would increased many new airplanes to increase to use fossil fuels of excessive emissions to the atmosphere to cause the effects of aid rain, poor climate change , destructive winds, rising sea levels and devastation of low lying areas by global warming bad consequences. Hence, it seemed that Ryanair airline had responsibility to concern how to protect natural environment due to its airplanes numbers and passengers were increasing to cause to increase to use more fossil fuels to cause the possible long term harmful consequences of excessive emissions to the sky to bring global warming occurrence nowadays. As I was this Ryanair airline marketing manager, I shall recommend Ryanair airline needed to consider this global warming socially responsible issue due to its airplanes spent too much fossil fuels to cause harmful consequences of excessive emissions to the sky. It would bring threats to developing countries people life and houses by global warming, so it concerned only how to raise itself interest marketing behavior of performance, but it neglect the serious global warming to cause bad influence to any developing countries people life danger, it was possible that passengers would feel it was not a socially responsible airline company, so it could not build a good image to whom in this airline industry and its further passengers would choose its other competitors (socially responsible airline companies) to substitute its airline service provision.

● Discussion

I should suggest Ryanair airline needed to control fossil fuel numbers to reduce to harm excessive emissions to natural environment seriously and it could spend much expenditure to buy good quality of fossil fuels to active the reduction of too much emissions to damage natural environment aim and it could shorten the sky flying distance to fly to other countries' airports from its airport to aim to attempt to reduce to use much fuel to pollute sky air per day and it could cancel some long flight flying routes and increased short flight flying routes to reduce flight spending hours to attempt to reduce to use fossil fuels to provide every airplanes to fly to pollute sky air every day.

Although, these marketing strategies would be possible to reduce airline income, but it would also attract many further passengers to choose to sit to its airplanes to go to travel if it could build good image to prove it was a socially responsible airline to serve passengers to let them to like to choose to use its flying service to go to travel willingly, even it could lead other airlines to follow it to use its marketing strategic methods to reduce to spend too much fossil fuels to pollute sky air to raise global warming problem seriously together. Hence, if Ryanair airline could attempt to achieve to reduce the fossil fuel numbers to use to airplanes to fly , it was possible that the other airline companies should follow it to do the same behaviors to aim to do social responsible organizations to concern how to reduce the global warming problem to cause to harm to our natural environment seriously for long term in the future.

2. The case study refers to apparent hypocrisy of clients who may claim to be concerned about the environment, but nevertheless continue to fly what might bring about a narrowing of this gap between what consumers think and what they actually do?

In fact, some apparent hypocrisy of consumers who may claim to be concerned about the global warming harmful natural environment problem due to airline companies, e.g. Easy Jet,
Ryanair etc. western countries' airlines which allowed fossil fuels produced harmful consequences of excessive emissions to atmosphere, but nevertheless continue to fly. However, I might recommend these methods to bring about a narrowing of this gap between what consumers think and what they actually do.
I think to bring a narrowing of this gap between consumers were happy to carry on airplanes to fly and it would not influence them to concern about climate change problem at the same time.

There was certainly a possible that governments would intervene. Such as the UK government and European commission had floated the idea of taxing aviation fuel and brought aircraft emissions within scope of the European emission trading scheme. Thus, if these western countries governments raised to charge aviation fuel taxing, it would possible to threaten any western airlines to shorten any flight routes hours and flight flying distance to fly to destination of the countries' airports from these airline companies' every country's airport, so which would not need to use more fuels for its airplanes to use if it had shorten flight flying routes distance to arrive other countries' airports. Hence, the airlines did not want to pay higher aviation tax to government, so which would attempt to shorten some flight flying routes from long distance to be short distance when their airplanes needed to fly to some other countries' airport to aim to buy less fuel numbers or which would not buy more airplanes.

Due to they needed to pay high aviation tax expenditure to their countries governments every year. Thus, it was possible that high fuel tax expenditure would cause airlines to shorten flight routes time. The most important, when some airlines decided to buy less fuels. These airlines might bring about a narrowing of this gap between what consumers think and what they actually do and these airlines were possible to raise their competitive ability, due to which would possible to persuade the concerned environment protective passengers who would choose to buy these airlines air tickets to more than to buy the other airlines' air tickets. Due to some airlines could not reduce to buy more fuel numbers to provide their airplanes to fly and which would increase air pollution to sky seriously, those airlines' spending excessive long hours (time) of every flight flying routes to fly to different countries' airports which would use more fuel to fly to cause air pollution to harm natural environment seriously and which would let these clients to feel unhappy to choose to buy air tickets to sit their airplanes possibly. Hence, different governments raised aviation tax would cause many airlines to reduce to buy too much fuel numbers to use possibly. It seemed that airlines needed have a social responsible duty to concern they needed to buy more fuels if they increased airplanes numbers, then they would raise air pollution to cause global warming problem seriously. Hence, I think passengers would not buy air tickets to fly to travel by airplanes when who would have long days of holidays. Otherwise, who would choose to stay at home or who would choose to go to travel by cruises on water transportation on their holidays. However, in western developed economies, legislation to enforce environmentally sensitive methods of productive is increasing, so airlines might adopt environmentally sensitive flight service processes to gain a competitive advantages. The challenges of using fuels resources in more efficient and less polluting way has achieved research and development, e.g. wind power research, solar panels, heat pumps and carbon capture technology have presented opportunities for airlines to improve the efficiency of fuels and airline marketing to business and individual group passengers.

Legal actions to place control over the emission of air pollutants have been instituted in several ways, such as the form of a public nuisance low. This is when conditions cause discomfort, inconvenience, damage to property or injury from airlines fuels to cause air pollution. The governments have also intervened in the protection of the public to threaten the airlines' fuels emissions pollute air in the sky. As a result of much research, devices for pollution control have been developed, guidelines for air quality were established fuels tax increasing incentives were introduced to enforce ordinances for restricting the emission from airplanes' fuels. For example, governments can pass the clean air act, legislation to reduce air pollution in their countries. In conclusion, airlines can co-operate environmentally friendly management to prevent global warming, it is as a part of its corporate social responsibility and makes company wide efforts to do by saving energy and reducing aircraft fuel emissions. Hence, global airlines ought plan to achieve to reduce to consume excessive fuel emissions to reduce a narrowing of this gap between what consumers think and what they actually do concerned about the environment pollution was caused by airlines if which still wanted to make travelers who prefer to choose to go to travel by flying more than other water or ground transportation etc. methods.

3. How would a company , such as Easy Jet airline measure and monitor consumer's attitudes?

Easy Jet airline has created environment problems, e.g. harmful chemicals sift down from smoky trails of low-flying jets. The scream of Easy Jet airline engines is constantly heard by

people who love near big city airports. It's aircrafts produce air pollution with consequent changes in climate.

It is a fact that many people prefer air travel rather than ground or water transportation, This has promoted a critical look at safety and quality control. Contributions to air pollution is a chief concern because of this revolutionary change in public transportation in the United States and around the world. The government must also establish standards for exhaust emissions. Thus, Easy Jet airline measure and monitor consumer's attitudes which needs to indicate to let them to believe that which suggests which airplane manufacturers are forced to develop low pollutant engines.

Due to the problem of air pollution from its airplanes involve a complex set of interactions among technical, social and economic factors. Hence, it also needs to measure it's emission from Easy Jet aircrafts, particularly on landing and take offs, are a source of bitter complaints from nearby residents. In a few airports visibility has been dangerously restricted by particulate emissions and photo chemical smog. Easy Jet airline also needed to have energy savings activities to its operations, ranging from procedural and flight plan improvement to reduce flight distance and attitude and weight management and it also needed to create energy through maintenance to achieve to continue to reduce co2 emissions by introducing high efficiency aircraft and through other measures to monitor consumers' attitudes . In line with its aim to be an environmentally friendly airline that harmonizes the needs of natural , humans and airline businesses. It aims to be respected by society , live up to its social responsibilities and make a contribution to society. Although emissions from aircraft are not included among greenhouse gas reduction targets, but it also needed to make systematic efforts to improve energy efficiency and reduce emissions by creating a road map to actively participate . Furthermore, Easy Jet airline also needed continually to pursue a management style that concerns nature, people and fellow corporations, even under the most severe conditions as a major practice toward implementing its environmental policy. Easy jet airline achieves environment goals to measure and monitor consumer's attitudes, such as minimizes energy and resource consumption and introduces up to date and fuel efficient fleet and engines and develops and apply energy efficient operation technique, it establish strict internal environmental standards to set internal standards that are stricter than general environment laws applied worldwide and minimize pollutants through systematic management and observance of standards. It systematically analyses the airlines' environmental impact and make the outcome to carry out reductions and evaluates the environmental impact of its aviation operations, maintenance and service and improves environmentally friendly processes and it continually improves environmental systems through feedback .

In conclusion, Easy Jet airline can increase the recycling of waste to reduce fuel consumption of resources and it can make systematic efforts to reduce emissions by creating a roadmap and actively participating in global warming by saving energy and reducing aircraft emissions through engine washing to aim to consume fuels efficiency and reduce emission to pollute air.

4. What might be the consequences for the marketing of a budget airline of Government policy measures which have the effect of doubling air fares in real terms?

If the country Government decided to raise higher flight fuel tax charge policy to budget airline. Due to the country Government hoped budget airline to reduce fuels consumption to provide to airplanes to use to reduce sky air pollution to cause global warning problem. In fact, budget airline needed to increase to use much fuels to provide to many flights to carry on passengers travel needs. Generally, budget airline would not like to choose to reduce to consume much fuels due to it's passenger numbers had been increasing. If budget airline decided to buy less fuels to reduce much fuels to consume for its flight needs. It would lose many passengers if it had not enough times of flights to provide airplanes to fly to different countries' airports to satisfy passengers' different flight route choices. However, the consequences for budget airline would also be passengers to choose to buy budget airline air tickets possibly if it decided to raise doubling air fares in real terms. Due to budget airline hoped to compensate its loss if it's country Government raised higher fuels tax to cause budget airline needed to pay high cost expenditure every year. Hence, budget airline needed to raise to spend two kinds of expenditure every year, such as purchasing more fuels expenditure and paying more fuels expenditure both. For long term, budget airline would choose to raise doubling or more air fairs in real terms in order to reduce to need to pay too much feel tax expenditure to compensate it's loss every year. In result, it's passengers would feel it's air tickets fares were not reasonable raised to compare it's other airline competitors, but it's flight services were not excellent to compare it's airline competitors specially. Hence, it's increasing air fares would cause many passengers to choose other airline competitors possibly.

5. Critically discuss how the marketing manager of a budget airline might respond.

Marketing manger might use cost benefit analysis to let budget airline to know how to invest in intangible asset, such as corporate social responsibility to give long term benefit to itself budget airline. I suggest this marketing manager needs to explain the reason why reducing fuel consumption is an investment in intangible asset to budget airline as below:

Airline transport has increasingly become a global technologically and dynamic growth industry. However, airline companies need to remain committed to satisfy the clients' growing demands in a sustainable manner when at the same time maintaining an optimal balance between economic progress, social development and environmental responsibility. The concept of corporate social responsibility is a challenge for who to face today's risky, competitive and complex airline business environment. There has been a need for airlines in the airline industry to develop an environment agenda and take measures to minimize the ever increasing environmental impacts created by their activities. The forms of corporate social responsibility in the airline sector includes working in partnership with local communities, socially sensitive investment as well as involvement in activities for conservation of the environment. The fact, airlines are spewing 20% more co2 into the environment then previously estimated and there is a tendency for amount to increase to 1.5 billion tons a year by 2025 year. So, airline industry must need to innovative, environmentally responsible industry that drives economic and social progress. It has risks (social, environmental, operational, threat, strategic and financial risks) that they have to deal with marketing managers airlines, such as budget airline marketing manager is responsible for the optional decision making about corporate risks in its daily business. Adrian, (P. 2012) indicated that the marketing manager of budget airline needs to indicate the benefits can be categorized into three namely to let budget airline to feel as below:

(a) Regarding the economic view, budget airline is essential for facilitating world business and tourism, it needs to create jobs and enables the expansion of trade across the global by opening
up new market opportunities. It also attracts businesses to locations all over the world, hence satisfying the mobility requirement of a growing portion of the world's population. It also aids in the movement of products and services quickly over long distance facilities economies and social participation by remote communities.

(b) From the social perspective, budget airline forms an unique global transport network that links people in different countries safely and efficiently. Air transport is increasingly accessible to a large number of people who can now afford to travel by air for pleasure and its business purpose.

(c) Lastly, in terms of the environmental perspective, there is a need for budget airline to minimize or contain the impact in its environment through the continuous improvement of its
fuel consumption, noise reduction and the introduction of new technologies. Budget airline marketing manager can enquire this question to whose company, such as how budget airline can quantify the benefits derived from such investments to do with how to quantify the benefits, so budget airline can be compared to the cost of

investments. Through budget airline has be different over the years to value many intangibles, such as corporate social responsibilities. Budget airline marketing manager needs to make choices among several alternatives: it is important to adopt a tool that with allow choices to clearly weigh and distinguish between the options available. So, budget airline marketing manager needs to persuade whose company to believe to maximize the gain, which may be either economic or social and may be beneficial to an individual, a group or society at large, e.g. reducing fuel cost can maximize economic or social benefits for long term. The measurement of benefits from corporate social responsibility policy includes gains from additional income to an increased quality of life or a cleaner environment.

On the other hand, the costs are made up of the opportunities forgone, internal and external costs and externalities. For instance, increasing the flying route for budget airline, the noise and air pollution are the externality when the secondary effect could be an increase in the cost operations. In this case, the pollution creates the new cost (externality). The budge airline business cost is the increase in the cost of operating the additional route. The budget airline's fuel consumption causes air pollution will influence whose client stakeholders' powers of seeing and thinking, cultural setting, experience is from the past and motivation at the time of sensing to the airline image to be poor due to who will feel the budget airline is not a social responsible organization. It aims to earn profits from passengers, but it neglects to take care other stakeholders benefits due to its fuel consumption to pollute environment to cause global warming problem. It seems that budget airline needs to considerate to use more fuel consumption to cause global warming problem more than doubling air fares in real terms if Government decided to raise more fuel tax charging to it to reduce its income.

I suggest marketing manager of a budget airline to reduce to use more fuels to pollute air, so budget airline does not decide to increase double air fairs charges to clients due to Government raises fuel taxation expenditure. Because it will cause clients to cancel its air tickets if who feel its air fairs are not reasonable to raise prices to compare other airline competitors. The marketing manager of a budget airline might respond to promote this navigation system to persuade budget airline does not choose to double air fares if Government raised fuel taxing charge. Innovation of flight operation on the optimum routes using (RNAV) Area navigation, as conventional airways and routes between airports were built by connecting ground navigation aids to the destination, the budget airline often became rather inefficient. On the other hand, RNAV can build routes connected any points with almost straight line by confirming aircraft position by means of global positioning system etc in addition to radio navigation destination of fuel consumption and CO2 emission through shortened flight time and distance. Other reducing fuel consumption include reduction of aircraft weight, use of new type point for aircraft painting to reduce emission of polluted to air . Hence, budget airline will spend less fuels to avoid to pay high fuels taxation expenditure to its Government and it does not need to charge double air fairs in real terms to cause many passengers who will choose to find other airlines to buy cheaper air tickets or who will cancel their budget airline air tickets due to who feel budget airline charges unreasonable air fairs. So, if budget airline did not achieve as above any methods to attempt to reduce fuel consumption, I believe that it will lose many passengers due to it decide to charge doubling air fares in real terms to compensate its fuel tax increasing expenditure .

CHAPTER XXVII

How can ethnographic research predict consumer emotion

Critically assess the role of ethnographic research as a means of learning More about buyer behavior. To critically assess whether the role of ethnographic research as a means of learning more about buyer behavior. I shall indicate what the marketers who use general methods to learn more about buyer behavior to compare to ethnographic research difference. In general, marketers learn buyer behavior who shall follow the simplified stages in the buyer decision process , such as the beginning is from need recognition to information search to evaluate to decision to the end of post purchase evaluation stage. Hence, the any buyers behavior shall be cycle stage to decide whether who shall repeat to choose to buy the company's product or use it's service if who feel the product or service had achieved their satisfaction after who spent. The marketers shall use questionnaires or marketing researches to enquire consumers to gather their ideas to analysis to get evaluation to assess whether how whose companies need to produce what kinds of new products style, design, color, price level and sale channels to achieve the most suitable marketing strategy to raise their sale competition. Otherwise, the role of ethnographic search is one different method to learn more about buyer behavior. In general, companies shall not need to arrange questionnaires to enquire participants to fill to answer questions to gather data to carry on evaluation and which do not need to follow the simplified stages to assess target client groups purchase decision process to carry on the sale and post purchase evaluation cycle to evaluate whether what are their product criteria or weaknesses which need to improve to raise their sale competition in their market. I think ethnographic research can get closer to the truth about consumer behavior. On behalf of companies' clients, which can seek to uncover hidden truths about the way their clients' lead their lives, by paying volunteers to be followed for days on end, being filmed and having their every more recorded. Companies will pay their target householder participant group to carry on an observational survey by digital cameras to be filmed record at home. One essential feature of ethnographic research is that it must not have any predetermined agenda.

There is little value in undertaking this type of research if the mind set of the researcher is expecting to see preconceived phenomena, it is the unexpected that is often of most interest, and which is so difficult to pick up through more structured forms of survey. In fact, participants in a survey may feel self conscious when who are being filmed, and the more interesting insights are likely to be observed when participants are feeling relaxed and off their guard .It is not just what people actually do that can be interesting, but what they almost do, and the body language used when members of the household are discussing an issue. It can take several hours of filming to yield just a few moments of true insights into participants' true attitudes and behavior.

One example of the company's ethnographic research in action was provided by a project commissioned by the footwear brand Dr Martens. It wanted to understand how young people used fashion brands in their every lives .

Why for example, did some brands, such as Nike trainers or baseball caps become popular in youth culture? The researchers identified groups of young people around the world who responded to Dr Martens' target market. In return for a payment, volunteers were followed for several days and their daily routines filmed with a handheld digital camera. In total, 180 hours of captured film was edited to just one hour of highlights showing the key drivers of youth culture which are relevant to the Dr Martens brand. It seemed that young people preferred fashions that allowed them to customize an item of clothing and in some way take ownership of it. The research drew the conclusion that iconic fashion items for young people had to have a distinctive label or style that made their wearers stand out as part of a tribe. Hence, ethnographic research seems to help this company to know why the young clients choose to buy other brand sport shoes, it is possible that they the other brands sport shoes' color or design can be accepted more to than to buy Dr Marten brand's sport shoes when they wear different style of clothing. Hence, it can use digital camera to observe the worldwide choice of paying target youth volunteers whose daily individual behaviors at homes to get the more actual evidence to evaluate what factors influence youth clients choose to buy other brands of sport shoes. Otherwise, if it use structured questionnaire surveys to enquire youth clients , it is possible that who can not give their feedbacks honestly. Otherwise, observable youth people whose daily activities can help this company to know it is possible that their design and color of clothing are one factor to influence their choice to buy preferable brands of sport shoes to wear if who felt the brand of sport shoe was suitable to wear to influence their clothing to be felt more smart in appearance. However, I suggest companies to avoid to tell householders what the research project is about, until it is over. That way, the chances of participants deliberately playing to the camera can be reduced.

Hence, ethnographic researcher ought not tell to participants why who needs to record their daily activities at home till to the end of observable survey finishing due to it is possible that the participants will not perform their actual behaviors if who knew the researcher's observable intention. However, if marketers need to understand how whose companies clients actually make purchase decisions to their products, who shall use structured questionnaire surveys for collecting large scale factual data, but it will have major weaknesses when companies can not understand individual's attitude. Complex sets of factors that influence their buying decisions can only rarely be captured by a questionnaire.

Qualitative approaches such as those using focus groups can get closer to the truth, but participants often still find themselves inhibited from telling the full story to the companies to know.

Ethnography is one of many approaches that can be found within social research. Ethnography was a descriptive account of a community or culture. Ethnography usually involves the researcher participating in people's daily lives for an extended

period of time, watching what happens, listening to what is said, and/or asking questions through informal and formal interviews collecting documents. In more detailed terms, ethnographic work usually has most of the following features: People actions are studied in every contexts rather than under conditions created by the researcher, such as in experimental setups or highly structured interview situations as well as data are gathered from a range of sources including documentary evidence of various kinds, but participant observation and/or relatively informal conversations are usually the main ones as well as data collection is for the most past relatively unstructured in two senses and it doesn't involve following through detailed research design at the start and the categories that are used for interpreting what people say or do are not built into the data collection process through the use of observation schedules or questionnaire to analysis.

Generally, fairly small scale, perhaps a single setting or group of people. This is a facilitate in depth study and the analysis of data involves interpretation of the meanings, functions and consequences of human actions and how these are implicated in local and perhaps also wider contexts what are produced for the most part are verbal descriptions, explanations and theories and statistical analysis play a subordinate role at most. How ethnography can learn more about buyer behavior. It means collection of data to pursue an answers to these questions more effectively and to test these against evidence. Collecting data in natural settings, in other words in those that have not been specially set up for research purposes (such as experiments or formal interviews). Where participant observation is involved the researcher must have some role in the studied and this
will usually have to be done at least through implicit and probably also through explicit, negotiation with people.
The methodological model for social research is physical science conceived in terms of the logic of the experiment. Ethnography was sometimes dismissed as quite inappropriate to social science on the grounds that the data and findings it produces are subjective. Hence, ethnographic research is the role to learn more about buyer behavior through marketers may have been listening more to consumers (e.g. through qualitative research), efforts have almost always been directed at controlling consumers; ranges of products or services pre determined by producers have been pushed through with little real involvement of consumers in the process at a time in which consumers are ever more aware of what is being done to marketers. Ethnographic field research involves the study of groups and people as who go about every day lives. There has two distinct activities. First, the ethnographer enter into a social setting and gets to know the people involved in it; who participates in the daily routines; develops ongoing relations with the people in it and observes all the approach. But second the ethnographer writes down in regular systematic ways what who observes and learns when participating in the daily rounds of life of others. Thus, the researcher creates an accumulating written record of these observations and experiences. These two interconnected activities comprise the core of ethnographic search: firsthand participation in some initially unfamiliar
social world and the production of written accounts of that world by drawing upon such participation. Hence, ethnographers are committed to get close to the activities and everyday people.

Getting close minimally requires physical and social proximity to the daily rounds of people's lives and activities, the field researcher must be able to take up positions in the midst of the key sites and scenes of other's lives in order observe and understand whom. In learning about others through active participation in their lives and activities. Finally, close continuing participation in the lives of others encourages appreciation of social life as ongoing processes. Through participation the field researcher sees how people do uncertainty and confusion, how meaning is through talk and collective action, how understandings change over time.

Consumer behavior refers to the behavior that consumers display in searching for purchasing, using, evaluating and disposing of products and services that who expect will satisfy their needs and it's behaviors that are directly involved in the action of obtaining, consuming and spending products/services, including the decision processes that precede and follow these actions. The knowledge of consumer behavior helps the marketer to understand how consumer think, feel and select from alternative like products, brands and the like and how the consumers' buying behaviors are influenced by their environment, the reference groups, family and salespersons. Most of the factors are uncontrollable and beyond the controls of marketers, but who have to be considered when trying to understand the complex behavior of the consumers. Consumers buying cycle processes involved when individuals or groups select, purchase, use or dispose of products or services or ideas or experiences to satisfy needs and desires.

In the marketing context, the term consumer refers not only to the act of purchase itself, but also to patterns of aggregate buying which include pre-purchase and post purchase activities.

Pre-purchase activity might consist of the growing awareness of a need or wants and a search for and evaluate of information about the products and brands that might satisfy it. Post purchase activities include the evaluation of the purchased item in use and the reduction of any anxiety which accompanies the purchase of expensive and infrequently bought items. The various factors include lifestyles and its impact on the consumer behavior. On the first hand, ethnographic research can learn more about buyer behavior as below: ethnographic research described the dominant, positivistic consumer perspectives and methodological and analytical overview of the traditional perspectives. There are two factors mainly influencing the consumers for decision making. Risk aversion and innovativeness. Risk aversion is a measure of how much consumers need to be certain and sure of what who are purchasing. Highly risk adverse consumers need to be very certain about what who are buying. Whereas less risk adverse consumers on tolerate some risk and uncertainty in their purchasing. The second variable, innovativeness is a global measure which captures the degree to which consumers are willing to take chances and experiment with new ways of doing things. Hence, ethnographic research can learn whether the buyer's shopping motivation is abound with which various measures of individual characteristics, e.g. innovative, variety seeking etc. different factors to the buyer behavior.

On the second hand, perception is a mental process, whereby an individual selects data or information from the environment organizes it and then draws significance or meaning from it. Perceived fit is an attitudinal measure of how appropriate a certain channel of distribution is for a specific product. Consumer's perception of the fit between a service/product and channel is very influential in determining whether who will consider using that channel for a specific service. In fact, perceived fit was found to be more important than consumer's preference for the distribution method or service. Product quality and packaging and brand awareness familiarity with a channel is a measure of the general experience who have with purchasing products through special channels , e.g. internets, newspapers advertisement factors let consumers to decide to choose to buy or not buy the specific product. Shopping motives are defined as consumer's wants and needs as who relate to outlets at which to shop. Two groups of motives, functions and non functional have been proposed with

time, place and possession needs and refer to rational aspects of
channel choice. The functional motives included convenience, price comparison. Otherwise, the non functional motives entailed recreation and it related to social and emotional reasons. Hence, ethnographic research can assess whether the product or service is the functional motive or non functional motive to cause the buyer's choice.

On the third hand, economic theory holds that of largely rational and conscious economic calculations. Thus, the individual buyer seeks to spend whose income on those products that will deliver the most utility (satisfaction) according to his tastes and relative prices. It aimed to simplify assumptions and examine the effects of changes in single variables (e.g. price) holding all other variables constant. (e.g. low price of product is the higher the sales. The identified the impact of price differentials on consumers' brand preferences; changes in produces on demand variations; changes in price on demand sensitivity and scarcity on consumer choice behavior amongst many others. The consumer behavioral perspective in contrast to the economic view which underscores the importance of internal processes in consumer decision making, the behavioral perspective emphasizes the role of external environmental factors in the process of learning, when which it is argued causes behavior. The behavioral perspective therefore focuses on external environmental, such as advertisement that stimulate consumer response through learning. Consumers must be exposed to information, e.g. advertisement of it is to influence their behavior. Hence, ethnographic research can assess whether the product/service is consumer behavioral perspective or behavioral perspective to cause the buyer's choice.

On the fourth hand, consumers were suggest that high involvement with a product results in an extended problem followed by an information search, alternative evaluation, purchase and post purchase activities. The process is aided by an active information processing sequence involving exposure, attention, comprehension, acceptance and retention. The choice is determined by the outcome of the information process aided decision sequence may have satisfying or dissatisfying outcomes. Consumer's motivation and intention and that unpredictable factors (such as non availability brand or insufficient funds) may result in modification of the actual choice made by a consumer. This model assumes that observed consumer behavior is preceded by intrapersonal psychological states and events (attitude intention-purchase sequence). Hence, the events are as outputs of the processing of information, taking for granted that consumers seek and use information as part of their rational problem solving and decision making processes. Hence, ethnographic research can learn why the buyer doesn't choose to buy the product whether it is unpredictable or predictable psychological factors.

On the fifth hand, personality perspective means some purchases have more personal relevance than others. When this partly reflects on factors, such as price, it also bears on the way in which some products enhance the consumer's self concept , e.g. possessions are considered to reflect on a consumer's image of whom. Personality in general is understood as a concept. Personality has also been understood as the unique way in which traits, attitudes, when individuals might not always be uniform and predictable in their patterns of choice in different situations, it might be possible to make sense of and to forecast the general reactions of broadly defined groups and classes of purchasers.

It is the concept of consumer general behavioral response patterns that forms the basis for marketing's personality based segmentation strategies. The possibility of using measures of personality to guide marketing action, for example in segmenting markets , tailoring new brands of innovative consumers and repositioning mature brands has encouraged a large volume of research. Attitude itself is a learning experience and can lead to a change in attitudes before buyers enter the buying process. Thus, attitudes don't automatically guarantee all types of behavior. They are really the product of social forces interacting with the individual's unique temperament and abilities and social influences are not all of the behavioral variations in people. Two individuals subject to the same influences are not likely to have identical attitudes, although those attitudes will probably more points than those of two and cognition. Affect refers to the way a consumer feel about an attitude object, behavior involves the person's intentions to do something with regard to an attitude object and finally cognition refers to the beliefs a consumer has about an attitude object.

Thus, ethnographic research can learn whether it is from external social factors more or internal personality factors more to cause the buyer's choice. The theory of cognitive information processing , attitudes are formed in the order of beliefs, affect and behavior. Attitudes based on behavioral learning follow the beliefs, behaviors and affect sequence and finally attitudes formed based on the experiential hierarchy follow the affect, behavior and beliefs route. A consumer who is highly involved with a product / service category and who perceives a high level of product/service differentiation between alternatives will follow the cognitive hierarchy (beliefs affect behavior). From the ethnographic research marketers perspective the sequence of attitude formation is from a communication point of views from a strategic point of view, such as it has proved useful in specifying the different elements that work together to influence buyers' evaluations of attitudes ; products or services may be composed of many attributes or qualities, some of which may be more important than others to particular people. So consumer's decision is to act on whose attitude is affected by other factors, such as whether it is felt other factors, such as whether it is felt that buying a product/ service would be met with approval by friends and family. The complexity of attitudes is underscored by multi attribute attitude models, in which sets of beliefs and evaluations are identified and combined to predict an overall attitude.

On the final hand, the situational influence perspective, a situation is defined by factors over and above the characteristics of a person and product or service. For example, situational affects may be behavioral (e.g. entertaining friends), experiential or perceptual (e.g. being depressed or being pressed for time). According to the behavioral influence perspective of low involvement decision situation, consumer decision making is a learned response to environmental cues, as when a person decided to buy something on impulse that is prompted as a surprise special in a store.

According to this approach, then ethnographic research marketers must concentrate on assessing the characteristics of the environment, such as the physical surroundings and product/service placement, that influence members of that target market. For example, point of purchase (such as product/ service samples) are particularly useful in inducing impulse purchases. Ethnographic research marketers focus on measuring consumers' effective

responses to products or services and develop offerings that elicit appropriate subjective reactions and employ effective symbolism. Situational effects can also be perceptive, e.g. there could be a number of ways in which mood can influence purchase decisions. For example, stress can impact information processing and problem solving abilities. In addition, time poverty can impact buying decisions. An individual's priorities determine whose time style. According, consumer buying change is not something which consumers do for themselves, rather it is a result of something that is done to them by some internal ,e.g. trait or external ,e.g. environment force over which they have little or no control. Thus, ethnographic research can assess what is the situational influence factors to cause the buyer to choose to buy the product or consume the service. In conclusion, conditions of competition are changing rapidly today and companies need strategies to react to those changes promptly to raise competition. Due to technological developments, physical differences of products/ services have decreased. Differentiation should be on the meanings products/
services bear instead of on their physical features and a successful brand differentiation can be possible by building personality. Hence, understanding consumer behaviors are related to marketing natures in the product sale or service provision to every marketer who needs to considerate to win whose competitors.

2. Discuss the ethical issues that are raised by ethnographic research.

Consumer research has been important to the development of marketing theory and practice. Consumers are seldom, if ever, involved in the research design and analysis processes which raises issues that go beyond ethics. Particularly, problematic when participant observation is employed , as little is and little could be addressed by research guidelines and codes of ethics relevant to marketing research. Some of the relevant ethical issues to participant observation that arise from the lack of the consumer in the research process as well as the potential issues that may be involved in participatory research designs, the shortcomings of the available ethnographic marketing research guidelines and codes of ethics as for as participant observation is concerned. Some argument regards the real time and nature of ethical circumstances at the field where the ethnographic researcher must often respond to unexpected situations immediately.

3. Why ethical ways of thinking it is important to recognize that are raised by ethnographic research.

It is possible that the issues of power that can arise ethnographic research as well as it is from the consequences of simply doing
research , even if the intentions are good and it is from the fact that ethnographic research marketers' knowledge system is necessarily linked to other forms of structural power (e.g. gender, race, development, the system). The ethnographic research marketers whose emotional and power issues present in ethnographic research relationships are also acknowledged to influence ethnographic results, and this is where the key issues of using research participants for data collection comes in. Ethnographic research designs that objectify and don't include research participants in the conceptualization of the research study through to data analysis have been widely criticized by ethnographic researchers and these issues must be considered within the scope of the ethics of care.

Researchers (ethnographers) need have moral responsibilities toward research, included informed consent, confidentiality, reliability and validity. In sum, ethical guidelines and codes of conduct can be beneficial in alerting consumer researchers of ethical ways of conducting research. However, participants needed rules to be aided by researchers' own ethical reasoning in the field. The ethnographic researchers need to highlight the importance of constant negotiation of participation in the different stages of research, how participants may not be willing (due to lack of time or even personal circumstances) to help ethnographic researchers in the data analysis process and how researchers' own deadlines and academic constraints may get in the way of the idealized research process of involvement between ethnographic research participants and researchers are well to their discussed topic. In general, ethnographic researchers need to know what who need to understand about ethics, such as harm, consent, data protection etc. recap of ethical approval what it is and what ethnographic researchers need to do and what further sources of
information and support need.

In ethic principles, ethnographic research should be designed, reviewed and undertaken to ensure integrity and quality. Participants must normally be informed fully about the purpose, methods and intends possible uses of research, what their participation entails and what risks, the confidentiality must be respected research participants must take part voluntarily, harm to research participants must be avoided in all instances and the independence of research must be clear and any conflicts to interest or partiality must be explicit and increasing stakeholder demands. The mature of the ethical consumer is educated, middle class or over emotional to decide what kind products who needs to buy and how many numbers are enough to buy. For example, with the environment dropping out of media attention, ethic provided new moral ground and campaigns or opening of a chain of ethical supermarkets, ethical image became a desirable commodity for the big retailers. Some ethical customers need to satisfy with fair trade marked products to buy from the ethical supermarkets. How morality may play a significant role in the performance of buyers' actions. It is concerned specifically with how rules, responsibilities and values centering on right or wrong influence the character of consumption. The idea that morality (ethicality) can have a considerable impact upon the consumption. Hence, I think business moral performance is needed to satisfy every buyer's decision of consumption and it is linked to the ethnographic research growing literature on ethical consumer behavior. Within psychology, for instance, morality can be seen as a process of cognitive learning where systematic punishment and reward help to educate individuals of their actions. Whether consumption is informed by at least some of the available moral perspectives to some of the available moral perspectives, so it caused ethical issues that are raised by ethnographic research. Ethical consumption is concerned with predicting market behavior, it included some kind of relationship between the attitudes, values and behaviors of a defined ethical consumer group. For example, ethnographic researchers have been interested in the effects of environmental concern on environmentally friendly consumer behavior. Depending on how ethical consumption is defined, it recognizes alternative forms of what are essentially moral values, attitudes and buyer individual behavior. Consumer behavior has been changed by external elements, such as economy, technology, cultures, religion etc. factors. It would be unfortunate to be great importance for an understanding of ethical consumption issues.

In conclusion, consumption behavior is the art of need for desire to, it could be thought of as directly influenced by certain core values held as sacred within society. For example, ethical buyer behavior may concerns about animal protection, environmental protection, human protection etc. life rights issue. Facts, knowledge and truth about morality in consumption are seen as being raised by ethnographic research. According, the relationship between morality and consumers behavior could be better through of as the products of a continued process of political, social, technological and religious re-organization of life. For example, capabilities of new digital , microchip technology enhanced many consumers with the delights of efficient, task-saving, small and shiny products. Simultaneously, and not unrelated turbo-charges cars, mobile phones, cock tail parties etc. high technological products are arguably reflected power, success and good living to influence buyer behavior ethically daily in our society. Hence, I believe ethical issues that are needed to consider by ethnographic research.

4. Discuss possible alternative approaches by which marketers may learn more about youth culture.

Market based trading -selling, buying and consuming has existed in our society. Human action and interaction and behaving in different roles in exchange markets and various trading situations which is a typical of consumers and market trading interplays of several actors in economic, societal and cultural contexts as well as consumer behavior and consumer culture and consumption which have close relationship. Individual youth consumer or a group of youth consumers who is described as humanistic economics where people, their values and culture are primarily analyzed. In general, research on brands and organizational issues of the marketing function defined the questions of how to sell more products or provide more services to speed up the general level of consumption in order to better the economic situation of a firm or a nation. Basically, individual youth buyer seeks to speed whose income on those products/services what will deliver the most utility, typically satisfaction, according to whose tastes and budget. In economic, consumer behavior is identified with rational decision making. Decisions are automatically translated into purchasing and consuming, The price and income constraints are generally accepted factors in an economic analysis of

consumer behavior. Consequently, consumers are seen as rational actors that purposefully optimize the production of their utility.

Sociological and macro and cultural perspective which focuses on consuming , emphasizes on emotions, multicultural new consumers aspects, cultural studies and the meaning of culture for consumer research surfaced also in the late 1980 years. For example, consumption symbolism, different aspects to property and possessions, political consumption, research and cultures and subcultures. In consumer studies can be traced to the mid 1990 years, when consumer culture was recognized as a distinct cultural entity. Consumption was seen as a society activity which above all others, unities economy and culture. The one alternative approach is that learning more about youth culture, there is a clear common sense about its influence on social youth consumption changes, and the importance of its analysis in order to understand modern youth consumption. For example, marketers may learn more how to make youth to cause excessive consumption nowadays. The influence of the means of mass communication and oriented medias has contributed to send promotion messages to different youth audiences, e.g. from children and teen ages to youths. To see themselves in real conditions why who need to buy products or need services before beyond their possibilities have been planned to buy electronics, cars and even a house etc. products.

The another alternative approach is that marketers may also learn what are youth consumer modern culture how to make them, such as symbol status and power how become habituated to consume familiar products/ services able to reinforce familiar image in youth cultural different target groups. The final alternative approach is that culture is sociological influence on client's needs, it is based on the individual's physiological and psychological needs, such as food choice. Maslow recognized that once individual have satisfied these basic physiological needs, such as foods and drinks, who may seek to satisfy social needs by cultural influence, for example, the need to have meaningful interaction with peers. More complex still, western cultures see increasing numbers of people seeking to satisfy essentially internal needs for self satisfaction, products therefore satisfy increasing complex needs. Moreover, food is no longer seen as a basic necessary to be purchased and cooked for self consumption with growing prosperity, youth people have sought to satisfy social needs by eating out with friend or family. Youth peoples' satisfaction of such social needs may influences on their foods sating basic needs. Hence, if the youth clients had afford to go to restaurant to eat more expensive and good taste foods. The high class food culture can change the youth client's food necessity to influence whose food choice. A young child is often considered society unacceptable, so such youth behavior is socialized out before the child reaches adulthood. The faculty cultural influences a child's perception of the world and the family cultural influences lasts into adulthood. For example of this effect on buying processes can be found in youth adults selection of a particular brand breakfast cereal because it is the one that who were brought up with youth individuals are surrounded by peer group/or reference groups with act as a guide for youth consumption of behavior peer groups can be primary and direct to influence their youth culture (e.g. colleagues at work and school), popular movie actors can secondary and indirect to influence to their youth culture (e.g. guideline or behavior provided by popular movie actors or media figures) ; youth individuals culture can also

identify with a social class and the values of this class can influence youth behavior, e.g. school culture or working class. However, culture in its widest sense influences youth buying behavior and deference to suppliers can differ significantly between different countries‘ youth culture to choose to sell their products or provide their services to the countries' youth markets. Youth needs are also influenced by the situation in which youth currently find themselves in their countries. The subjects of age and socio-economic status can have profound effects on youth buying behavior at different youth age market segmentation, such as youth client groups can divided to any companies to concentrate on selling, e.g. between 20 ages to 40 ages or between 10 ages to 20 ages etc. different age groups.

In conclusion, marketer may learn more about youth culture from different countries‘ family life cycle stages of change which have sought to take account of their increasing complexity to influence to estimate the countries' youth buyer numbers. The family relationships can include single parent family, married parent family, no children family youth buyer groups of family life cycle youth buyer changing numbers in marketers‘ target countries. Due to all different countries family life cycle youth buyer numbers can indicate the countries' youth individual needs changing numbers and the target countries' youth buyer numbers are likely to change their purchase tastes and needs as youth culture goes through life. Hence, marketers can measure the target countries youth age segmentation estimate numbers to decide how many products or how much services to supply to them to satisfy their needs accurately.

CHAPTER XXVIII

Marketing research methods

Critically evaluate the relative merits of quantitative and qualitative approaches to data collection for a large retailer.

The marketing research process needs to follow these steps: defining the problem and research objectives, developing the research plan, collecting the data, analyzing the data, then presenting the findings.

In general, the specific marketing research major activities include: Research into customer needs and expectation and a variety of qualitative techniques are used to study the often complex sets of expectations that customers have with respect to a purchase. For example, when buying a personal computer, what are customers' expectation with respect to reliability, after -sales support, design etc? Customer satisfaction surveys indicate customer areas of satisfaction or dissatisfaction; how spending money on various forms of communication, such as advertising, sales promotion, and public relations; researching similar industry studies about competitors in completely unrelated business sectors how to improve own marketing effectiveness; researching key client studies about number of customers how to make special efforts to ensure that these customers are satisfied with its standards of service and prices; researching into intermediaries, such as agents dealers are close to consumers to gather information about consumers' needs and expectation. For example in relation to reliability, delivery times and after sales services; researching front line employees their attitude towards the company and researching environmental scanning changing on trends to influence the company development in the future. Structure of market research includes spending on market research, types of market research and potential problem. Market research means researching the the immediate competitive environment of the marketplace, including customers, competitors, suppliers, distributors and retailer. Otherwise, marketing research includes all the above and companies and their strategies and markets of whose products sale or services provision and the wider environment within which operates (e.g. political, social, economic etc factor influences). Hence, marketing research means the systematic design, collection, analysis and reporting of data and finding relevant to a specific marketing situation facing the organization. In general, the ten most common market research activities for a large retailer data collection, include determination of market characteristics, measurement of market potential, market share analysis, sales analysis, studies of business trends, short range forecasting, competitive product studies, long range forecasting, pricing studies and testing existing products.

The reasons why a large retailer needs to conduct that research in new product development include the product must appeal to the customer, timely market research can help the large retailer to predict its client's needs/wants, market research tends to point out success and failure before its product is launched for real and it can save its money and time. A large retailer's market research can be sources by either primary or secondary or both and it can use either qualitative or quantitative or both methodologies and it can achieve objectives either exploratory or descriptive or causal experimental.

The primary source is collection of data specifically for the problem or project in hand and the secondary source is based on data previously collected for purposes other than the research in hand. e.g. published articles, governments etc.

On the quantitative benefits hand, it is cheaper to sample
size ; probabilities in depth motivations and feelings, it allows managers to observe real client reaction to the issue, e.g. comments and associations regard a new product fresh from the laboratory. It often used precursor to quantitative research, it can give the research department a low cost and timely sense of which issues in quantitative research. Quantitative research is designed to gather information from statistically representative samples of target population. The sample size is related to the size of the total population being studied, the variability within it, and the degree of statistically reliability required, balanced against time and cost constraints. It includes these skilful analyses such as below:

Correlation analysis means two phenomena are associated with each other. For example, whether change in household income is associated with the amount that a household spends on eating out of or firm's advertising expenditure on a product and sale revenue for it's relationship. Regression analysis means to use to build a model of causes (independent variables), which lead to an effect (the dependent variable). Companies shall use a historical database to test models that are assessed for the amount of variance in the dataset that they explain. Analysis of variance is used to test hypotheses about differences between two or more means. It is widely used in experimental frameworks where the researcher wished to examine the effects of two or more treatments on customers.

Conjoint analysis can provide valuable information for market segmentation, new product development, forecasting and pricing decisions and it can analyze the real life trade off that shoppers make when evaluating a range of features that are present in a range of product. Cluster analysis is frequently used in segmentation studies, but does not provide the marketer with a unique solutions.

Neural network analysis splits a dataset into a training set and a testing set. However, quantitative analysis techniques can suffer from a number of weakness , such as sampling error, measurement error, significant estimation of sample population error, inappropriate estimation of population may be validated statistical tests and inappropriate interpretation of results can highly subjective.

On the qualitative merits hand, large retailer can get merits, such as many sample size and questions and information per respondent and much application of questioner's skill, analyst's skill and type of analysis. Qualitative techniques essentially seek to recreate the listening ear and interpretative mind that so many entrepreneurs use so well. Qualitative marketing research involves the exploration and interpretation of the perceptions and behavior of small samples of individuals and the study of the motivators behind observed actions. It can be highly focused, exploring in depth, for example, the attitudes that buyers have towards particular brand names. The techniques used to encourage respondents to speak and behave honestly. However, it is difficult to assess the validity of qualitative research techniques, and the tests for significance that are available for most quantitative techniques are largely lacking for qualitative techniques.

The quantitative and qualitative approaches to data collection for a large retailer its merits can achieve objective is either by exploratory, it means preliminary data needed to develop an idea further, e.g. outline concepts, gather insights, formulate hypotheses; it is either by descriptive, it means to describe an element of an ideas precisely, e.g. who is the target market, how large is it, how will it develops ; it is either by causal, it means to test a cause and effect relationship, e.g. price elasticity is by experiment. Moreover, the quantitative and qualitative approaches to data collection can help a large retailer to find methods how to solve problems to raise competition confidently. In the beginning, of the market research process step, it needs to define the problem and objectives, such as it needs to distinguish between it's research type needed, e.g. exploratory descriptive or causal . Then, it needs to develop the research plan, such as deciding on budget, data sources, research approaches and instruments, sampling plan and contact methods. Next, it needs to collect information, such as information is collected according to the plan. Following step, it needs to analyze the information , such as statistical manipulation of the data collected, e.g. regression or subjective analysis of focus group. Final step, it needs to present the findings, such as overall conclusion to be presented rather than statistical methodologies.

Data collection gathers for a large retailer, it can gather syndicated data from householders, it is gathered either by psychographics and lifestyle, advertising, evaluation etc. styles of surveys and use panels or both sources. Primary data is originated by a researcher for the specific purpose of addressing the problem at hand, the collection of primary data involves all six steps of the marketing research process as well as secondary data has already been collected for purposes other than the problem at hand. These data can be located quickly and inexpensively. The intention to uses of secondary data for a large retailer, it aims to identify the problem and better defines the problem, develops an approach to the problem, formulates an appropriates research design, for example by identifying the key variables, answers certain research questions and test some hypotheses and interprets primary data more insightfully.

On qualitative merits to secondary data collection for a large retailer. The criteria aspect, this data collection method can give merits of response rate, quality and analysis data, sampling technique and size, questionnaire design, fieldwork benefits to a large retailer, so it's data should be reliable, valid to the problem; on error and errors in approach, research design, sampling , data collection and analysis and reporting, so it can assess accuracy by comparing data from different sources. On currency aspect, this data collection method can assess time lag between collection and publication, frequency of updates, so census data are updated by syndicated large retailer; on objective aspect, secondary data collection method can help large retailer to judge whether the data collected were needed to used for which parts of market strategies benefits for consumer research, so the objective determines the relevance of data; on nature aspect, this data collection method can define key variables, units of measurement, categories used, relationships examined, so it can reconfigure the data to increase a large retailer market strategies benefits usefulness and on dependability aspect, this data collection method provides expertise, credibility, reputation and trustworthiness of the source, so it's data should be obtained from an original source to raise market research benefits to a large retailer. Hence, internal secondary data collection can help large retailer department project to store project to analyze sales by product line, by major department, e.g. men's wear, by specific stores by geographical region, by cash versus credit purchased, sales in specific time periods, by size of purchase and trends in many of these classifications were also examined.

Secondary data collection can include demographic data, which is type of individual household level data available from consumers, such as identification, e.g. name, address, telephone , sex, marital status, age, income, occupation etc. as well as psychographic lifestyle data, such as consumer personal interest. Hence, a large retailer can get this quantitative and qualitative data to judge whether who is segmentation target to compete in its business market. For example, market research demands cooperation and trust between the client commissioning a study and the company carrying it out.

The reputation that a market research agency has built for itself
is particularly important where qualitative research is involved as well as qualitative research techniques are utilizing quasi quantitative technique in order to enhance their credibility.

In conclusion, large retailers are reliance on customer's view due to many experienced larger retailers are relying more on interactive development with lead clients. Because traditional market research for truly innovative new products have frequently proved misleading. Hence, quantitative and qualitative approaches must need to use to gather to assess how to achieve marketing strategies timely and objectively and relevant to win whose competitors nowadays.

2. Discuss the limitation of statistically based consumer databases of the type discussed here. Do qualitative approaches based on small groups offer any advantages?

Any large retailers need to follow this process to use marketing information system to gather data from consumer databases. First step, which need to gather data either from internal data or external data source or both. The internal data includes enquires, orders, customer complaints etc. as well as the external data is from customer panels, intermediaries etc. Next step, the marketing information system will carry on processes as data collection and analyzing internal data. Final step, the marketing information system will produce outcomes, such as input to decision support system and data for decision makers to evaluate and storage of data in a data warehouse outcomes. A large retailer can collect consumer data computerized database, from online bibliographic database or from internet numeric databases, full text database or offline directory databases, special purpose databases. Hence, computerized published external secondary sources can help large retailers to identify individuals or organizations to collect specific data, for example, consultants and consulting organization directory, directory of market research reports, studies and surveys and research services directory and gather indices to help in locating information on a particular topic in several different publications. Hence, large retailer can collect classification of computerized databases include bibliographic databases are composed of citations to articles, numeric databases contain numerical and statistical information , full -text databases contain the complete text of the source documents comprising the database, directory databases provide information on individuals or organizations and services and special purpose database provide specialized information. Hence, large retailer can get syndicated service to collect and sell common pools of data of known commercial value designed to serve a number of clients and syndicated sources can be classified based on the unit of measurement (households/consumers) and institutions two groups. Syndicated services of householders/ consumers include surveys, data collection is from psychographic and lifestyles, general and advertising evaluation as well as it also include panels data collection is from purchase and media of volume tracking data and scanner diary panels as well as it also include electronic scanner services is from scanner diary panels with cable television.

Potential problems to limitation with market research of statistically based customer data bases include, small groups do not know when and how to do research from database and problems exist with research buyers and suppliers and it needs frequent techniques and small groups exist problems with traditional market research effort. On limitation of when and how not to conduct market research issue, it includes lack of resources, closed mindset, poor timing arrangement in marketplace, research results are not actionable, late timing is process, unclear objectives and cost outweighs benefits limitation. On the lack of resources occasion issue, If quantitative research is needed, it is not worth doing unless a statistically significant sample can be used, On the research results, small groups' clients are difficult to get psychographic data from statistically based consumer databases to analyze to carry on market research. On the closed mindset limitation issue, when research is used as a preconceived idea. The statistically based consumer databases needs long time to gather data to analyze to carry on marketing research in its process. It cause poor timing to give clients to find marketing research result, if the client wants to know whether who ought to invest to develop the new product to promote to the marketing to sell from statistically based consumer database in the short time.

On cost outweighs benefits limitation, the statistically based consumer databases expected value of the information gathering time and resources spending cost should outweigh the cost of gathering the data from normal marketing research method.

On the limitation of problems with research statistically based customer databases , qualitative limitations include narrow concept of research, unrealistic view of timeframe, as well as variable quality of market researchers and it is possible that market researchers have not own sufficient technical to apply statistically based customer data bases. For example, market researchers will feel difficult to find facts from statistically customer data bases and who will spend much time to define research result from finding.

The qualitative approaches based on small groups offer any

advantages from statistically marketing research customer databases only, but small groups can not offer any advantages from statistically market research customer databases. The reason is due to market research is about determining the characteristics of a market, for example, in terms of its size, requirements, growth rate, market segments and competitor positioning. Otherwise, marketing research is broader and is about researching the whole of a company's marketing activities. In most organizations, such search would probably include monitoring the effectiveness of its advertising, intermediates, and pricing position. Hence, small groups need to focus on marketing researching its company's internal marketing activities, such as pricing strategy, advertising method. Due to small groups are not large organizations, which did not focus on market research to external marketing environment, such as growth rate, market segment etc influences. However, statistically based customer databases also have these qualitative approaches to small groups offer advantages include, easy of completion, realism, comprehensive, per-testing, questioner training, respondent motivation, repetition, cultural issues, bias in formulation and sensitivity of question etc. qualitative approaches.

3. What effects do you expect the development of interactive electronic media to have on retailers' collection of marketing research information from consumers?

The effects that I expect the development of interactive electronic media to have on retailer's collection of marketing research information from consumers. Limited use of market research indicated formal market analyses continue to be

useful for extending product lines, but they are often misleading when applied to radical innovations. Problems, with traditional market research has allowed prominent product failures and wrong predictions; markets are increasingly becoming micro-segmented, e.g. sports shoes aimed at fashion conscious women specifically for aerobic, so mass market research becomes correspondingly irrelevant; it is helpful for improvements, but traditional market research method is less for radical innovations and is less for more accurate targeting. Thus, I expect the development of interactive electronic media effects to have on retailers collection of marketing research in formation from consumers. It may be advantageous to analyze continue to be useful for expanding product lines in the most short time and it will not mislead to businessmen when who applied this electronic media on retailers collection of marketing research method to get radical innovations accurately. For example, predicting whether who are major targeting segments for the sport shoe company to sell in the short time accurately, such as between 10 ages and 30 ages young male client group or young female client group or between 31 ages to 50 ages adult male client group or adult female client group.

On the evaluating internet resources for retailer's collection of marketing research legal hand, it needs to indicate the content of a resource must be reflective. If there is change, the resource must promptly reflect that change; if a law has been amended, any discussion on the web must reflect the law as amended. Otherwise, the internet resource is not qualified for citation in legal marketing research; research specialization and achievement, institutional and professional affiliation, medium of communication, e.g. professional journal and publishers are all useful criteria to evaluate credibility; questions to ask include: Is it a reviewed articles? Is it a law review journal? And does the author exhibit critical assessment of a resource? ; Copyrighted work means that an individual or an institution could claim ownership, responsibility and liability for the resource. It also publication and therefore users may have to comply with the principle of fair value; resources with citations journalistic ones. Researchers should therefore accord higher preference to resources with citations; many web resources disappear with the resources who contain. For instance, an electronically published law report must not only be current but also be continuous for it to be a dependable source for consultation, it is important to examine whether a resource reflects the attributed of misinformation half truths prejudice; a marketing researcher needs resources that can be connected to individual retailer or company's resources. In general, online market researchers know that search engineers vary in how who select ranking of results. With the advent of search engine optimization and the role of online marketing search engines, results are impacted by things other than returning results that are customized to rank higher sponsored links, with the page owner paying advertising dollars to get their site ranked higher. General search engines can be helpful when getting started or determining the scope of a particular question. Search engines like Google, Yahoo can be powerful tools. It is good practice to not rely on only one general search engine. General research engines, like Google, also have power helpful in narrowing large search results.

An old librarian advertisement page is that customers can have something quick, cheap and accurate but who can only pick two out three. Therefore, choosing the top two most important factors will help consumers decide between conducting an open web marketing search and using specialized commercial databases. However, law firm librarians need to play important roles in helping their firms and staff members locate, manage and use Internet resources efficiently and cost effectively and who need to understand not only the needs of their firms and clients, but also the specific types of information available online as well as offline to meet clients' unique needs and who also need to help business firms grow and strength their client services by taking advantage of the rich information online. For instance, law librarians need to lead the form in creating the best and most comprehensive combination of knowledge and information re-sources, including capturing and preserving reliable free and low cost internet resources, that accommodates the firm's budget and user needs, maintain the firm's intranet, further enabling cost effective online legal research, promote free and low cost online resources and research techniques, whenever, feasible to help attorneys and staffs improve research efficiency and cost effectiveness, manage electronic subscriptions which now generally account for a large annual spending than books and newsletters, educate users and conduct training sessions on online research skills, provide tailored content for individual users or groups to facilitate intelligent filtering of the abundance of available information online, provide guideline on the usefulness and reliability of legal resources, guide attorneys as well as consumers in finding information from the internet efficiently.

On evaluating internet research surveys marketing research hand, there have advantages of internet research surveys, rather than mailing a paper survey, a respondent can be given a hyperlink to a web site containing the survey or in an email survey, a questionnaire is sent to a respondent via electronic mail, possibly as an attachment . Electronic media survey is as an alternative to conventional survey modes , e.g. the telephone, mail and face to face interviewing. For example, a web survey can relatively simply incorporate multi-media graphics and sound into the survey instrument, automatic branching and real time randomization of survey questions and/or answers into self administered web surveys. However, unlike when phone and mail surveys were first introduced, concerned exist about whether these internet based surveys are scientifically valid and how they are the best conducted. Because internet can offer possibility of multimedia and interactive surveys containing audio and video, convenience samples to respondents email address. As a result, quick polls and other types of entertainment surveys have become increasingly popular and widespread on the web marketing research.

On the web marketing based surveys had particular three of benefit assumptions to attract companies to choose to do marketing research: (a) internet based surveys are much cheaper to conduct, (b) internet based surveys are faster, (c) when combined with other survey modes, internet based surveys yield higher response rates than conventional survey modes by themselves. In general, companies shall consider the following key characteristics of surveys choices: Response rate, timeliness, data quality and cost .

(Adrian, P. 2012) indicated that in response rate hand, web surveys respondents that can or will answer via the web may not be sufficiently large to compare mail surveys possibly. However, a company AT& T employees surveys experiment indicated to report a 63% response rate via email (63 returned not of 100 sent by email) compared to a 38% response rate for postal mail (14 returned out of 40 sent by mail). Interestingly, it indicated the response rates to the fast that, at the time, At& T employees received a lot of corporate paper junk mail yet over the internal email system, they received little to no electronic junk mail. I expect the development of interactive electronic media market research survey can achieve responses from a convenience sample might be useful in developing research hypotheses. Responses from convenience samples might also be useful for identifying issues, defining ranges of alternatives or collecting other sorts of non inferential data.

On timeliness hand, survey timeliness is increasingly stressed. The length of time it takes to field a survey is a function of the contact, response and follow up modes. the relevant measure is not average response time, but maximum response time (or perhaps some large percentage of the response time distribution) since survey analysis generally does not begin until all of the responses are in. However, simply concluding that internet based surveys are faster than mail surveys ignores the reality that the total amount of time for survey fielding time is more than just the survey response time. A complete comparison must take into account the mode of contact and how long that process will take and the made of follow up allowing for multiple follow up contact periods. For example, if email address of respondents are unavailable and a probability sample is desired than respondents may have to be contacted by mail. In this case a web survey only saves time for the return delivery of the completed questionnaire and not for the contact and follow up, so that the resulting time savings may only be a fraction of the total survey fielding time. For example, a internet survey company, knowledge networks has indicated that to achieve 70 to 80 % response rates they must leave a survey in the field for about 10 days. This period comprises one workweek with two weekends because they find that most respondents complete their surveys on the weekend (Adrian, P. 2012).

In conclusion, the delivery time of an internet based survey is faster than the delivery of a survey by mail, it does not necessarily follow that the increased delivery speed will translate into a significantly shorter survey fielding period. Two points are relevant: dramatic possible for specialized populations and even for populations in which all electronic surveys are possible.

On the quality hand, the primary purpose of a survey is to gather information about a population , the information is useless unless it is accurate and representative of the population. When survey error is commonly characterized in terms of the precision of statistical estimated, a good survey designing seeks to reduce all types of errors, including coverage, sampling, non response and measurement errors. Data quality includes unit and item non response, honesty of responses , particularly for questions of a sensitive nature, completeness of responses particularly for open ended questions and quality of data transcription into an electronic format for analysis of requires by the survey made. Data quality is usually measured by the number of respondents with missing items or the questions, longer answered are usually considered more informative and of higher quality email surveys may incur a higher percentage of items missing than mail surveys. Other quality issues for internet based surveys resulting from some sort of sampling errors are generally the same as for conventional surveys. However, such accuracy may be misleading if non response biases are not accounted for and researchers need to carefully consider the trade offs between smaller samples that allow for careful non response follow up and larger samples with less or no follow up. Web surveys can be programmed to conduct input validation as a logical check of the respondent's answers.These types of checks improve data quality and subsequently save time in the preparation of the analysis file. This will eliminate errors and from the respondent's point of view, simplify the process of taking the survey.

On cost hand, designing a survey fundamentally involves making trade off between the quality and quantity of data and cost. For smaller research surveys that are not subsidized in any way, a major component of total survey cost is frequently the researcher's time for survey design and subsequent data analysis. The labour cost of the personnel who actually execute the survey. It depends on the size of the survey and the complexity of the design either researcher labour cost, survey personnel labour costs or a combination of the two will likely dominate the survey budget.When lower costs are often of the benefits, of internet based surveys, Couper et al. (1999) found no cost benefit in email compared to postal mail surveys in their work. In a large and comprehensive survey effort of different government agencies. Couper et al. compared an all email survey (contract, response and follow up) versus an all mail survey. They found that evaluating and testing the email software took over 150 hours almost 4 times as much as they budgeted.

For the mail survey, costs for printing and posting were $1.6 per reply and data editing and entry cost about $1.81 . For the mail survey , managing the email cost $1.74 per completed case. In addition, they handled over 900 toll free call of a technical nature when the printing and mailing costs were eliminated for the email survey. Couper et al.(1999) found that the cost of evaluating and testing the email software, additional post collection processing and the cost of maintaining a toll free phone line which was largely dedicated to responding to technical questions related to the email surveys offset any savings. For example, email survey was designed so that respondents would use the reply function of their email program so the resulting replies could be automatically read into a database upon receipt.

I expect web marketing based surveys can reduce errors to avoid to mislead companies to find the wrong marketing strategy to compare paper surveys from every time of individual group customer questionnaires researches from internet. Moreover, I also expect web marketing based surveys can reduce cost to compare paper surveys from every time of group customer questionnaires researches from internet. In conclusion, I expect the development of interactive electronic media to have on retailers collection of marketing research information from consumers, the internet companies need to consider the electronic surveys response rate and time and quality and cost and legal responsibilities issues to let any companies to use their electronic media to carry on marketing research from customers to feel more satisfactory to compare to traditional questionnaires market research media if internet companies still hoped business companies still chose to use whose service to do marketing research in the future.

CHAPTER XXIX

England wine bar segmentation case study

Critically evaluate the bases that bars may use to segment their markets.

The United Kingdom bars market is a mass marketing, it means a strategy that presumes these is one undifferentiated market and that the bars wine drinking service provision will appeal to all consumers in that similar bar market. Marketing matching strategy divides segmentation, it means act of dissecting the marketplace into submarkets (segments) that require different marketing mixes, then targeting, it is the process of reviewing market segments and deciding which one(s) to pursue finally positioning, it needs to establish a differentiating image for a product or service in relation to its competition. segmentation variables may divide geographic, demographic, psychographic and behavioral variables.

In general, marketers may use a single variable or two or more variables. Geographic segmentation is based on the location of the target market, people living in the same area have similar needs that differ from living in other areas, climate, population, taste and micromarketing. Demographic segmentation is based on factors, such as age, gender, marital status, income, occupation, education, ethnicity. Psychographic segmentation is based on lifestyle and personality characteristics. Behavioral segmentation is based on attitudes toward or reactions to a product/ service and to its promotional appeals, usage rate, benefits sought from a product/ a service and loyalty to a brand or a store.

There are three basic market targeting strategies, such as undifferentiated, differentiated and concentration. Undifferentiated strategy ignores differences between groups within a market and offers a single market mix to the entire market and it works when a product/service is new to the market and there is minimal or no competition. Differentiated strategy means targeting two or more segments with different marketing mixes for each, concentration strategy focuses on one sub-market. Most British towns would had many small bars, all looking fairly similar to each other, with relatively few point of differentiation. Thus, if the UK bars do not use to segment their markets. I believe these UK bars will face much competition between themselves. In general, the market for drinking in pubs was fairly homogenous, comprising mostly male, who went to the pub mainly to drink and only very rarely to eat.

Now, UK pubs, clubs and bars continues to be a popular leisure activity in UK and pubs have benefits from a growth in eating out.

But, pub operators face challenges , including taxes on alcohol, growing competition from supermarkets for off sales, a smoking bad introduced. Pub operators have had to focus the design of bars on meeting the needs of smaller and smaller market segments. No longer is the pub market dominated by males going out to drink-professional women and families are among many segments and the professional and families segments, who seems dislike loud music or big screen television, who like to drink good quality coffee served more than beer, who like to enjoy bright and airy decorative in bars, who like to drink served to the table rather than queuing at the bar. These may have been design features that were unsought or unwanted by the traditional male heavy drinker segment. Hence, it seems that UK female professionals and families shall be the popular segment in this UK bars market. However, segmentation can not be based simply on where people live, and must recognize their mobility and movement patterns. Therefore, for some sites located in town centers or on busy roads, an understanding of people's work patterns and commuting habits can be crucial. Being near a train station may be crucial for attracting a target market or urban professionals who want somewhere to stop off to meet friends before catching a train home. I think the UK bars may use to segment their market. Segmentation is essentially about identifying groups of buyers within a marketplace who have needs that are distinctive in the way who deviate from the average consumer. Some consumers may treat satisfaction of one particular needs as a seek to satisfy any of needs from a car purchase total market, the possible factor that might influence and individual's choice of car, car market segment targeted includes status, safety for families, a particular image, a cost effective transport, seeking environment by buying a green car and a company buyer saves tax client groups. Hence, British bars are fairly similar to each other, with relatively few points of differentiation. The market for drinking in bars was fairly homogenous and British supermarkets can sell wines and the comprising mostly males who went to the bar mainly to drink and only very rarely to eat. Today, the bar scene in any British town centre is much complex. Hence, I think British bars ought to segment their markets if which wanted raise their competition.

On the first hand , the UK bar owner can choose professional women and family segment, in upmarket local, low density housing areas, it is likely to offer high quality food, no loud music or big screen television, good quality coffee served more than beer, bright and airy bar environment, drinks served to the table, rather than queuing at the bar, due to the proportion of women using these bars is higher than most of the locals.

On the second hand, the UK bar owner can choose male segment, in basic or mid market locals, that were unsought or unwanted by the traditional male areas; trade is focused on regular drinkers and tend to be met lead with little food. Beer, cider and spirits are the big sellers. Most show televised most offer some sort of food. There may also be themed evenings, quizzes, darts or pool. Customers tend to use the bar to meet friend and relax.

On the third hand, the bar can choose young local customers aged 18 to 30 secondary and university students segment. Amusements including pool tables and machines with feature and chart music and video screen will be prevalent.

On the fourth hand, the bar owner can choose city local to workers and shoppers segment, such as non office labors and supermarket buyers clients, it will offer basic bar food and snacks as well as centrally located in town centers but offering high levels of food, city dry led bars target the same customers as city locals, but focus on office labor clients mainly and it tends to be large and it may have function rooms and restaurant areas.

On the fifth hand, the bar owner can choose office workers and shoppers both segments. It may locate in centrally city location, but it needs to change from day to night to attract different types of customers. It can provide coffee bar attract in the day serving office workers and shoppers, but provide wine attract to young people's bar with loud music by might.

On the sixth hand, the bar owner can choose bar is located on or near the young non student people's circuit. Expect loud music, possibly a dress code and door staff and food is less important.

On the seventh hand, the bar owner can choose adults no children targets, in more upmarket areas. Restaurant quality food served for whose premium dining aim.

On the eight hand, the bar owner can choose family with children target, it again focuses on food these bar offers good value for money dining during the weekend and early evening.

On the final hand, the bar owner can choose to meet point for a specific customer group for example bikers, sport client segment in bicycle areas. It may be live music or entertainers to drink whose wine after who ride bicycle to need to find restaurant to sit down to relax and eat food needs. Hence, UK bar market is such as car sale market to follow family life cycle, gender and household composition, age, ethnic group, social class, individual income, lifestyles, individual attitudes, values benefits sought, the bar loyalty, the bar geographic location etc. the client internal psychological factors or the external environmental factors to divide different segments to sell in the market. However, I suggest the UK bars market segment ought to analyze to target young adult wine drinkers mainly. Bar consumer segmentation in the wine industry takes on many forms: demographic, geographic, behavioral and others. For the bar wine industry, this group currently fits the legal drinking age range of 21 to 28 ages. With the recent oversupply of wine bars on the UK local market, so UK wine bars competitions are very high. Due to this situation, I recommend who need to focus efforts on finding new populations of wine existing consumers, rather than just redoubling efforts with existing clients.

I think wine bar marketers in the United Kingdom have primarily focused on the existing population of wine bar old consumers, which are the very large baby boomer young generation. This was an effective strategy for many years, when the wine supply and economic conditions were stable. Now, however, one of the most promising of the new wine bar consumer segments in the UK is that of the boomer generation. Generally viewed as children of the baby boomers. This segments group is considered whose consuming power and represented the future bars market for most wine brands drinking in UK bars. The children of the boomers who are young and who ought like to meet friends to go to bars to drink different kinds taste of wines and play entertainment in bars during who have school holidays. UK bars market segmentation means the process of dividing which different drinking wines taste into meaningful, relatively similar and identifiable segments or groups. In general, UK bars market segmentation is useful for two major reasons. First, it assists bars marketing searchers in analyzing the needs of a specific customer segment. Second, the resulting data, it allows bars marketing campaigns to be focused on these identifies needs. In the long run, this allows bars to spend their marketing and advertising budgets wisely when at the same time meeting the needs of the drinking wine customer. Ideally, this should result in efficient, effective and profitable bars marketing and sales efforts. There are multiple types and levels of segmentation used in various industries, but those used most frequently by the wine bar industry are those that also fall into for four classic marketing segmentation bases. There are geographic, which is based on where the customer lives, such as big cities or small cities, demographic, which is based on age, gender, income, social class, psychographic, which is based on lifestyle and personality and behavioral which is based on occasions, benefits, usage rate , readiness to purchase stage.

In bars business, the wine taste is main factor to influence the clients choose to come to the bar again. In general, there are five consumer segments, such as conservative, knowledgeable wine drinkers; image oriented, knowledge seeking wine drinkers, basic wine drinkers, experimental, highly knowledge wine drinkers and enjoyment oriented, social wine drinkers. Anyway, psychographic factor can influence people choose to go to bars, the psychographic wine segments identify five major wine lifestyle, such as relaxed lifestyle, dining ambience, fun and entertainment, social aspiration and travel lifestyle. Hence, psychographic factor and wine taste knowledge factor are reasons why people choose to go to bars to drink wines instead of who choose to go to supermarkets to buy wines to drink. Regarding geographic segments in the wine industry, it includes individual wine bars or organizational wine bars or supermarkets or stores wine sale methods in UK country. Regarding wine consumption behavior is another factor, it includes five segments: Super-core, who consume wine daily; core, who consume wine at least two or three times per month; marginal, who consume wine at least two or three times per quarter ; non adopters, who don't drink wine, but drink other alcoholic beverages and non drinkers who don't on the areas where are not close to supermarkets or stores and the living people who are super core to consume wine daily in the areas. The bar has more chance to increase client numbers, it is unconsidered whether the bar's wine taste can satisfy its clients needs. However, the young age market segment has very high consuming power. They don't only have a lot of money, but who influence family purchase. Many perform the grocery shopping for their families and have been given parent co-signed credit cards at a young age.

A key question in market segment analysis for this group is: What drives their purchasing behavior regarding wine? Young people can spend on average of 16.7 hours per week on the internet, excluding e-mail. They use it for shopping, in chat rooms, for research and to keep up is their primary source of information and who trust it. Because of this focus, wine bar marketers are urged to use integrated media to reach young people and not use only traditional channels. Online technology is a critical part of this,, but also offline locations where, such as music clubs, wine bars magazines, cable television and outdoor posters. E-mails targets at online interest groups and cell phone marketing are also useful. However, wine bars advertising that ought includes diversity of race and gender. In addition, young people are highly influenced by minority cultures in terms of music, sport, dress and language. The wine bars marketing implication is that advertising should show a variety of diversity in terms of race and gender. Another consideration is to emphasize values and focus on cultural values when targeting specific ethno-centric segments of young people population in UK. I believe why wine bars can attract more young people, it is due to their focus on wine brands and who like to attempt different new or old wine taste, young people are very wine brand conscious and seek wine brands that provide quality, but at a fair price. Anyway, young people market segment characteristics is their belief in fun and responsibility, who tend to believe that life should be fun and enjoyable, but at the same time who do want responsibility and challenge on the job, who want to make sure that who take time out to enjoy life and believe that certain activities, so I feel young people accept to drink wine in base , the possibility is more than old people or adult ages people.

In conclusion, I think this UK bar market is an undifferentiated mass marketing, due to any bars characteristics can only give places to provide similar tastes of wines or coffees drinking or foods and entertainment for clients to enjoy to single formulation of its food provided services, to bars have traditionally offer one standard of food service delivery to all of their domestic or foreign customers. Due to UK small, middle and large size bars and supermarkets and restaurants are increasing to cause competition seriously. Overtime, however, bar consumers' needs tend to fragment into segments of different needs. Where UK bar markets are competitive, a bar may no longer to able to ignore the bar clients whose special needs of small groups of its customers, because if bar owner sold similar taste of wines, coffees drinking and foods to its competitors of bars and restaurants and supermarkets, I believe the non segment bar will lose many clients to compare the segment bar in UK bar drinking wine restaurant industry.

2. In the context of bars, discuss the relative merits of quantitative and qualitative approaches to market segmentation.

In UK bars market, I think it had the relative merits of quantitative and qualitative approaches to bars market segmentation. As UK bars market segmentation, the UK bar owners need to identify groups of bar customers who have similar needs and respond in a similar way to a given marketing stimulus to raise their bar competition. Hence, UK bar owner may use segmentation to measure whether whose bar ought to choose to locate where location (areas) to provide which kinds taste of wines, coffees, foods and entertainment to attract which kind of bar client group mainly, e.g. if the bar target client group is professional office female, it can locate at upmarket location in low density housing areas. It is likely to offer high quality food because there are many professional office female clients are in these low density housing living. However, bars market segmentation should be regarded as the bar wines and coffees drinking and entertainment service provision of critical thinking rather than as some pre-determined set of procedures.

It shall follow that to let the bar owner to know what is an appropriate basis for the bar segment and one client group market may not be appropriate to all bar client groups in the UK bars market. To aware of the criteria by which the effectiveness of any UK bars segmentation basis can be assessed. I shall indicate those four important criteria to measure the relative merits of quantitative and qualitative approaches to UK bar market segmentation which can earn. The four important criteria include the usefulness to the UK bars marketing planning; the size of the resulting to the UK bar segment; the UK bar measurability and the UK bar accessibility four criteria. On the usefulness to the UK bar's marketing planning criteria hand, it needs to ask this question before which chooses who is whose bar target client group and location and wine and food taste. Is the basis of bar market segmentation useful to the bar owner? It is easy to develop bases for market segmentation when losing sight of the purpose of the exercise. Essentially, the exercise is worthwhile only bar segmentation allows the UK bar owner profitably to penetrate a greater proportion of UK bars market then would have been the UK bar market case if the exercise had not been undertaken. UK bar market client groups identified as homogeneous bar market segments must be just that: Similar in terms of the needs of tastes of wines or coffees drinking and entertainment consumption behavior of the domestic or foreign individual client who contain. The UK bar shall fail in whose segmentation exercise because its assumptions about homogeneity within a bar segment, e.g. male or female or young student or young non student or family with children or family without children or bicycle sport client or office of non office segment, who overlooks some critical differences within the bar segment which leads to varied responses to the bar service offering that has been specifically targeted at the bar client segment. For example, a bar segment for the office workers target client group, instead of the bar owner needs to consider the location whether it is located to close to whose office, who also needs to consider these factors such as, what kinds of foods , wines, coffees drink taste and what kind of entertainment and service price charge and their habit consumption time. To be more effective, bar market segmentation must recognize the diversity of needs within this bar target client group. Hence, the bar can measure to quantify and quality its bar target client group to produce its bar market planning effectively.

On the size of the resulting to the UK bar segment criteria hand, the UK bar owner ought need to ask this question: Are the segments of an economic size to whose bar business? Any basic for bar segmentation should yield segments that are of a size that the bar can profitably exploit, because as the bar segments
get smaller who get closer to achieving the marketing philosophy of satisfying each bar client's needs as though each one were the center of the bar's attention. The problem for the uneconomic to provide for what a reasonable size of bar segment is varies from one UK bar market to another and is constantly changing over time. In the bar market , it is possible to provide quite unique tastes of wines or foods to target very small segments of the UK bar market. For example, if the bar target client group is professional female office worker clients. I think it ought need to locate its bar in the office areas location and the office and the office can not be close to supermarkets because supermarkets will have different style of wines and coffees to sell and its provision of cup of wines and coffees drinking and foods tastes must be different to supermarkets wines and coffees and foods tastes and the bar needs to consider what the entertainment is the professional female worker clients who need to enjoy in the quiet or noise bar environment. Because this factors will influence the bar's female professional workers' psychological needs and satisfactory needs. If who feel the bar's drinking and food and entertainment service provision which can't satisfy whose demand, who can choose another bars to close to office areas to cause the bar female client numbers will reduce. On the UK bar measurability criteria hand, the UK bar owner needs to ask this question: Can the bar market segment be measured? Ideally UK bar should be able to know the precise size of its identified bar market segment(s).

This is imported in order that the bar segment(s) can be compared and its profit potentials assessed. Unfortunately, UK bars clients data are often not available to the UK bar quantity market segments. So the UK bar owner should believe the areas of bar clients exist but can't measure or the bar client numbers should define bar segments only on the basic of what it can accurately be measured, but the different areas (location) bar clients may have litter bearing on the homogeneity of bar consumers' needs and consumption aims or reasons. The UK bar market segments information have include, e.g. the age profile of an area, number of people per household etc. However, bar owner also needs to assess of individuals psychological subjectively factor, such as whose attitude and lifestyles, e.g. if the professional female worker who does not like to drink coffee or wine drinking, even the bar location is close to the professional female worker office client, it will not persuade who to enter the bar. Hence, the UK bar owner needs to find the areas where people whose lifestyles and attitudes to bar enjoyable feeling, then it may decide to measure whether the area (location) may have which bar target group(s) is/are the largest numbers to choose which kind taste of wines, coffees drinking and foods provision and which kind of entertainment to satisfy the bar's identified target client group(s) needs. Finally, on the UK bar accessibility criteria hand, the bar owner ought to ask this question: Are the segment(s) accessible to where bar business? There is little points to define the UK bar owner segment(s) of the UK bar market whose those bar segments are not accessible to the bar segments are not accessible to the bar owner or ever likely to be inaccessibility can come about for a number of reasons. Such as the UK bar owner may be prohibited by law from opening to locate whose bar in certain areas in UK geographic location (areas) or the UK law prohibits UK bar to sell some kind of taste of wines in whose country. Hence, the UK bar owner needs to know UK law prohibition to which kind of taste of wines drinking sold and where location (areas) to open its bars before who decides where to open its bar to sell wine to whose target clients segment(s) in British country. In conclusion, the UK bar owners can earn the relative merits of quantitative and qualitative approaches to market segmentation from these four criteria consideration.

CHAPTER XXX

P&G body and skin product marketing strategy case study

How would you explain the success of the fairly brand?

P&G fairly brand which mainly sold low value consumer goods, such a household detergents from bar of soap washing products to sell in UK country supermarkets in the beginning. Then, it innovated to produce liquid soap washing products to sell in UK country supermarkets. Further, it continued to innovate to produce soap products, such as the power of four for price of one, launched this low bulk, high concentration soap product to sell more cost effective to sell in supermarkets, even overseas supermarkets. P&G predicted domestic dishwashing machines instead of liquid of soaps , so it innovated to produce dishwasher cleaning fluid detergents products to let housewives to clean their dishwasher after every family used dishwashers to clean their plates to aim to keep their dishwashers to feel more clean to compare to clean by hand washing. Even, P&G will continue to innovate to produce potential anti-bacterial food washes to satisfy consumers' increasing concern over resides on the surface of fruit and vegetables.

In fact, P&G can predict what the new washing products will sell in this washing market, who will be its direct competitors, which are generally similar in form and satisfy customers' needs in a similar way as well as who will be its indirect competitors, which may appear different in form, but satisfy a fundamentally similar need. Such as P&G sold bar soap washing products in the beginning, it aim to satisfy families wash body to feel more clean needs. But, P&G felt it's direct competitors can sell similar bar soap products, so it innovated to produce new liquid soap washing products to raise its washing unique products and was different to its body washing product competitors. On the other hand, P&G also predicted domestic dish washing machines instead of liquid of soaps , so dish washing machines shall be which indirect competitors. Due to housewives can use dish washing machines to wash plates, so who will not use hands to wash plates after eating, it will cause who reduce to use bar or liquid washing soaps to wash their hands. So, P&G innovated to produce dishwasher cleaning fluid detergents products to let housewives to clean their dishwashers after every family used dishwashers to clean their plates to aim to keep their dishwashers to feel more clean to compare to clean by hand washing.

Even, P&G will continue to innovate to produce potential anti-bacterial food washes to satisfy consumers' increasing concern over resides on the surface of fruit and vegetables. Hence, P&G had attempt to raise its competitive ability in fruit and vegetables food and dishwasher machines cleaning market instead of bar and liquid soaps human clean market. It seems P&G threats of new entrants and threats of substitute clean products. In fact, P&G considers it soaps or other washing products whether which will cause chemical harmful to human skin or foods or dish washers after consumers have used its washing products. In the absence of that safety relationship of P&G social responsibility, its brand can act as a substitute in managing buyers' exposure to risk. P&G branding simplifies the decision making process by providing a sense of security and consistency of buyers which may be absent outside of a relationship with a washing product supplier.

P&G brand addresses a number of dimensions of purchase risk which have been identified as: physical(Will it's soap or washing products cause consumer skin harm or foods harm or dish washers harm?); psychological (Will P&G soap products or washing products satisfy consumer's needs for safety of mind?); Performance (Do P&G soap products and washing products work in accordance with consumers' satisfactory requirement?); Financial (Will P&G soap and washing products provide adequate performance with consumers' budget?). Due to consumers will compare P&G soap and washing products to its competitors' risk level to choose which brand washing products can give the minimal risk to harm to their health to decide to buy from supermarkets. Hence, P&G brand needs be built objectively measured (bar or liquid soap products or washing products are such as unique shape and smell and reliability) and the subjective values that can be defined only in the minds of its consumers (such as perceived personality of P&G brand is unique compare to other washing products brands). It means that P&G will be recalled that its brand processes functional and emotional attributes. P&G brand has been variously described as having personality that are ' fun', 'reliable ', 'traditional' and ' adventurous' and it needs to let consumers to feel it can give no harm to whose health after who use P&G soap or washing kind of products. In fact, P&G developed a single strong P&G brand strategy to sell different kinds of washing products, such as bar soaps, liquid soaps, dishwasher cleaning fluid and anti-bacterial food washes etc products, It aims to let consumers who choose to buy to use these kinds of washing products, then who must remember P&G brand. One approach to P&G branding is to apply the same brand name to every washing products which produces. The big advantage of this approach is the economic of scale in promotion. Instead of promoting many minor brands through small campaigns, it can concentrate all of its resources on one campaign for P&G one brand. But, the main disadvantage of this approach is that P&G can pose significant risks of confusing the values of it's brand. If P&G positioned its bar soaps, liquid soaps, dish washing fluid and anti-bacterial food washes etc. products range as premium priced, top quality, confusion may arise in consumers' minds if it applied the same brand name to a budget version of its washing products. Does P&G brand still stand for top quality? This is a particular problem for P&G new washing product, such as anti-bacterial food washes and dish washer cleaning fluid products which are of unproven reliability. Hence, P&G sells in low price strategy in supermarkets to let many families can buy its different washing products to do trial test whether its innovative washing products which are better quality to compare to other brand washing products to satisfy who to choose to buy P&G brand washing products for every families to use long term.

In fact, UK soaps product is a imperfect competitive market. The different soap manufacturing companies produce similar color and shape bar or liquid soap products and they build different brands and they are targeted at specific segments, such as family group and they need promotion to promote their brands and soaps price is premium sustained. Hence, P&G needs a differentiated product may have significant monopoly power in that it is unique, but if it fails to satisfy customers' needs, its uniqueness has no commercial value. However, P&G had innovated it different bar soap products to liquid soap products, even it also launched dishwasher cleaning fluid detergents products, due to dish washer machines reduce housewives to use hands to wash plates to use soap to clean whose hands after eating

as well as it launches
potential anti-bacterial food washes to satisfy consumers' increasing concern over resides on the surface of fruit and vegetables. Hence, P&G aims to be any new cleaning products leader to raise its cleaning market share effort.

The soap and other detergents manufacturing industry of Procter & Gamble (P&G) trends and characteristics who its primary intended is target client group(s). I think families (householders) or student individual daily consumption are P&G main target client groups. Soaps are personal care products. Consumers will compare different brands of soaps to decide which brand soaps ingredients can give health to them to wash their bodies and skins. The soap industry includes (P&G) and other soap manufacturing companies primarily engaged in making soap, synthetic organic detergents, inorganic detergents and crude vegetable and animal fats. In general, skin care soap sales include bar soap, body wash and liquid categories which can sell in supermarkets and discounting retailers and drug stores. Traditional , bar soaps, which are considered a mature category, exhibit very low growth, when newer products (shower gels and body washed) substitute products are launched. However, natural soaps still have opportunities for growth if which can be launched to raise care to skins and bodies health to human. The soap and personal products industry is being driven to a large extent by the changing age composition of the population, specifically, baby boomers have established anti-aging preparation as the chief benefit of health products aimed at correcting or improving the physiological condition of the skin. They have led the broad personal care sector of the economy to focus on the potential in aging consumers. Growth is occurring in a variety of age-sensitive product markets from soaps and skin creams to massagers and body fat analysis machines. As baby boomers lives get busier, stress relief soap products will become more important to carry on launching their skin care health quality for human benefits in daily washing. The group composed of 45 ages old to 54 ages old females is responsible for the highest amount of sales of body care and bath products in mass stores, who can influence householder families members spending effort in soaps consumption. P&G soaps are displayed to supermarkets to retail, the supermarkets' shelves are remained unaffected by the changing population in the personal care products sale areas. Even retailers like Brook stone and Sharper Image expanded their interest in branded personal care items. Not only was more retail dedicated to the personal care products, but they were often placed in specific "spa shops" within the store, with displays used extensively to merchandise the personal care category. Body boomers are not, however, the only group important to the growth of this personal care industry. The number of personal care products designed specifically for children is increasing. Health and beauty aids suppliers are using licensing to tap into the growing spending power of children. The traditional soaps manufacturers must carefully review their marketing and other business strategies in order to adapt to the transformed market. The changes also create better opportunities for new personal care product companies to enter particular market segments. The mass bath and body care category has made recent introductions reflective of several trends that department stores, salons and special boutiques have been offering for years. The world consumers are changing their personal care demand to cause a result of soap product innovation, so P&G also needs to replace older well known soap products with newer ones that contain special formulations. New product activity and the increasing popularity and liquid soap increase competition in this personal care market.

A growing perception among consumers that who must deal with problem skin and rising levels of concern about germs are helping drive sales of personal soap. Although, traditional brands such as Dove, Dial and Irish Spring still hold the largest portion of the toilet soap market smaller special soap manufacturers are increasing their market shares. Hence, P&G needs to focus on concentrating who its specialty soaps. In general, consumers want a soap that fits their particular needs and specialty soaps, often made with natural ingredients to protect bath and hand skin health. However, some competitors choose to sell soap substitute products, such as oils, bath blends, perfumes and fragrances in supermarket. Hence, these personal care products can also influence P&G company liquid soap sales in overall soap retail market. In soap manufacturer industry, the naturals trends is also evident in the ethic segment of skin care.

Ethic consumers are seeking multi-functional products full of botanicals and vitamins butter natural ingredients. So, I think P&G needs to launch this kinds of new class of skin care product to raise its skin class of skin care product to raise its skin care health care to increase consumers' confidence. Due to personal care products market competition is increasing, such as one stop shopping stores can offer for a variety of health related items, healthy foods, dietary supplements, prescription and over the counter drugs, skin care products and other natural personal care products. In addition, smaller natural skin care manufacturers are staying competitive by targeting skin-related over the counter drug markets. Moreover, internet retailing of personal care products has grown rapidly. Web site can offer can be nearly limitless. One important advantage held by online sellers over stores with physical locations is the constraint caused by a lack of shelf space. The characteristics of online sellers allow them to stock a much wider variety of the products consumers want, if also provides an opportunity for small or large manufacturers audience of consumers. One of the greatest difficulties faced by a firm wishing to enter a consumer products market is persuading retailers that they will benefit by dedicating scare shelf space to the manufacturer's products to online selling reduces that problem.

A potentially important negative aspect of electronic commerce for personal products is that inability to feel and especially, smell the merchandise. Many personal care products list fragrance as an important characteristics. To the extent consumers are already familiar with a special products, this is not a problem, but such as P&G getting a new liquid soap products might be more difficult. Soap industry needs to launch to improve soap qualify to satisfy consumer need. It must need enough workers to help P&G to manufacture enough different kinds of soap to sell to different countries soap market. I think its workers include these kinds , such as packaging and filling machine operators, first line production supervisors, cleaning, picking equipment operators, hand packers and packagers, hand material movers and soap researchers because it needs these workers to help it to produce different kinds soaps in the manufacturing process in factory, so it needs to give training to raise whose proficient skills to prepare to produce any new kinds of soap efficiently and it needs to consider the labor supply to soap manufacturing market , e.g. who needs to know what the difference between chemicals and all natural ingredients to prepare to produce its soaps ethically. Because if they have errors in the manufacturing process to cause consumers feel to use P&G soaps to have chemical negative health response. These workers shall influence P&G health soap products image negatively.

Hence, P&G needs to consider its workers' working attitude ethically. However, P&G was the largest soap maker and it did not own the most part maintain in house chemical manufacturing capabilities. P&G must therefore purchase new materials from other suppliers, so P&G needs to consider its raw materials suppliers market to measure whether who can give it the largest benefits and the cheapest costs both, Thus, giving the raw material suppliers global marker to choose who remain a greater incentive to provide superior service to P&G. I think P&G needs to spend time to choose who is its raw material suppliers who can provide the best natural health quality and the least chemical ingredients to cause consumers to use to feel uncomfortable response to their skins negative influence. Hence, I think P&G ought innovate its soap products quality to satisfy to avoid to use any cheap chemicals ingredients to produce its old or new kinds of soap products to sell to consumers unethically if it still wants to a sale leader in this personal care product market.

2. How do you think Procter & Gamble has been able to increase its market share at a time when competition from supermarkets' own-label brands has intensified?

Procter & Gamble operates mainly low value consume products, such as household detergents are among the most competitive and building successful brand is key to long term profitability. Differentiating one product from another in the minds

of consumers can be extremely difficult, with one packet of detergent looking very much like another and performing similarly. It seems that it can not be unique to sell in supermarket. However, then it innovated new liquid soap products, it seemed to adopt to change in consumer preference, and maintaining consistent standards when exploiting new market opportunities. Adrian, P. 2012) showed that Fairy liquid was rated as Britain's number one cleaning brand by Marketing magazine and in 2010 accounted for 3 percent share of the UK washing up liquid category by value. The brand has been a regular household feature since the name first appeared in 1898 year on a bar of soap. P&G first launched Fairy liquid in the UK market I think Procter & Gamble (P&G) has this marketing strategy to supply its soap products to supermarket retailers. A supermarket is not only supply to likely to encounter a massive range of products, such as food , drink, homecare, personal care, luxury products etc. Consumers can see categories and see how much the offering changes, the range , the packaging , the branding and advertising or promotion of any brand products sale at shelves. Hence, such as P&G manufacturer in 1960 year. At the same time, the market for washing up products was still in its infancy, with most consumers using solid soaps, and only 17 per cent of households using liquid soap. But P&G gained most from a change in consumers' habits. It educated the public of the benefits of using washing up liquid. The launch of Fairy liquid soap products involved distributing 15 million trial bottles to about 85 per cent of household in the UK. Creating early awareness and trial of the Fairy liquid soap innovative products led to Fairy gaining a market share of 27 per cent by 1969 year. It had a proud positioning as a slightly more expensive product which is better value and worth. So, it created brand values of a soft, caring, homely image by advertisement promotion. It also attempted to adopt in response to changing attitudes, for example, a commercial in 1994 year for the first time used a father instead of a mother at the kitchen sink. During the first twenty years of the brand's life, product innovation had been relatively modest. However, an increasing competitive market, customers have forced P&G to innovate in order to maintain and strength its market share.

Adrian, P.(2012) showed that with emergence of many 'me-too' competitors from supermarkets, Fairy needed to offer additional unique advantages to raise its competition. In 1984 to 1985 years, P&G introduced a lemon variant of Fairy and its total market share increased to 32 per cent. By 1987 year the market share had increased to 34 per cent, with the newly introduced lemon variant accounting for one-third of sales. In 1988 year, a new formulation was launched , offering 15 per cent extra mileage, as well as more effective grease eradication. In 1992 year, the original Fairy Liquid was replaced with Fairy Excel, which claimed to be 50 per cent better at dealing with grease. This helped to increase the market share to 50 per cent . In the following year a concentrated version of Fairy Excel Plus was launched, with the slogan ' The power of four for the price of one'. P&G launched this low bulk, high concentration product to retailers, such as supermarkets, who were tiring of filling their valuable shelf space with more and more variants of basically low value products. Excel Plus offered supermarkets more cost effective and profitable use of their shelf space. Increasing ownership of domestic dish washing machines posed a threat and also an opportunity to Fairy. The threat came from a relative decline in sales of liquids used for hand washing of dished. The opportunity arose from increased demand for dishwasher cleaning fluid and the Fairy brand was extended to dishwashing detergents. In 2006 year, P&G introduced Fairy Active Bursts for dishwasher. Excel Plus was launched in the UK, Denmark, Finland, Germany, Holland, Ireland and Sweden etc western countries' supermarkets to help it to sell.

Innovation and reliability have been at the heart of Fairy's branding strategy, in a market which has been contested by other manufacturers' brands, and increasingly by supermarkets' own label brands. Preferences for new scents of detergent are continually emerging and provide an opportunity for innovation. Following a series of food safety scares, some observers of the market have pointed to a potential market for anti-bacterial food washes which would satisfy consumers' increasing concern over resides on the surface of fruit and vegetable.

Its innovative liquid soap products, it needs supermarkets where which compete with other soap product manufacturers for the attention and hopefully the purchases to shoppers choice. It's a soap products from bar soap to liquid soap kind of products. P&G brand have been a player in the household and consumer personal care products market for nearly 200 years. They started life making candles at a time when there were still a common source of domestic lightly. But they moved on from those to other related products, soaps and cleaning products. Today, P&G have around 300 brands, including Crest Oral Care brand, Pampers Nappies brand and Baby products, Tide and Arial brand washing powders, Tampax Sanitary products etc different brand in this personal care market. To keep a range as wide as this refreshed and to develop new and improved produce to feature on the supermarket stages around the world needs a powerful innovation engine. P&G had built a world wide research and development operation which involves some 7500 scientists and a spent of around USA$3 billion per year. It might be not as much as the high technology pharmaceutical industry, but still very impressive for its sector. P&G had some very effective systems and structures to ensure efficient soap products innovation project selection and progression . P&G had an impressive record on new product launches and many of their new categories billion dollars brands, products magic whose annual sales could be high as US$150 to US$200 million. But, in the late 1990 year, there were concerns about this approach to innovation. When if worked there were worries, not least the rapidly rising costs of carrying out research and development cost. However, I think P&G should not raise its new kinds of soap products sale price, such as liquid soap products. Even it had spent too much research and cost development expenditure. Hence, I think it still needs to keep competition to attract different countries consumers to buy from different countries consumers to buy from different countries supermarkets globally. Hence, low sale price is its major market strategy in supermarkets sale make. For long term, I suggest P&G chooses to outsource its research and development internal business department to one or more than more external technological research and development consultant company/companies to carry on researching any new soap products to avoid spending too much expenditure to raise soap products sale prices to reduce its competition to sell in supermarkets. P&G 's pioneering use of advertising, direct distribution , marketing research , brand management and produce innovation strategies to raise it's growth throughout the 20th century. Diversification, globalization of it's brands, innovations in distribution and supply chain management and P&G 's technological and product innovation strategy continues to drive its success into the 21st century. P&G had pioneered a series of strategic innovations had sustained its competitive advantage in a number of highly competitive market and its primary focus was process innovations in many areas.

Firstly, background on P&G was from its origin to 2008 year briefly reviewed. Next five strategic innovations were each reviewed along with its competitive implications in the areas of direct to consumer advertising, direct product distribution, marketing research, brand management and technological and product innovation. Hence, P&G soap products innovation was divided to two stages of two different periods to aim to satisfy consumers' body and skin health needs of bar soaps choice to use liquid soaps choice in this personal bath and washing care market.

Adrian, P. (2012) showed that in 1915 year, P&G opened a facility in Canada representing its international operations. A chemical division was created during 1917 year and 1918 year which was responsible for research and development of new products. To sell these new products. P&G created a market department in 1924 year. The purpose of this department was to study consumer preference and purchasing inhabits (Data monitor, 2008:7). In 1926 year, a perfumed bar of soap was introduced. By the end of the 1920 year P&G had no longer produced candles, thereby signal a major shift in its core business . Then, 1933 year, the acquisition lead P&G into hair care products. In the early 1940 year, P&G established a drug products division which also developed and sold a variety of toiletry items.Then, P&G introduced new products and entering new markets, it had not stopped innovating on its established products , such as tide liquid soaps was launched in 1984 year. During this time P&G also purchased Blendax a popular tooth paste brand in Europe. As the 1980 year, P&G made a significant move in Asia by entering into a joint venture to produce products in China. In 2007 year, it invested US$35 to US$50 million in its Gillette manufacturing facilities in South Boston, USA. At the same time, it announced a restructuring whereby P&G. Beauty and health division would be managed under the P&G purchased HDS cosmetics laboratory skincare line that focuses on specific skin conditions that require more attention than general cosmetics. P&G 's history of marketing innovation began in 1980 year with Ivory soap on what had been promoted around the world as the floating soap (Dyer et al., 2004).

Ivory represented P&G 's first attempt to brand a product through the use of advertising to connect with customers. Direct to consumer advertising was an innovation P&G pioneered with its customers and as such was a major innovation versus the traditional practice of advertising to wholesalers and practice of advertising to wholesalers and other distributors. During the 1800 year's soap was cut from huge soap slabs at the local grocer. Soap was a classic commodity with each manufacturer's product virtually indistinguishable from others. It is believed that P&G 's technological innovation was making Ivory out of Palm and Coconut oils, both less expensive than olive oil that was the basis of better soaps of the soaps to be mass produced and felt of finer higher quality soap (Dyer et al., 2004).Unlike other soaps of that, Ivory ingredient was lathered, easily and floated in water without melting. The unique blend of the soap meant that P&G could sell the soap in a premium market, such as supermarkets. However, since it used less expensive inputs, this led to higher margins. Those higher margins provided the mass to pay for advertising to raise the profile of the soap (Dyer et. al., 2004), thereby creating the brand and the beginning of a product differentiation strategy to sell in supermarkets.

3. To what extent can the principles and practices of brand management used for fairy liquid be applied to other goods and services, such as televisions and package holidays?

I think the brand management principle used for P&G brand, fairy liquid soap products sale which is more similar to apply to any television brands management products sale. Otherwise, the brand management principle uses for P&G brand, which is not more similar to apply to any package holidays travel services. Firstly, televisions and liquid soaps which have similar characteristics, such as they are products and it can be touched, seeing it existence and they are needed to launch to adopt consumers' taste, e.g. consumers link to accept to use liquid soaps more than bar soaps popularly as well as consumers like to watch colorful and clear image of televisions more than black and white image of televisions. Hence, any soaps and televisions companies which need to launch high technological televisions or more health ingredients of soaps to satisfy consumes' needs seriously if which wanted to build their brands famously and which wanted to retain old consumers and attract more consumers to buy their products in this skin care and television entertainment markets. Otherwise, if some companies did not continue to launch their television or soap products. I believe these companies brands will be not popular, even consumers will forget their brands existence due to other companies continue to launch their televisions or soaps to build strong brands in those skin care and television entertainment both product markets competitively.

Anyway, any one travel agent's package holidays travelling service is not similar to P&G brand fairy liquid soap products characteristics. Due to package holidays travelling services which can't be touched and can't be seen, the package holiday visitors who can only feel the travel agency whether whose travel journey itinerary arrangement, e.g. travelling destination, travelling date and time, travelling living apartments, hotels, restaurants, leisure activities, air tickets prices, airlines choice etc. whether this package holidays travelling is suitable to him/her only or whose family or whose friends with her/him together. The most importance, package holidays travel services are not similar to soap or television products which need to often launch whose skin care and seeing entertainment products to adopt consumers' needs. Although, the travel agencies sometimes need to reorganize new travel journal itinerary , e.g. seeking England, United States fresh and unique travelling places or cheap hotels who travelers choose popularly. But, travelling industry is seasonal period leisure business, it means that public holidays will have many consumers. Hence, basically, the seasonal periods are limited to travel agencies to build whose brand easily. It means that the client numbers are influenced by the seasonal periods, their numbers will not have much changing, even the travel agent often spend much effort and time to seek any new and unique travel journey itinerary holidays package. Although, travel agencies do not need to spend much money to invest to launch its package holidays travel arrangement service. But, they are existence in one competitive travel market. Every travel agent package holidays travel service price is controlled by the seasonal period whether the period is holiday or is not holiday and what the travelers' feeling to the country, e.g. safety extent, shopping places and prices extent, air ticket prices extent, accommodations and restaurants prices extent. These factors are controlled by the travelling countries. Agencies are difficult to differ their packages holiday travelling services to win other travelling agent competitors to build strong brand management famously. Due to which cannot control external factors to influence their price competition easily, such as airline companies air tickets prices, the destination (country) which hotels, restaurants, leisure services and transportation prices which are controlled by the travelling destination country's businessmen directly. It implies any travel agencies are difficult to build unique strong brands to attract many travelers who choose to find which to help them to arrange packages holiday travelling services to earn more commissions easily. However, if the travel agency had owned only concentrated on arranging packages holiday travelling services experiences and it had many prior packages holiday travelling consumers who feel that it can arrange the most suitable packages holiday travel arrangement services to let them to satisfy all different packages holiday services. I believe who will only choose this travel agent to help them to arrange any packages holiday travel arrangement services again, even who will introduce its packages holiday travel arrangement services to their friends to know the travel agency's brand by mouth speaking individually.

It seems that a new or an old travel packages holiday travel arrangement services agent who ought need more old customers who can speak to whose friends to know how it can give excellent travel packages holiday travel arrangement to them individually, so television or radio or newspapers media travelling advertisement channels do not need promote long time if whose old consumers feel which can provide excellent packages holiday travel arrangement services to make them to enjoy satisfactorily. Hence, it's old consumers‘ feeling whether who satisfy or who do not satisfy its packages holiday travel arrangement service which will influence the travel agent to build its brand successfully in this packages holiday travel arrangement market. Otherwise, a new or an old television products brand sale company needs more magazines, radios, televisions advertisement to promote which television products for long time due to every family who have different demand to choose to buy the television products, e.g. size, design, manufacturing history and manufacturing country's price. It implies the family can't influence to whose friends to decide to buy or not buy the television brand easily. Due to every family has different demand to choose which kinds of television company brand. The television brand's any different style of television products of the family to choose is not same to or influence to whose friends television brands, so the television brand's buyers speaking will not influence whose friends whether to choose or not choose to buy the television brand easily. Furthermore it will take a closer look at the motivational world of the travel agency staff and how both groups interact. These questions will be analyzed with regard to its significance and applicability in brand management. The results of a neuropsychological systems of package tourists and travel agents with a psychological test.

When investigating the travel market it must be taken into consideration that it is subject to considerable changes due to , for example new dynamic production processes, price comparing systems, the growth of online providers etc. Every travel agent needs to make each brand unique and distinguishable in its perception . The key issues discussed where: Why do package tourists buy? Which scopes and potentials are there ? When positioning style brands? How can potential customers be better addressed and won as a customer? Central question concerning travel agents where: What is there main motivation (commissions, incentives) ? How can travel agents be addressed more effectively? How can travel agents help to increase the sale? Sensing versus intuition concerns perception itself, thinking versus feeling are decision strategies based on perception and judging versus perceiving relate to the handling of these decision . Because individual travel agent needs explain why their choice of packages holiday arrangement is the best suitable to every consumer considerately when the consumer is the first time to contact the travel agent , so the travel consultants need have professional image to make whose visitors to believe whose packages holiday arrangement is the most right to satisfy them to travel in their journeys. Otherwise, one of television brand seller who does not need to build more professional image, due to who is only the television company brand representative, whose duties are needed to explain what the television features and functions to let whose customers to compare to other brand television products when who enquires any one of television brand seller. However, travel agent must need to seek any packages holiday travel informational to let any consumers to choose to let them to compare whether which packages holiday arrangement service is the most suitable to who from the travel agent immediately. Hence, a package holiday travel agent seems to be a travel economist, who needs to compare which packages holiday arrangement is the most right and the most reasonable price to follow travel data gathering to adopt to every customer needs after whose customer spends whose packages holiday arrangement to feel satisfactorily if who want to help whose travel company to build famous brand of providing excellent packages holiday arrangement successfully in this travel market. Hence, any packages holiday businesses which travel consultants seem to be individual mouth speaking advertising to every visitor when who enquire whose packages holiday arrangement ideas to achieve aim to let every visitor to feel travel consultant can suggest the useful packages holiday arrangement because who must not have confident to arrange their travel plan by himself or herself. It seems that a new or an old travel packages holiday arrangement service agent which needs more old customers who speak to whose friends to recognize its existence to build its brand for long term. So television or radio or newspapers travelling advertisement do not need to spend long term if whose old customers feel which can provide an excellent packages holiday arrangement service to them to enjoy satisfactorily. Hence, its old consumers' feeling whether who satisfy or who do not satisfy its packages holiday arrangement service from the first time, they shall influence whose friends or relatives who decide to attempt to enquire the travel agent successfully.

Otherwise, any one of television brand sale persons who do not need to build more professional image, due to the sale persons are only the television company brand sale representative, whose duties only need to explain what the television features and functions to let the customers to compare to compare to other brand television products to decide whether who ought to buy the brand television or ought not to buy the brand television. However, any travel agents must need to seek any packages holiday information about airline air tickets prices, itinerary journey and hotels, transportation, restaurant meals, leisure activities of the travel destination country to let any consumers to choose the different packages holiday arrangement programs to compare whether which packages holiday arrangement program is the most suitable to their travel needs immediately. So, their satisfactory extent to the packages holiday arrangement from the travel agent's consultant who can influence their friends or/and relatives to feel whether the travel agent can help them to arrange packages holiday satisfactory. Otherwise, a new or an old television product brand company needs more advertising from magazines, radios, televisions to promote which television products for long term, due to every family who have different demand to choose to buy the television products, e.g. television size, design, manufacturing history and manufacturing country and prices etc factors which can influence every family choice. It implies the family can't influence to whose friends or/and relatives to decide to buy or not buy the television brand easily. Due to every family members who have different demand to choose which kinds of television company brand. Furthermore, it will take a closer look at the motivational world of the travel agency staff and how both groups interact. These questions will be analyses with regard to its significance and applicability in brand management. The results of a neuropsychological study, which measured the implicit personality systems of package tourists and travel agents with a psychological test. When investigating the travel market , it must be taken into consideration that it is subject to considerable changes, due to , for example, new dynamic production processes , price comparison systems, the growth of online providers etc. Every travel agent needs to make each brand unique and distinguishable in its perception. The key issues discussed where: Why do package tourists buy? Which scopes and potentials are there? When positioning style brands? How can potential customers be better addressed and won as a customer? Central question concerning travel agents where: what is there main motivation (commissions, incentives)? How can travel agents be more effectively? How can travel agents help to increase the sale? Sensing versus intuition concerns perception itself, thinking versus feeling are decision strategies based on perception and judging versus perceiving relate to the handling of these decision. Because individual travel agent needs to explain why whose choice of packages holiday arrangement is the best suitable to every consumer considerably when the customer is the first time to contact the travel agent , so travel agent is needed more professional travel knowledge to arrange the best packages holiday to serve every visitor to enjoy their holidays satisfactory to build their brand. Otherwise, any television brand company sale representatives who only need to introduce what the style of television product which feature to let the visitor to know to decide to buy or not buy it. So, any television product brands which need more different kinds of advertising to help them to promote to build their brands long term.

In conclusion, P&G fairy liquid soap brand management principle, which is more similar to apply to television product brand management principle, which need to launch their different style products to satisfy clients needs. Such as P&G brand company needs to continue to change its product ingredient to let many customers to feel to use safely , e.g. it launches bar soap products to liquid soap products as well as any television product companies to launch how to change television images and colours to be more clear to attract many customers to choose to buy whose television brands products. Otherwise, packages of holiday arrangement tourism service, tourism consultants need to own professional travel knowledge to help whose visitors to arrange any the most reasonable price and the most safe and the most unique journeys to attract any visitors to choose whose packages of holiday services. In fact, travel agents who do not need to spend much money to invest to carry on launching their travel service to raise time to gather travel information to increase whose ideas to achieve to persuade every visitors to choose packages of holiday arrangement successfully. Hence, it seems P&G fairy liquid soap product brand management principle which can not apply to packages of holidays travel arrangement service clearly.

CHAPTER XXXI

Mobile phone company marketing strategy case study

Critically evaluate methods that mobile phone companies could use to assess buyer's likely response to new features, such as video on demand.

Mobile phone is a product to satisfy customers' verbal communication needs during who leave home to need to communicate with anyone urgently . Mobile products are only bought for the verbal communication benefit. In other words, a mobile phone product is of value to someone only as long as it is perceived as satisfying some extra need, instead of verbal communication, such as watching video demand from internet when people are sitting on buses, or trains , or drive cars to watch video entertainment from their mobile phones. So, a mobile phone can be a material product, it can also provide an intangible service, such as verbal communication and watching video or sending email from internet by an 3G or 4G telecommunication fast speed internet service provision channel when who leave their home, who can also enjoy to watch video and call anyone and send email such as staying at home. However, mobile phone is a high level of emotional involvement communication product by the buyer due to there are many different and similar style of mobiles to provide to customers to choose to buy, so I think the mobile phone can provide watching video from internet feature is prefer to buyer to choose more than the mobile phone can not provide watching video from internet , even it's price is more than the non video watching mobile due to young people like to watch video instead of going to cinemas to see movies, it is possible who have no time or who feel movie tickets prices are expensive. Mobile phone is low level of accessible product, due to buyers can use home telephone when who stay at home or who can use any restaurant phone if who is walking on the street , it's location is near to restaurants. Mobile phones are shopping goods, due to consumers generally put a lot more effort into choosing shopping different style of mobiles to buy. Their evaluation include price, credit facilities, guarantees, after sale service, email or video entertainment from internet service.

Different brands of mobile products are distributed through fewer retail outlets and therefore there is likely to be a higher margin for the retailer. Customers are usually willing to travel to an outlet to find a brand style of mobile, rather than expecting it to be available on their doorstep. Large amounts of money may be spent on advertising to develop strong brands, such as 3G and 4G telecommunication provision service to watching video or sending email from mobile internet. In fact, mobile product needs to provide intangible service, such as verbal communication , watching video, sending email. Hence, many mobile users ought prefer to buy the brand of mobile company which can provide these kinds of services because who feel these services are whose basic needs, specially the students like to use mobiles to watch video entertainment or working people like to use mobiles to send email to their offices to keep communication when who need to leave offices to work outdoor. However, watching video on mobiles is one new idea to focus of whether who need this service, it can be unclear who the customer is and it can be difficult to conceptualize the exchange that takes place between the provision video watching service of mobile buyer and the mobile seller of the idea. Hence, mobile phone companies need to do market research to evaluate who are the preferable ages segment group and what factors which will cause who do not choose to buy their mobile brands of watching video mobile products. Mobile phone industry is a product innovation industry.

Nowadays, mobile phones have these features, such as cameras, MP3 players and web-browsing. The life cycle of mobile phones as a broad product category is now at the mature stage, some would say saturated. But when individual product formats are examined, a pattern of continual development, launch, growth and eventual decline is evident. Mobile phone companies vision is to affect people, process and technology by enhancing workflow, improving access to knowledge, increasing the speed of business transactions and providing better modes of video watching feature. Some mobile phone companies are already using mobile applications to deliver video image to increased client matching feeling satisfaction. The mobile phone video watching speed convenient availability and price is factor to influence individual client to choose the mobile phone company's style video mobile or chooses another mobile phone to buy.

Some mobile companies have complex products that need to be maintained at the client's premises. Photocopies are a good example. The quality of field service and support is an obvious factor is establishing customer satisfaction as well as in building the kind of customer loyalty that leads to repeat business. The mobile companies have leveraged the potential of wireless support tools are gaining ground in the marketplace. I think mobile phone is not seen simply as a way to communication function. It ought to spend on carrying on researching and development on internet to deliver email message communication and it also needs to provide on line video watching entertainment service new features when every individual client is using every mobile phone company's different style of mobile phone if the mobile phone companies still wanted their mobile phones can sell to clients in this global mobile phone competitive market. Today, mobile phone is popular communication tool to every family. Due to beyond the rapid consumer adoption and usage of mobile phone is the opportunity mobile phone companies offer for brands to connect more meaningful and personally with consumers. Considering it every individual direct line and immediate connection with audience when who is leaving at home to communicate easily.

Most brands spend less than one percent of their marketing budget on mobile. The argument is that the one percent spend level is too low, given the fact that most consumers devote about 10% of their media attention to their mobile device.

During the 20 century, marketers employed mass-market media channels-Television , radio. The result was that brands created marketing massages that out of necessity had to appeal to a broad spectrum of consumers. It implied that watching video had been every person's habitual behaviour everyday. If mobile phone can provide video watching feature to satisfy every client's seeing enjoyment. I think the individual client will choose to buy the mobile phone, which can provide video watching feature more than the mobile phone which can't provide video watching feature, even the individual client feels the owing video watching feature of mobile phone which price is higher than the lacking video watching feature of mobile phone. Because there are many people like to bring their mobile phones to watch video when who are leaving at home.

I shall suggest to do one marketing research of open to close survey method to new features, such as video on demand by whose mobile phone.The survey questions can be conducted , such as whether the client will determine to buy mobile phone with video feature more or who will determine to buy mobile phone without video feature more when the client need to buy one mobile phone to use; whether the client shall compare all different style of mobile phone with video feature which price, size, design and functions before the client determine to buy one mobile phone with video feature; whether what the factor is the most importance to influence the client choose to buy the mobile phone style with video feature, such as function, design, price, colour, size, quality more durable use production of year; whether what factors influence the client to buy other companies' mobile phone with video feature, such as cheap price, unique indifferent design, attractive colour, smaller size or larger size, production of year, whose friends or family introduction, advertisement promotion, convenient availability more durable use and quality; what kind of mobile phone with video feature, the client won't accept to use, such as screen picture is small size, image lacks clear color, too big size or too small size mobile phone feeling difficult to control . Hence, after any mobile phone had gathered their questionnaire researchers idea, then which can analyze whose data to carry on evaluating to estimate whether video features on mobiles demand on the difficult countries' consumer numbers. For example, every country sample of 100 people whose ages were between 10 ages to 20 ages segmentation group, a sample of 100 people whose ages were between 21 ages to 30 ages segmentation group, a sample of 100 people whose ages were between 31 ages to 40 ages segmentation group, a sample of 100 people whose ages were between 41 ages to 50 ages segmentation group, a sample of 100 people whose ages are between 51 ages to 60 ages segmentation group etc. If the 10 ages to 20 ages segmentation group had 50 people out of 100 people who prefer to buy video feature on mobile. It can estimate the country's this age group whose people numbers whether how many population shall prefer to buy video feature on mobile in the country. Hence, market survey research method can identify to measure every country's different age segmentation of client numbers who prefer to buy video feature on mobile clearly.

2. In terms of a new product development process, how could the development and launch of Tele point services have been improved in order to avoid the problems that were experienced ? What lessons can be learnt for the development of 3G (or 4G services)?

Adrian, P.(2012) showed that Hutchison is not new to taking big risks in the mobile phone market. It was behind the Rabbit network of semi-mobile Tele point phones launches in the UK in the 1980 years. These allowed callers to use a compact handset to make outgoing calls only, when they were within 150 meters of a base station, these being located in public places such as railway stations, shops, petrol stations, etc. As in the case of many new markets that suddenly emerge, operators saw advantages of having an early market share lead. Customers who perceived that one network was more readily available than any other would all other things being equal be more likely to subscribe to that network. Operators saw that a bandwagon effect could be set up to gain entry to the market at a later stage could become a much more expensive market challenger exercise. Such was the speed of development that the

Tele point concept was not test marketed. To many, the development was too much product led, with insufficient understanding of buyer behavior and competitive pressures. Each of the four companies forced through their own technologies, with litter inclination or time available to discuss industry standard handsets which could eventually have caused the market to grow at a faster rate and allowed the operations to cut their costs. The Rabbit network came with the announcement by the UK government of its proposal to issue licenses for a new generation of personal communication networks, these would have the additional benefits of allowing both incoming and outgoing calls, and would not be tied to a limited base station range. By 2006 year, the next generation of mobile phone services were under development, with Japanese trials of 4G faster than 3G telecommunication service. 3G phones were also challenged by the development of alternative wireless access services, notably Wi Fi. Many companies, such as T-Mobile had began offering mobile Wi Fi services, which allow users to log on a local access points and gain access to their email and browse internet. Subscribers to VOIP telephone services could also effectively make the free phone calls from a Wi Fi access point. For many business travelers, using their laptop, Wi Fi access seemed a more attractive and less expensive option than using a 3G phone connection to check for email. It was likely to become even more attractive, with development of longer range Wi Max services that extended beyond the very limited 50 meter or so range of Wi Fi. The pressure of 3G telecommunication services was intensified when the UK government announced in 2006 year that it would license the development of a national Wi Fi network.

It seems that 3G and 4G telecommunication service can be capable of speeds faster then Tele point Rabbit telecommunication in any places conveniently. It causes Tele point Rabbit telecommunication becomes obsolete to mobile to use. From 2003 year, mobile phones industry seemed that the new digital technology would be a third generation of mobile phones (3G). By 2008 year, work was well with the development of the next generation of fourth generation

mobile phone (4G) telecommunication service. In terms of a new product development process, the mobile companies need to consider the development and launch of Tele point services have been improved in order to avoid the problems that were experienced. The mobile product mix comprise range of mobiles that a company offers to the mobile market. Tele point service launching whether it is the individual mobile is with its core or secondary and augmented elements to influence consumers to buy mobiles essentially. I think the external factors, such as UK mobile phone companies whether which can sell the augmented mobiles or the secondary level mobiles or the core mobiles which can influence Tele point service demand, such as if the mobile company can only provide the core benefit, but it's style of mobiles which lacks the better characteristics in the secondary level to attract consumers, which shall reduce mobile sale numbers, features are such as mobile design, color, shape, reliability, texture, packaging , even if it lacks the augment level competitive effort, such as after sales service, brand name, credit facilities, speed of delivery and warranty. Thus, even Tele point service launching is useful to mobile buyers, if the consumers feel the mobile products prices are expensive and they are not valuable to attract them to buy mobiles. Tele point service is not the main factor to influence the buyers to choose to buy mobiles in UK mobile market when this mobile phones are launched to

sell in the beginning. The another factor is that Tele Point was new telecommunication service in 1980 in UK mobile telecommunication service market. There is likely to be a lot
of promotional effort by Tele Point service to promote to mobile markets to secure sales.

It is likely that the network of semi-mobile Tele point phones telecommunication service needs have high costs in the development of its service, costs that in the early stages may not be covered by revenue. Potential customers for a new network of semi mobile Tele point phones telecommunication service may be few and far between and therefore sales in early stages may be quite slow. This stage is known as the introduction stage. However ,Tele point phones telecommunication network service had this limitation. It only allowed callers to use a compact handset to make outgoing calls only, when they were within 150 meters of a base station, these being located in public places ,such as railway stations, shops, petrol stations, etc. If it's service proved popular, more people will show an interest and start purchasing it. However, due to many other mobile network telecommunication competitors who copied Tele point network telecommunication service technology to launch more fast speed and no location limitation and they can make incoming and outgoing calls both functions, even 3G or 4G telecommunication internet service is provided to mobiles. Hence, Tele point telecommunication network can not adopt to consumers demands.

Although, Tele point is the first network telecommunication service to adopt to handset in UK, but it handset network innovation can't identified as a source to mobile users' long term competitive advantages in this mobile phone network competitive market. Due to other telecommunication network companies can improve or revise to Tele point network service to launch more advance telecommunication service to provide mobile users to use more conveniently. Tele communication network fails due to mobile consumers useful demands are raising, its existing telecommunication service may no longer satisfy their needs, telecommunication technological change may make Tele point existing network service obsolete, telecommunication network service competitors can provide more convenient telecommunication network to mobile phone users and the social and economic environment may have changed, creating new mobile users needs in the global mobile telecommunication network service market.

The development of information and communication technology (ICTS) with mobile can bring the benefits of within each of virtually all the world's people social communication, such as Japanese mobile phone focusing on 3G technology. Factors promoting it can be summarized as follows: Deregulations by government/ mobile number portability and collocation; competition among carriers, such as introduction of new change plans; technological development, such as connection speed and contents and applications. Dynamic models are based out only on the assumption, such that carriers don't instantaneously adjust to satisfy their long term demand but also on network externalities. The Japanese mobile market has shown a remarkable growth with more than 106.2 million 3G subscribers and 4.4 million 2G as of Dec. 2009. The 3G diffusion rate accounts for 90% followed by that of Korea and this implies the market is almost saturated. Another remarkable transformation is found in its usage: Data communication exceeded voice services. Japanese 3G(4G) mobile phone originally had much variety of functionality other than voice service, being based on supply and demand side of the services: The founder is 3G technology which enabled new services, such as m-commerce and e-entertainment while the latter is due to existence of consumers who are willing to utilize various services. Although, the global mobile phone market has reached to the saturation stage and the growth rate of subscribers has been slowing down. Moreover, the recent development is found in the fact that data communications exceeds traditional voice communication and being the first phenomenon in the world. However, the effects of price elasticity and product differentiation of various carriers and network externalities increase the demand for mobile phone. Hence the technological innovation , such as electronic payment, high speed access and consumers‘ attitude toward entertainment and m-commerce are important factors for the success of 4G telecommunication service need is more than 3G telecommunication service need to every mobile phone users popularly. Moreover, new business models including a flat rate charging plan can play an increasing important role. Operators under these circumstances are confronted with competition due to the short product life cycle and the pressure to differentiate. Although, 2 G networks are adequate for voice, there was a growing interest in shifting from 2G to 3G even 4G based on a number of important drivers. First, the higher speed of 3G technologies translates into added convenience, capacity and functionality for the user. Second, there is much excitement over adding internet protocol (IP) capability and hence internet access to the mobile phone. In developing 3G standards, international

telecommunication union worked with regional organizations and industry associates to reduce a large number of initial proposals to a smaller number of global standards.

In accordance with the development of mobile technology services already provided on 2G mobile phone , such as upgraded and consumers needed not feel difficult when using those services including email services (electronic mail, phone mail and video mail), web access and download music, movie and game. Moreover, carriers provide their customers more innovative functions, such as video mail, video-clips, video phone , broadcasting type video program, walk navigation, ringing tone songs, high speed internet connection, digital television broadcasting etc. via 3G mobile phone. In short, 3G services add multimedia facilities to 2 G phone by allowing video, audio and graphic application. Since 2G mobile had technological limitation of networks and handsets data transmitted via 2G was mainly text when due to development of networks and handsets, pictures and flash moving pictures are available and some handsets enables to view HPS for personal computer. Google and Yahoo started mobile search engines. Thus, 3G mobile becomes platform to use mobile contents, such as games and mapping services etc. Data communication , such as viewing web showed remarkable increase in 3G mobile phone, but monthly changes also increase and this became serious problem.

In case of the internet in fixed communications, the flat rate changes are already introduced.

In addition, mobile carriers don’t adjust to satisfy clients’ long term demands and than dynamic model approaches are available . Especially, network externality or network effect has to be considered in telecommunication. Mobile telephone is the most widely used form by communication in the world today. Mobile communication boost the earnings of many users change the local economy and even significantly, raise the GDP of many countries. The mobile phone has a number of benefits but there is a huge gap in 3G mobile phone why there is the case only two countries . Japan and Korean have more 3G than 2G subscribers. Similarly, why do leading nations like the USA, UK and Germany have 3G penetration rates of less than 30%?

The conclusion, we obtained technological innovation were achieved first, than based on this various service innovation were followed. It should stress that the former includes innovations in handsets as well as those relates to networks and IP technologies. The diffusion on new services depends on how they meet clients preference and needs, but behind services innovations those always technological innovations. On the other hand, some other social backgrounds, such as consumer's attitudes, economies and businesses systems are required. For example, the Japanese and later other service providers solved the first start up problem for mobile internet (mobile internet uses 3G with entertainment content that was supported by a micro-payment system) . In conclusion, Tele Point telecommunication service failure was due to it felt it was the telecommunication service provider to Unite Kingdom people to use mobile, it believed UK people, even any countries‘ people ought only chose to use its telecommunication service monopoly. So, in this mobiles market, it did not continue to develop and launch its telecommunication technological service. However, due to its telecommunication service had geographic location distance limitation and out calling only limitation to every mobile UK and overseas users in different countries. Hence, many mobile users who would feel inconveniently. However, then other telecommunication service providers copies it's telecommunication technology to launch and research to develop 2G, even, 3G and 4G telecommunication technology, its competitors can provide no geographic location distance limitation and in calling and out calling both to every mobile user who can use conveniently. Finally, Tele Point telecommunication service was not accept to choose to use to its old mobile customers popularly, even the new mobile customers would choose to use any telecommunication service providers, due to which telecommunication service could give more advantages to compare it's telecommunication service.

If Tele Point telecommunication could spend time and technology to continue to launch to improve its telecommunication communication time speed, raised incoming call function and reduced no geographical location distance limitation difficulties (weaknesses). I believe that Tele Point telecommunication ought attempt to continue to launch to improve its weaknesses of such as above weaknesses to adapt mobile consumers' demand easily, then it ought continue to keep its competitive position in this global telecommunication market till to nowadays.

3. Consider how the launch of 3G services in a less developed country with a less sophisticated telecommunications infrastructure may differ from a launch in a western developed county?

The growth has 3G telecommunication service in less developed country risk for the companies involved, especially where new technological displace the technology which went before them, calling for ever increasing capital investment, and no chance of a return from customers until long after the initial investment has been made in new capacity. Mobile phone companies need to predict the less developed countries, such as Africa country which has how many people who need mobile phone usage whether Africa has high businessmen who can support place, promotion, people and service to assist mobile phone companies to launch 3G or 4G telecommunication service. I think mobile phone companies need to let Africa country people to know mobile phone 3G telecommunication service technology is as the key to a whole new world of mobile telephone in which the mobile phone would be positioned not just as a device for voice communication, but a vital business, leisure, and information tool. So, mobile phones can assist Africa people to communicate in any places conveniently. A less developed country is a planned economy, the government makes all decision for society. Producers only make what they are instructed to make. The main benefits are that most workers are employed and most people enjoy a similar basic lifestyle. The problems cause to launch 3G mobile telecommunication service include that a planned economy gives little capacity for development, so growth and investment is limited, the infrastructure is usually under-developed as government spends on other areas, such as defense, wages are state controlled, so people have less motivation to perform at higher levels, mobile charges are fixed by government, consumers often can't afford luxury products, such as computers or mobile pones which are taken for granted in developed countries. Otherwise, a western developed country is in market economies (also known as free enterprise), the government's role is limited to providing legislation to protect businesses and consumers and making sure or organization restricts competition. It also provides essential services (like policy defense) and ensures the developed country's money supply is stable .

Thus, businesses are motivated by profits to make products that clients will buy. Customers' demand for products and services affects the levels of supply and the pricing, if clients don't less be more efficient or produce on alternative product. For example, During 2003 year, the Hong Kong based Hutchison Whampoa became the first company to launch a 3G service in the UK, with its 3G telecommunication network. The launch was accompanied about the wireless internet and video capabilities. The world was going to be transformed by streaming of video and football matches live to customers' mobile phones and a whole new world of mobile advertising media would open up. However, launching 3G or 4G mobile telecommunication service to developed country , such as United Kingdom or less developed countries, such as Africa , I think the mobile phone companies need to consider what kinds of needs are the country people who prefer to get needs mostly. UK is a developed country, the people will need to get video entertainment, internet extra service from their mobile. Otherwise, Africa is a less developed country, the people live very far. It seems that location technology was value added data services. Even the emergency services stood to benefit from 3G's ability to precisely pinpoint a caller's location. By 2004 year, 60 per cent of calls to the UK emergency services were made mobile, but in instances callers did not know exactly where they were and ambulances and fire brigades only had very approximate locations. A less developed country is developing economy . It often face great difficulties in improving its economy. For example, in a planned economy, assets like land or property are owned by government. Individuals and businesses are not used to make decisions and operating to make a profit. Developing economy likes a less developed Africa country may also be market economy. But share features, such as the population lives on very low incomes, poor infrastructure , such as transport (roads or railways) or local government, poor communication systems, low levels of basic health and education and a low gross national product (GNP). Over 75% of the country's workforce is in agriculture which can be affected by the climate. Telephone landlines are scarce, expensive and difficult to install . It has less bank branches which are based in cities and tourist areas. Many Africa people are self employed business people, such as small farmers. The impact of mobile telecommunication technology on developing countries. The connectivity provided by mobile phone technology supports economic development. Its impact on a developing country likes Africa country has been extremely positive. Many families live in remote areas of the countryside . Installing landlines over those distances is expensive and difficult families are often separated as the main earners are forced to live in order to earn enough to keep their families. Many are self-employed small farmers or trades people such as plumbers and builders. For small business, better access to mobile technology means that who can advertise to a wider audience and don't have to rely for work on word of mouth. They can be sure that clients can contact them with ease. Due to far remote distance between houses and mobile phone companies, to launch in less developed county, any a mobile company must need a mobile network is quick and easy and secure to install and less expensive than landlines. For example, in a less developed country as Africa country, any mobile phone companies need to provide 3 G telecommunication service to any customers when who go to an accredited shop and in return for cash which has credit registered on their mobile to pay rather difficult than a pay as developed country mobile clients top up their mobile card.

So developed countries mobile clients must pay their charge more convenient to compare to developing country mobile clients. Hence, mobile phone companies need to locate mobile card payment stores in developing country, such as Africa country's petrol stations, supermarkets and retail bases stores places. Hence, any mobile phone companies ought need to spend more capital expenditure to launch rapid commoditization of 3G or 4G telecommunication equipment and rising separation of network and service provisioning are pushing the operators to adopt multiple strategies with network infrastructure sharing in the core and radio access networks to improve network costs to a less developed country, such as Africa country more than a developed country, such as Hong Kong country. However, Africa is a potential mobile phone market. Due to limited land line availability, the cell phone is becoming Africa's computer of choice. Never before has a technological innovation been adopted as quickly as the introduction of cell phones in developing countries. Africa county mobile market will be larger to compare to fixed telephone lines, broadband, computer in home telecommunication markets.

By international telecommunication union (2011) source indicated that global mobile usage, 2011 yr. of mobile subscriptions per 100 inhabitants statistic, Africa region had 53, Asia & pacific had 74, America had 103 and Europe had 120 inhabitant numbers. It implies Africa, less developed country had the least inhabitants to compare to any developed countries, so its mobile market will be large (Sullivan, 2007). In conclusion, extensive cell phone networks already are in place throughout the developing countries. These networks constitute and infrastructure providing clear solutions to many problems with building mobile transaction systems. These networks are not exist, but the majority of those in these nations, such as Africa country now uses cell phones for conventional voice communication and text messages to availability of inexpensive handsets and reasonable industry pricing structures. The features of mobile phones transaction systems in developing countries, include interface, network type, date, storage, power source for recharging cell phone, telecommunications provider, financial institution transactions of cash in/out receipt service.

CHAPTER XXXII

England NHS public hospital patient price structure of marketing strategy case study

What do you understand by the concept of a pricing model? Critically discuss their relevance to a public sector service ,such as the NHS.

A price model reflects the fact that companies can generate revenue through a variety of combination of the basic price and prices charged for optional additional items. Some price models may be sustainable by giving away a product at very low price initially, but then charge higher prices for essential items that are needed to make the product function. Sometimes, the dominant pricing model in a market is challenged by a new entrant, with the result that consumers' expectations are changed. The price model can occur in perfectly competitive market or non perfectly competitive market. A perfectly competitive market characteristics include there are many producers supplying the market, each with similar cost structures and each producing an identical product. No single supplier on its own influence the market price because it is not monopoly, water and electricity is managed by government to control the public utility company which can not charge high fee to every householder user at the reasonable price ; both buyers and sellers are free to enter or leave the market and there are no barriers to entry or exit and there is a ready of information for buyers and sellers, for example about competing alternatives, e.g. oil products and stock markets where shares are bought and sold are exist in perfectly competitive market. In perfectly competitive markets, firms are price taker and their ability to set prices is limited by the level of demand and supply within the market they serve. If the total demand go up, all other things being equal, the going rate of prices in the market for their product will rise. Likewise, if there is a drop in total supply for whatever reason (e.g. because of bad weather, there will be further pressure for prices in the market to rise. The final price paid in the market will reflect the balance between supply side and demand side factors.

The model of perfect competition presented the forces of competition may be ideal for consumers because the tendency of market forces to minimize prices and/or maximize firms' outputs. But in such markets, suppliers are forced to be price takers rather than price makers. in a perfectly competitive market, firms are unable to use marketing strategies to affect the price at which they sell. At a higher price, buyers will immediately substitute identical products from other suppliers. Lower prices would be unsustainable in an industry where all firms had similar cost structures. Otherwise, an non perfectly competitive market, firms are able to use marketing strategies to affect the price at which they sell. Such as UK medical service market , private hospitals and public hospitals and clinics which can raise their service fee to their patients to follow their patients demand due to their doctors and nurses service performance, medicines quality and price and patient beds supplies factors to influence their service charges to their patients in UK. Hence, NHS needs to provide different and excellent medical service to its patients to make them to feel it's service is better to other private hospitals and clinics if it wanted to apply price model to its car parking or hospital phone system service charge to its patients because it is a public sector medical service organization. It ought not charge extra service fee to its patients in its hospitals. If it charged extra service fee, such as car parking and hospital phone system service which are same or higher or lower than other private hospitals or clinic , which need to ensure which medicine quality, doctors and nurses performance which are better than private hospitals and clinics and its patient beds need have enough supply to any patients when who feel need to sleep in its hospital. Because NHS image is a non profit medical organization to any UK poor patients, who choose NHS medical service are due to its medical service charge is cheaper than private hospitals and clinics and who feel it can provide free car parking and free hospital phone system service.

A market is defined here need not be a physical location where exchange takes place (as happens in retail and wholesale grocery markets). A market in the economist's sense refers to all individuals and firms who wish either to buy or sell a specific product. A market is defined in terms of products or service and geographic description, so the UK soft drinks market refers to all individuals in the UK who seek to buy soft drinks and the suppliers to that market. The UK medical service market structure can describe as the number of consumers, such as patients and medical providers , such as private hospitals and public hospital , such as NHS (National health service) and clinics; the barriers that exist to prevent new private hospitals or clinics or public assistance hospitals from entering the UK medical service market (or prevent UK patients do not prefer to choose NHS medical service); the extent to which the supply medical services is concentrated in the UK small number patients normally and the degree of collusion that occurs between patients and/or private or public hospitals or clinics medical service providers in the UK medical market. Governments often seek to regulate the prices of key products and service, such as electricity and telephones and public hospitals medical services, so it is important to understand how firms can reconcile the sometimes conflicting approaches of market forces and regulation, such as NHS public sector medical service in United Kingdom. Of course, if NHS public sector medical service planned to charge some non major service fees, such as car parking and hospital phone calling service to its patients and hospital visitors and staffs which are same to private hospitals, it needs to consider pricing model should never be seen as an isolated element of hospital's marketing decision making. It needed to consider its service performance of its doctors and nurses, its social responsibility of public medical service image whether it is better or worse than private hospitals that it had created and NHS 's distribution strategy whether it's patient beds supply numbers are enough to patients and whether it's medicine quality and supplies and prices which are reasonable to compare to private hospitals or clinics in this medical service market in United Kingdom. Private business organization with a broad range if products or services are often price different with their portfolio in quite different ways. They may have developed a price model, which describes the way that it uses pricing of its portfolio to maximize its overall revenue. Hence, one product or service may be charged at a very low price, on the assumption that it can raise higher price if many clients choose to buy its product or consume its service. In some sectors, a number of different pricing models co-exist. For example, in the emerging multi-channel television broadcasting market, some channels are provided free of charge to users, but make revenue from selling advertising space, when others charge to users, either on a monthly/annual basis or a pay to view basis. The idea of a pricing model is familiar to private sector organizations, but do they have a role to play in the public sector? In the UK, pricing models are increasingly being discussed and developed for services which have previously been considered a vital service and available freely to all.

Adrian, P.(2012) showed that the National Health Service (NHS) has a long and proud tradition of providing health service to all, according to an individual's need, paid for out of general taxation, according to individuals‘ means. Pricing has historically had very little role to play in the NHS. However, from the mid-1990 year, individual NHS trusts began exploiting charges for ancillary services as a means of boosting their revenue. One of the first targets for charging was users of hospitals' car parks. Trusts argued that providing car parks was not central to the mission of NHS trusts, and conveniently, government was encouraging more people to use public transport and leave their cars at home. Critics argued that patients were essentially captive and public transport was not a realistic alternative for most people. However, it showed that at one hospital in London, a patient who attended A&E on the advice of her GP, was charged UK$3.75 for the first two hours‘ use of the hospital car park and UK$7.5 thereafter. She was ten minutes over the two hour period and therefore had to pay higher charge. She also questioned the fact that charges were reduced to UK$1 per hour after 6:00 PM, when many hospital departments were closed. For private sector service, a lower evening price, when there is not much demand from customers, and plenty of spare capacity, it quite common. But is it right that a hospital should only charges lower prices at the not busy time when much of the hospital itself is closed? If lower prices are designed to stimulate additional demand, it this a realistic prospect when many hospital departments are only available between 9:00 AM to 5:00 PM? Another source of revenue exploited by many hospital trusts from the use of bedside telephones by patients. Many trusts entered agreements with private telephone service providers which allowed incoming and outgoing patient calls only through the officially appointed system, which used a premium rate number. A proportion of the revenue was retained by the hospital. Conveniently, hospital trusts pointed to evidence that mobile phones could harm sensitive medical equipment , and therefore used this to eliminate competitive pressure from patients' mobile phones, forcing them to use the hospital's own telephone system. The ethic of hospital telephone pricing was challenged by the House of Commons Health Select Committee, which accused some trusts of using excessively outgoing call, adding to patients‘ costs, and boosting hospital revenue. It cited a hospital in Essex where people wishing to telephone patients were being charges 49p per minute at peak time and 39p off peak. By comparison , a typical household rate for a long distance phone call was around 7p in the peak and 2p in the off peak. The select committee also expressed doubts about whether a ban on mobile phones in hospitals was actually a result of possible interference with medical equipment and recommend visitors should be able to use mobile phone within certain areas of hospitals. So, it seems that UK private hospitals patients phone calling service fee is below than householder phone calling service fee and it is not every patient must need to use phone when who stays in hospital as well as the visitors should able to use mobile phones and who should not use hospital phones within certain areas of hospital, who will not interference with medial equipment. Otherwise, by banning mobile phones, had private hospitals been more concerned about creating a monopoly environment for pricing their telephone service, than any possible risk to their equipment? However, I think National health service (NHS) which is one public government assistant hospital, it can not be same to private hospital to charge unreasonable car parking fee or hospital phone service fee to its patients, due to these ancillary services is not hospital main income source and it is one non profit hospital, it needs to provide the fair and non expensive medial charges to its poor patient segment because who are not rich, so who will prefer to choose NHS medical service to compare to choose private hospital services in United Kingdom.

National health service (NHS) is a privatization, fragmentation and market competition of health care provision supposedly to cut costs and improve the efficiency of the health service in England. The NHS was set up in 1948 year to be a free and accessible care, publicly owned and funded sector service in England. NHS needs to consider to redefine its relationship with health service, limiting the quality and quantity of care it can expect to receive, how it access that care, who is delivering if and even how it is paid for. The result will be poorer, fragmented services with larger differences in quality and access. Services/treatments will cost more and the public will increasingly have to pay for aspects of its care that used to be free at the time of treatment. Traditionally privatization has been through the sale of public assets and services to private owners through the mass sale of shares, e.g. the sale of telecoms, railways, energy or water services. These companies than own the services and are able to make profits from them like any other are able private businesses. In the NHS until now, this model of privatization is taking place through a combination of the reduction of the role of government in regulating health provision, the transfer of services to the private sector through commissioning from any qualified providers, such as independent sector treatment care centers, outsourcing of parts of services to the private sector, the creation of market mechanisms for the distribution of funding within the NHS (e.g. commissioning, payment by results mechanisms, the purchaser-provider split and so called patient choice policies). The use of private finance initiatives that use private money to build new buildings and infrastructure and then the state has to pay, the creation of foundation trusts that are run much more like private businesses and have the ability to raise funding through private patients that pay for services, allowing services to become not for profit organizations, such as social enterprises, cooperatives or mutual and thus leave public ownership, limiting access to certain services previously provided by the NHS. Provided healthcare tends to cost more. It requires a large bureaucracy to operate, with huge transaction costs that come with contracts, billing and litigation. In general, as the proportion of private spending on health care rises, so does the overall cost. The creation of healthcare market can also impact upon the continuity of care people receive. There is always the threat that the private sectors or other providers who take on a service that doesn't secure the expected financial returns may cut losses and withdraw from the provision of that service. NHS is under increasing financial pressure. For example, surgery like hip and knee replacements are more expensive areas of care, the results cause the loss of training opportunities for junior doctors expenditure spending and other health professionals as ever large shares of routine surgery and medical procedures are diverted away from the NHS. Centers for research and medical innovations are also threatened. This can lead to service being out. NHS hospitals will therefore fail financially and be pushed into greater debt. This could lead to hospital mergers, closure or the private sector coming in to run the service on profit making contracts. NHS will bring poor health care service if it will not increase its service charge price to patients. The poor service will be caused, such as permanent damage may have been inflicted on patients with serious conditions due to the lack of follow up care after treatments. In a second worrying example dangerous delays affected the patients of a privatized out of hours. A competitive market system leads to greater rationing and gradually drives patients to take on more responsibility for funding their own care. It seems this already in the privatization of long term care and dentistry. Patients may soon have to top up the cost of their hospital care in the same way that many already do for community health services. The concern is that the NHS will provide a less comprehensive range of treatments. For the private sector, the aim is to make a profit from every contracts, which is not the same as providing the best service . For example, Southern Cross, where the need to make profit lead to the rapid closure of care homes, leaving old people with no home. Hospital people with learning disabilities and challenging behavior were subject to physical and psychological abuse. Privatization will lead to fragmentation of the health services. This is a process on a commercial footing and redesigning the system along market lives. With different organizations delivering different service in different locations, it is also likely to lead a new health service with some area receiving much better care than others, hardest, leading to greater health inequalities. Fragmentation of services leads to worse clinical outcomes as staff have less opportunity to work in a fully integrated dynamic multi disciplinary team. Patients with complex needs can be particularly considerable. The impact of privatization on current NHS staff, who are transferred from NHS employment to non NHS organizations would be changed terms and conditions at the time of transfer. These terms and conditions could be changes at some time in the future, staff would no longer be covered by the national negotiating arrangement in the NHS, meaning they would not be entitled to any future pay uplifts or agreed charges to the change terms and conditions of service . If staff moved from this employer to another outsourced community service, who would lose their entitlement to access the NHS pension scheme and would be treated as new staff rather then former NHS staff, the new service provider could argue that the service who will be providing is so different that they will not be requiring staff to transfer. Those staff will than be made redundant. In conclusion, NHS is one public medical service non profit organization. It's pricing model ought be public service price model, such as no price discrimination and non competitor based pricing aim. It may be difficult or undesirable to implement a straightforward price-value relationship with individual of public services for a number of reasons: Such as NHS public sector medical service pricing can be actively used as a means of social policy, subsidized prices are often used to favor particular patient segment groups, such as car parking fee charges to visitors or hospital staffs only as well as hospital phone system service charges to visitors only or prescription medical service charges favor the very ill and unemployed patients and low income patients and students patients.

2. What factors should influence the level of charges at an NHS car park?

Principles for fair hospital car parking, such as NHS is important because its car park service represents the hospital reputation. Charging for car parking is often necessary, but needs to be fair, providing a travel plan for users of all types of transport, controlling parking fairly, with concession for those whose health conditions or work commitments mean they have to park frequently or at anti social hours, showing car park and transport costs and how charges are invested, thinking about the environment and how transport can reduce the NHS 's impact , being open and involve patients and the public. It is important to get car parking and transport policy and it is communication, right to ensure fair access, good patient and staff experience and to protect hospital organization , such as NHS reputation. Clinical and social changes as car ownership to patients, staff and visitors to hospital sites has increased. For services with rural or urban , as public transport infrastructure is less convenient and reliable . When for specialist treatment, some patients need to travel greater distance and modern hospitals have often been located on the edge of population centres.

Car parking is also a factor in patient's experience of using healthcare. When much progress has been achieves to improve the patient environment inside the hospital, including cleanliness and new buildings, patients frequently report dissatisfaction with transport and parking arrangement. Visitors concerns both cost of car parking and also the availability of space for people with an essential need, illustrating the competing demands that managers need to balance. Patient experience is an important objective for hospitals; poor experiences can undermine confidence in clinical quality and stress can be worsened by poor transport and parking policies. Car parking can have a major impact on the local and national reputation of the NHS hospital . As patient choice increases, reputation and loyalty will be key drivers for provider's commercial sustainability. It seems car parking is one important factor to influence patients who choose hospital more than location/ transport/ easy to get to/ reputation of consultants factors. Ensuring that patients can access hospital when they need to is an important part of healthcare delivery. Many patients who need to travel to hospital by car, either because of mobility or illness, a lock of alternatives or through choice. However, providing a car park is not the only component of a travel plan. Access to healthcare should be considered in terms of service planning, decisions on location of services, building design, access routes and the other transport modes. One of the factor of the current changes to the way that NHS hospital services are delivered is that healthcare should be localized where possible. In many cases, people who used to have to travel to hospital are being treated in community health centers. The NHS hospital can also ensure services are accessible. Most notably, ease of access has recently been improved by reducing waiting times and by enabling patients to choose and book their appointment at a time and location that is convenient to them. Another of factor is whether NHS hospital had or had not ran a bus service from a nearby park and ride car park that runs every 15 minutes. The service has proved popular and is now run by the UK country council. The hospital is been to extend the shuttle service to the other three park and ride car parks which serve the city. The other factor influences NHS hospital charge includes the control parking fairly with concessions for those whose health conditions or work
commitments mean they have to park frequently or at anti-social ours. In order to ensure that those patients who really need to access hospital by car are able to NHS often need to ensure that car parking space is available on site. Space is usually constrained, NHS hospital is in city or town center with high land costs and planning constraints. Charging some patients, visitors and staff to park can manage demand for space when ensuring that those who really

need to park are able to access services. Where charging is required to manage demand, the overriding principle should be to ensure that where possible those patients who have the greatest need to park are prioritized. Where managing demand is a reason for charging for car parking, there may be scope for varying rates for different times of the day and the week, for example, increasing charges for non essential users in peak hours but applying a minimal charge at night when there is less reason to ration space. As well as prioritizing car access for those with greatest needs restrictions on car parking may also be required to deter non hospital traffic, particularly where NHS hospital is located in controlled parking zones, near shopping centers or other facilities that might need to illegitimate required use of NHS hospital grounds. In these cases , NHS hospital may be required to be charge the same as local car parks to avoid abuse by non visitors. However, alternative arrangement could also be explored, including day permits for people with appointment. NHS car parking fair policies should need to be fair application. This is often a cause of concern for patients and visitors. Concessionary schemes and season tickets should be well publicized and available, since a patient may not known in advance low frequently who will need to attend a clinic in the next month. Penalty charges, or towing away should only be applied extreme circumstances with a presumption of good faith that no patient or visitor chooses to stay in hospital longer than necessary and may how on arrival how long who will have to wait for treatment. Running a car park can be expensive. These are maintenance, security, insurance and running costs and the NHS hospital has to pay for
the space the car park uses. Costs are particularly high where land prices are high or there is increased risk of crime. At the same time, patients and the public rightly don't expect healthcare to suffer to pay for parking. The transport costs of non car owners are not subsidized by the NHS budgets to provide subsidized free car parks . To make car parking fee would be to penalize those using public transport. Therefore, fair charging is often the most sensible answer to adopt these two demands. Climate charge and pollution and congestion factor also have health impacts. Reducing car dependency is also a public health objective in order to reduce traffic accidents and increase physical activity.

These NHS organizations have a number of environmental and health reasons to seek to encourage people to use other modes of transport. Parking charge together with the expansion of alternative bus an cycling options to encourage a modal shift from cars to alternative transport. Patients , visitors and staff need to be made aware of these aims. NHS hospital can achieve a travel plan to develop to its car parking with the aim of during a period of busy time reducing single occupancy car journeys by 15% over three years, ensuring tat patients and visitors do not have to search for a space for more than ten minutes at peak times, encouraging the number of direct bus routes to the site to increase reducing staff parking spaces per employee by 10% as staff numbers grow. Car parking charges were introduced as part of the plan with certain categories of staff on exempted from charges (night and weekend staff, disabled staff, volunteers, car sharers and tenants of residential accommodation. From an environmental perspective, NHS travel plan supposed to reduce numbers of cars arriving at the site and the numbers of bus car raise. It aims to improve bus services to cause air pollution at the busy car parking period and cycle parking spaces and improved cycle facilities have encouraged staff to commute by bike. Additionally, a park and ride scheme aims to reduce car traffic of the NHS hospital in the busy time.

Moreover, it is absolutely wrong to charge cancer patients regardless of income, for unavoidable parking costs. From a staff point of view, NHS hospital car parking is an indirect tax on healthcare. However, most unions also support the aim of reducing car usage, as long as policies are fair. Because NHS hospital needs to develop transport policies for patients requiring regular cancer treatment. This approach has potentially negative publicity into a positive image to public. These ought be free parking for the duration of a cancer patient treatment or as often as is needed.

3. If you are studying at a university or college, critically reflect on the pricing strategy that it has adopted for ancillary services.

The development of a costing and pricing strategy will provide an university staff with greater access to price information, thereby providing a more accessible platform from which to base negotiations with commercial organizations. As prices will be informed by cost, the university will be seeking to apply

pricing strategies that maximize university as opposed to maximizing income. In fact, any universities is education industry which is different to common businesses which provide service or product to raise price when client numbers are increasing easily. Due to if an university which planed to increase school fee to charge students, which needed have unique courses to attract students to choose to study and its lecturers educational experiences and education methods needed to make student to raise learning interest and feel the courses are useful to choose to study the university subjects, so who shall compare the university subjects to other universities subjects, then to evaluate their school fees and lectures educational experiences and qualifications to decide whether who ought to choose the university or another university to study. So, I believe that the university can not raise its school fee easily if it has no more confident its subjects and lecturers which can make students to study to feel more satisfactory till to graduate. Otherwise, it will reduce student admission numbers if it still increase school fees, due to it has not researched what the subject contents are students who like to learn. Hence, any universities can't increase its school fee easily.

However, university ancillary services have primary paths to reduce internal cost to raise competitive advantages, such as services differentiation, low internal cost or internal span structural advantage. I shall recommend these price strategy to

adopt to reflect some university ancillary service (non major) service. The pursuit of a service differentiation strategy to an university advantages. The university needs truly understanding its unique core service (value) and then focusing resources on its ancillary services. An implicit part of having a focused

price strategy is not only defining what the university is going to invest in, but is also clearly articulating what the university is no going to do. For example, if the university investigated its students did not like to eat some foods taste, which ought to change some foods taste which could satisfy its students eating needs in its university canteens. Even the university could charge cheaper student parking fee to compare outside public car parks when they park their cars in university parks from the morning to afternoon studying busy time. It could only permit students to

park their cars in its students private car parks. Hence, university staffs and visitors could not permit to drive whose cars to park in university private student car parks, so university staffs could park whose cars in university staffs car parks as well as visitors could park whose cars in university visitors car parks. However, who also needed to pay cheaper parking fee to compare outside public car parks to buy
car park tickets to park their cars in university staffs and visitors both car parks in any limited time. Even, the university book shop could sell lower second hand books and new books prices to compare other private book shops to attract students to choose to buy studying books from university bookshops. However, if the university tried to pursue too many areas of service differentiation, which was likely to invest too broadly and thus reduced the return on investment for previous capital possibly because it needed time to research whether which aspects of it needed to change to adopted students tastes to satisfy their needs, then it needed time to change its services and it also needed time to evaluate whether it's changed services which can satisfy its students demand to make decision to raise its service prices. Hence, it ought concentrate on changing one aspect of ancillary service to ensure it's changing was right to adopt students' taste to attempt to raise service price. Then, it could attempt to evaluate whether what ancillary services which needed to change to achieve price raising possibility. University recognizes that focusing on the core is hard to do, given the history and culture of university. But the worst case scenario for an university is to be relatively expensive and completely undifferentiated. Whether will who pay high school fee per year to go to an university that is completely undistinguished on any ancillary service?

An university looks to areas where which can make cuts and achieves efficiencies, an university should start farthest from the core of teaching and research ancillary services. Cutting from the outside in and building from the inside out. Growth in programs and research, increasing faculty and student demands and increasingly compliance requirements have all contributed to the growth of administrative costs. The reasons are often very legitimate. But as new programs are added, old programs often are closed down in some university ancillary services, e.g. unimportant administration internal service . The resulting breadth of campus activities creates too much complex it for staffs to manage with any efficiencies of scale in university. Units don't trust one another or the center to provide ancillary services. Data center management is a good example of fragmentation on campus. At the university, the central information technology group managed fewer than half of the servers on campus in its data center. For the servers located in the colleges, fewer than half were managed by college information technology groups, the rest were considered hidden at the department or faculty level. Despite the internet data and security risk of having too many unmanaged serves on campus in the university's central information technology department. In similar cases, outsourcing data centers would be a good solution. Third party data centers could provide more solutions, higher levels of securing, greater flexibility in capacity and lower cost than internal solution. Redundancy, an university is an many other campuses, it was managed at the department level, there were no product standards and each department negotiated its own vendor contracts. A sample of purchase order showed that the same item was being bought for as much as e.g. 36% more in some departments than in others. By centralizing end, standardizing more if its procurement to expect to save more expenditure. An university hierarchy, most campuses have too many middle managers. Before it reorganized , an university has average spans of control (the number of employment). Campuses engage to save cost. An university campuses engage in too many activities that require to broad a skill set to effectively deliver in house. Take information technology application management for example, not only does it need to support classrooms and research needs across a diverse set of disciplines (history, music, law, engineering, biomedical science etc. different subjects), it also has to cover functions (finance, human resource, research, administration, student registrar, libraries and student services etc. functions). It weren't enough, information technology also has to serve industries beyond the core academics, including bookstores, retail food, debt cards, total museums, publishing houses. A single IT group would have a hard time managing all it that well, given the expertise required, leading to either poor service delivery, sub scale and costly delivery.

Outsourcing more of non core activities would reduce campus complexity and cost. Third party provides have greater scale capability and skill because the outsourced service is their core business, enabling them to deliver the same or better service at a lower cost. In order to reduce aministrative costs without diminishing service and perhaps even enhancing it's campuses will need to subscale operations by creating shared service or outsourcing improve processes by eliminating low value work and automating much. Better manage university assets to whether it is real estate, physical assets or intellectual property, a number of activities where partnership with third party providers would allow for financial relief and improved performance. Hence, an university can also invest its intellectual property to build its build to raise its market value for long term to raise its sale price for long term.

In conclusion, an university can attempt to use these two kinds of price strategies to adopt to reflect to its ancillary services. Such as the first is competitors price strategy, the university can set its students and visitors and staffs car parking fee by examining what its competitors such as, it's close public car parks are charging their car parking fee services whether they are similar in terms of the university car parking service characteristics fee to satisfy its parking car users' needs as well as the university can set its canteens meals price by examining what its competitors, such as it's close private outside restaurants meals price whether they are similar or different taste and low meal price to attract students or staffs or visitors to choose to eat their meals . The another is demand based pricing strategy, the students are prepared to pay represents the upper limit book numbers to the university's every year studying books. Such as the university book shops can decide every years different subject second hand or new teaching books price to follow the students demand. For example, if the subject second hand or new teaching books supply numbers is less than the student demand numbers, the university can raise the subject books sale price. Otherwise, if the subject second hand or new teaching books supply numbers is more than the student demand numbers, the university needs to reduce the subject books sale price, even it needs to reduce their prices to be lower than outside other private book shops marketing price to sell in the year. Hence, it seems that any universities can adapt price strategy to reflect to their services or products prices.

CHAPTER XXXIII

Tesco supermarket value chain strategy case study

Identify the elements of the value chain involved in the supply of fresh fruit and vegetables to Tesco stores.

The place(P) of the traditional marketing mix decides about channel intermediaries or middlemen to use an outdated, yet user friendly, term and the management of physical distribution. Placing products involves managing the process supporting the flow of goods or services from producers to consumers.

The process has sometimes been described as developing the best routes to market for a firm's products. Products must be made available in the right quantity, in the right location, and at the times when customers wish to purchase them. Marketing channels can perform an important role in the later stages of a value chain, in particular outbound logistic (e.g. order processing, storage and transportation); marketing and sales (e.g. market research, personal selling, sales promotion) and after sales service. However, it depends on which kinds of business to need outbound logistic, such as Tesco supermarket only needs ordering fresh fruit and vegetables from local farmers, then these foods need to be stored in refrigerate in warehouse and transport these foods to different supermarkets by vans. So, Tesco value chain only needs outbound logistic activity, but it does not need marketing and sales and after sale service to sell its fresh fruit and vegetables to its clients from its supermarkets (stores). In fact, Tesco stores is such UK farmer's intermediaries which can add value by breaking bulk. This might involve purchasing in large quantities of fruits and vegetables from UK local farmers and then selling smaller, more manageable, to keep volumes of fresh food stock in warehouses, then its vans will deliver these fresh fruits and vegetables to different stores daily. Discrepancies of fruit foods quantity are reduced by Tesco (intermediary) who provides every store clients with individual preferable fresh foods items that suit their needs daily. Tesco stores can offer superior knowledge of a target market compared with farmers, for example by ensuring which kinds of vegetables or fruits foods numbers are stocked in every store to match the economic and lifestyle needs of Tesco store shoppers who live in the area. Probably the most important gaps between Tesco store shoppers and UK local farmers in channel management are indicated at those of location and time. A location gap occurs owing to the geographic separation of farmers and the store shoppers of their fresh fruit and vegetables foods. UK farmers generally want to grow their fruits and vegetable food in one central location (farming), but farmers' food buyers typically want to buy their growing foods locally. A time gap arises when the UK local farmers' fresh foods buyers want to buy whose fresh growing foods at a time when a UK local farmer may considerate it inconvenient to make the available. UK local farmers may like to grow fresh fruits and vegetable foods at night from 8:00 PM to 12:00PM, then who will collect these fresh foods from 5:00 AM to 7:00 in the morning, but their buyers may want to buy in the evenings or at weekends afternoon. Tesco stores (intermediary) need to facilitate vans to transport these fresh fruits and vegetables foods from farmers' farming to its one central warehouse to deliver to different stores to sell the budget numbers of different kinds of foods to every local store consumers more exactly (Adrian, P. 2012).

Tesco stores is one of the world's largest retailers, it has social responsibility to protect fresh fruit and vegetable to sell to clients. It had attempted to predict customer behavior about hope much fresh fruit and vegetable and what kinds of fresh fruit and vegetable whose consumers will buy from data statistic in warehouse. It aims to reduce excess fruit and vegetable stocks in warehouse to cause perishable. In the winter might have seen choice reduced to basic items such as potatoes, cabbage, apples, supplemented by canned fruit and vegetables. Look in a Tesco supermarket today, and clients may find difficult to tell the season of the year or the distance from the countryside, simple based on the fruit and vegetables with are on display. In UK supermarket sector is intensely competitive, and has seen continuous innovation in the way it seeks to satisfy customers' needs. As consumers have become wealthier, the supermarkets realized that buyers would no longer be content with the staple foods such as cabbage and potatoes in the depths of winter-significant numbers of them now wanted excitement on a plate, and all year round. Furthermore, if they were planning a menu, they wanted to be sure that when they went to their local supermarket.

By and large, supermarkets have been key drivers of the value for the groceries that they sell. They have been close to their customers and identified their changing needs. They have built confidence with their customers, who can trust freshness and provenance of food they sell and the reliability of supply. It is therefore the supermarkets who have gone seeking sources of supply, rather than growers aggressively seeking to sell the produce that they have available. Before, the development of very large supermarket chains, retailers were more

fragmented. They did not have the power or resources to innovate with new product lines which they could then commission a grower to produce. Today, supermarket such as Tesco invest heavily in their food technology laboratories, and can then go to suppliers and place large orders with exacting standards with regard to price, quality, and delivery. Above all else, supermarkets have put themselves at the center of a slick distribution system which connects an international networks of growers through transport networks of trucks, ships and planes to put fresh produce in their network of stores, every day, all year around. The efficiency of the logistics, and the bargaining power of the supermarkets has often led to the price being charged at a British supermarket being lower than the price changed in supermarkets thousands of miles away where fruit and vegetables were grown. Tomatoes grown in Bulgaria and sold in Britain can be cheaper in Britain in local Bulgarian shops. The bizarre situation has occurred where the supermarkets import apples from France to be sold in Kent, the traditional home of British apple growing, plums from Poland to be sold in the grown product in Lincolnshire. Supermarkets argue that sourcing from overseas is not just an issue of cost saving more importantly, the supermarkets seek a continuity of supplies from large growers who can guarantee to deliver a specified quantity at a specified quantity at a specified time and place. The supermarkets capable of achieving this. British supermarkets are among the most efficient in the world, and their desire to ensure that customers can always get what they want may explain the mass transport of food. Local farmers' market may could environmentally friendly, but they rarely guarantee a continuity of supplies. As part of their drive for efficiency, supermarkets have a tendency to move food , such potatoes could being transported several hundred miles between distribution centers before they end up on a supermarket shelf just a few miles from where potatoes were grown. The environmental campaigning group Sustain has estimated that the average children travels 2,000 between the farm where it was grown and the supermarket shelf and furthermore the distance products travel from farm to end customer increased by an estimated 25 per cent between 1980 year and 2007 year (Priesnitz 2007).

Global warming had become an important issue with many clients and there was growing concern that supermarkets' practice of transporting fresh produce long distances around the world was irresponsibly adding to greenhouse gas emissions. Hence, distance travelled was one of value chain factor Terso supermarket needs to consider their fruit and vegetables food to keep fresh in refrigerate to transport to retailers to sell in UK. The most contentious food miles are clocked up by fresh fruit and vegetables flow in by plane from overseas. Although, air freighted produce accounted for less than 1 per cent of total UK food miles, it was the fastest growing way of moving foods around. One response By Tesco was to introduce a greatest proportion of local produce. To achieve this, it placed buyers and marketing teams in the regions in order to get a clear picture of local markets and to develop relationships with suppliers. By 2007 year, Tesco claimed to have 7,000 regional lines from throughout the UK, which were promoted as local produce, supporting local growers and reducing greenhouse gas emissions. Throughout its history, Tesco has demonstrated its ability to listen to what customers want, and this has been true in respect of its distribution system. The weaknesses of commodity systems are particularly for major customers, such as Mc Donalds, commodity systems do not lead to reliability in supply, quality, quantity or price nor high rates of innovation on which they can differentiate their offer from their competitors. The opportunity and challenge of fresh food product differentiation, so Tesco stores need to innovation to give rise to a number of strategic options to keep vegetables and fruits to be fresh in the short time to sell full numbers. If a firm, such as Tesco is the lowest cost producer than commodity market strategy can be an attractive strategic option. As Tesco stores fresh food sale that it's larger competitors shall find difficult to copy. Otherwise, Smaller size stores can sometimes be a competitive advantage.

Tesco stores (fresh food retailer) need to co-operate with suppliers and fresh food growers to align the whole chain to the changing needs of consumers. The food chain strategy aims to deliver superior value to specific groups of customers.

Tesco stores work closely with its fresh food suppliers to develop specific products for each range. Both the supplier and growers understand the Tesco marketing strategy and their role in the innovation process. Tesco is actively seeking new

chain ideas and is prepared to pay for such efforts. From a primary producer and supplier perspective the range of brands enables Tesco to work with suppliers to market the total crop .

2. Critically discuss the factors influencing Tesco's sourcing of fresh fruit and vegetables.

At a time when the media enjoyed the big supermarkets, such as Tesco, being seen to source fresh fruit and vegetables food locally and being good to the environment helped to restore. One observe from Friends of the Earth noted the local produce sold at a branch of Tesco in Excess had in fact travelled served hundred miles as it was moved from the grower to a regional processing center, then to a regional distribution center, and finally back to the supermarket where it was sold. There has also been debate about where sourcing fruit and vegetables locally actually reduces greenhouse gas emissions. There is an argument that Tesco supermarket would be better for environment to grow them in countries where fresh fruit and vegetables need less heating and fertilizers than if they were grown in British. The greenhouse gas emissions resulting from growing them locally in Britain may be more than the emissions associated with transporting them from warmer countries.

The first factor influences Tesco's sourcing of fresh fruit and vegetables is the main stages of horticultural value chain are as follows: The first stage is inputs elements needed for production, such as seed, fertilizers, agrochemicals fungicides and pesticides, farm equipment and irrigation equipment, production for export includes the production of fruit and vegetables and all processes related to the growth and harvesting of the produce, such as planting, weeding, spraying and picking, packaging and cold storage means grading, washing, trimming, chopping, mixing, packing and label are all processes that may occur in this packing stage of the value chain . Once the produce is ready for transport, it is chilled produce is ready for transport, it is chilled and placed in cold storage units ready for export, processes fruit and vegetables include dried, frozen, preserved, juices and pulps. May of these processed add value to the new foods by increasing the shelf life of the fruit and vegetables and the final stage is distribution and marketing means the produce is distributed to different channels, including supermarkets and small scale retailers and wholesalers and food services.

The second factor indicates several basic conditions must be for a country to enter the fresh fruit and vegetables value chain. These include climate allowing for year found supply, adequate road and transport infrastructure, such as ports and airports, essential for moving fragile foods to market efficiently, establishment of sanitary and to prevent disease spreading. The value chain needs to upgrading into the packing segment and processing segment. Upgrading into parking is dependent on understanding the market needs investment in capital goods and availability of supporting activities within the country, such as United Kingdom. Maintaining open lines of communication regarding demand preferences in fresh foods, quality, packing and fostering buyer involvement is critical in all stages of the value chain. For example, organize trips to key markets and they observe interactions at the point of fresh food purchase, a wide variety of equipment to attain very high standards of hygiene within the pack house operations as well as on site laboratories for fresh fruit and vegetables research and staff health tests, horticultural sector has been greatly inhibited in its upgrading along the value chain by the lack of fresh food quality packing materials. Much of produce destined for the Europe is shipped to neigh countries where it is repackaged, resulting in a significant of value. However, upgrading into the processing segment of the value chain has been difficult to achieve for low income developing countries since the processing of fruit and vegetables is cost prohibitive at low levels of crop production. Therefore, countries must gain a level of expertise during the production stage to increase output to a level that will enable the country to upgrade to the fruit and vegetable processing stage. For example, given the importance of ability to read pesticide labels and understand barcodes amongst others, standards have led to additional training initiatives to improve adult literacy. Skills training must be carried our in all job categories of value chain to maximize growth and upgrading opportunities. Investments in training are required for all job categories, from farm workers to managers, such as farming activities and the workforce within the agriculture sector, packing and storage positions and the processing stage in which workers are classified under the industrial workforce. Hence, fresh fruit and vegetables packing and processing services, such as washing, chopping, mixing as well as bagging, branding and applying bar codes are often carried out at the fresh foods source rather than at the end market destination. These processes which were previously based in the developed country, such as UK have created considerable new employment opportunities in developing countries.

The third factor influences Tesco's sourcing of fresh fruit and vegetables, which indicates today, the fruit and vegetables sector operators as a buyer driven value chain and large supermarket chains are the leading actors both in key export markets with controlling market and shares across the Europe and United States as well as increasing in emerging markets. These buyers including Sainsbry's Marks and Spencer and Walmart seek enhanced cost competitiveness, consistency and product differentiation, such as convenient, ready to eat fresh foods from their global supply chains. It causes considerable value chain method how fruit and vegetables are produced, harvested, transported, processed and stored to achieve how fresh fruit and vegetables characteristics of quality, size, pesticide use and the social and environment conditions of cultivation and post-harvest handling will influence buyer behavior decision. This ensures that the perishable food reaches its destination in good condition cold storage units are used throughout the chain to keep the produce fresh and both air and sea freighting supported by the cold chain are key elements to ensure timely delivery. Export is divided between production for fresh and vegetables and fruit consumption and production for processed fruit and vegetables that are not accepted for sale as fresh produce are as well as inputs for the processing stage, but in order cases, such as orange juice or preserved peaches a specific variety and grade quality is required and production occurs separately. The next segment is packaging and cold storage unacceptable low grade produce will be redirected to processing plants or the domestic market. Washing, trimming, chopping, mixing, packaging and labelling are other processes that may occur in this stage of the value chain. Once the produce is ready for transport it is chilled and placed in cold storage units ready for export. Packaging usually requires economies of scale due to the high costs of cold storage and other capital investment necessary at this stage .Processed fruit and vegetables include dried, frozen and preserved produce as well as juices. Processing plants purchase fruit and vegetables inputs from the producers. These firms may export their products under their own brands as well as under the buyer's brand. The last stage of the value chain before consumption is distribution and marketing. In this final stage, the produce is distributed to different channels including supermarkets, small scale retailers, wholesales and food services. Air freighting for horticultural foods and more cold storage segment of value chain in order to increase their access to key markets and avoid competition form new countries entering cold storage technologies allow suppliers to adapt to geographic constraints, such as size and distance to market.

3. Assess the level of power that Tesco exercises in the supply chain for fruit and vegetables.

The themes identified were the perceptions of freshness, having good relationships with growers and suppliers , good quality of fresh fruits and vegetables, competitive and pleasant environment for shoppers. Globalization of the fresh fruits and vegetables, retailer system has impacted on the distribution and marketing of fresh modern supply chain outlets now dominate the fresh food retail market. The increasing population and rising personal income is resulting in significant shifts in fresh food demand. Supermarkets are perceived to be the place where more wealthy consumers choose to shop. Consumers purchase almost everything there including fresh fruit and vegetable, meat, children and fish and other household supplier like dry food, bread, detergents, stationary and toys in supermarkets, such as Tesco stores, not choose to buy from fruit and vegetable markets or food retailers. The traditional markets and grocery stores comprise wet markets, fresh markets, farmer's markets are popular among consumers when purchasing fresh food are the oldest food distribution channel.

The traditional market has been defined as a market with little central control or organization that lacks refrigeration and doesn't process fresh foods into brands foods for sale where each vendor specialized in one fresh food line (meat, fish, fruit or vegetable) or in a sub line (fruit and vegetable). A fresh market and/or wet market generally occupies one or two floors of a building that is located adjacent to a housing area where there is a high population density and high traffic flow. The ground floor is normally rented to retailers who sell fresh food or ready to eat items. The upper live level is occupied by retailers who sell ready to items or non food products/ These stores are family owned retailers that sell a limited variety of foods ,such as fish, fruit and vegetable, bread and milk, stationary , toys and household supplies. However, consumers may limit their purchase from these stores due to the high prices and limited product lines. Another distribution power level to Tesco supply its fruits and vegetable to deliver to its clients in the short time. Tesco faces its customers occurred with respect to its home delivery service. With the launch of its Tesco online service, it effectively extended the supply chain right through to customers' own homes, adding value to its product offer by avoiding the need for customers to even visit a supermarket. Was it good for the environment to have fleets of delivery vans around town and countryside? Simple evaluations were difficult to make supermarket buyers again, Tesco was keen to be seen as a good citizen in this final leg of its chain, for example by launching electric delivery vehicles which Tesco decided to reduce global warmth when its vans do not need to deliver fresh foods and vegetables to different supermarkets from its warehouse in the long distance. Tesco stores is a retailer to UK local farmers that buys their fresh fruits and vegetable for the purpose of reselling them to end consumers in its different local stores daily. The Tesco stores are large, self service stores carrying a very wide range of different kinds fresh fruits and vegetable foods to sell in its different local value chains from UK local farmers supply daily. For example, Tesco stores are often the first with new store shoppers initiatives such as loyalty cards and low fresh food prices are based on large scale efficiency to sell in Tesco smaller independent stores to match. Hence, the factors can influence Tesco stores channel selection power include that the expectations of store shoppers who expect to buy local stores or who prepared to travel to a retailer that the farmers' fresh fruit and vegetables keep to save more than one day or more days to buy. This might mean taking into consideration factors such as a geographical preference to buy locally, or a tendency to feel more comfortable visiting a particular type of store; Tesco fresh foods attributes can be important, fresh produce that is highly perishable requires fairly short channels. Bypassing channels, a UK local farmer may seek to cut out intermediaries , such as Tesco stores by dealing directly with the public and Tesco may feel difficult to open up any new local stores for the farmers. Over saturation, a farmer may be accused of using too many fresh fruits and vegetable food distributors within a given geographical area, making it difficult for any individual distributor to achieve a satisfactory level of fresh foods sale , such as Terco stores. Too many links, in the supply fresh foods chain, Tesco stores may be required to buy excessive fresh fruits and vegetable foods from any farmers daily, who may be perceived as a fresh food farming competitor, rather than a cooperative channel member. New channels, these can have a similar effect to bypassing an intermediary, for example, many UK local farmers have opened up internet sales channels, thereby taking fresh food sales away from established intermediaries, such as Terso stores. Cost cutting, in order to increase volume fresh fruit and vegetables food sales, a UK local farmer may seek to distribute through higher volume, low cost intermediaries, which may make it more difficult for a smaller, full service intermediary , such as Terso stores sell the farmers' any fresh foods and UK local farmers can give incentives and rewards to other intermediaries to help them to sell in UK any stores to raise Terso's competition in UK foods supply market.

Chapter 11

A national chain of restaurant mobile advertising strategy

1. Critically assess the likely opportunities and problems
of mobile advertising for a national chain of restaurants.

A global crisis in the advertising industry largely linked to the impact of the internet is transforming the business models of media industries, the content they create and distribute, and the audiences who consume that contents. Such as consumers can use whose mobiles to find where the chain of restaurants are located and meal and drink prices and meal and drink types and
restaurant opening and closing time etc. information for the national chain of restaurants from internet advertising when who leave at home conveniently. The opportunity to mobile advertising for a national chain of restaurants, it can expand its national chain of restaurants brand to different countries visitors and instead of its self country visitors to let them to know whether where its chain of restaurants can provide what kinds of food or drink to serve to them to eat before they prepare to go to any one of the national chain of restaurants immediately. Hence, when visitors travel to its country, it will be more easy to let them to remember where any one of the national chain restaurants are located in the nation when who enter the national chain restaurants website or enter yahoo website to type" national chain restaurants" word, then who can seek any one of the national chain restaurants from whose mobiles easily.

In fact, if a national chain of restaurants chose to use television advertising, due to the national chain of restaurants which locate at itself country locally. It is only concentrate on promoting it's country's domestic eating consumers target to know it's existence when its country's domestic eating consumers are watching television at homes. Usually, working people need to work and students need to go to school to study from morning 9:00AM to 6:00 PM at night. Hence, the national chain of restaurants can only advertise at night time. Furthermore, the overseas travelers watch the nation's television when who are staying in the nation's hotels at night time. Hence, the national chain of restaurants can only use television to advertise to attract the largest numbers of local and foreign visitors to watch its advertisement at night time possibly.

Due to mobile advertising exists, television advertising is more difficult to attract the durability of audience segmentation models to build upon demographic and it also lacks new opportunities to implement psychographic and behavioral models for understanding audiences. Such as, many young people who accept to use mobile to communicate, so it implies every family usually has a mobile to use and mobile advertising also have much opportunity to help any businesses to promote whose services or products to let many families to know whose advertising. In fact, mobile users can use mobile to watch movies or news, so who ought to link internet to watch during who are sitting on any transportations or walking, so when the nation's people who feel hungry, who can use their mobiles to link to internet to seek any restaurants to decide which restaurants are the most close to their locations to choose. As a national chain of restaurants, it is more effective to advertise it's different chain of restaurants' locations to let any it's different locations of national mobile users to seek its any one of chain restaurant conveniently when who are walking on the street if who feel hungry who can turn on mobile to find map to seek the national chain of restaurants immediately. In fact, the global households who the average viewing audience composition, the number of global households using the television set and the various times it is in use, the average audience (home viewing during an average minute of a
program) and the total audiences (homes viewing the program in excess of minutes) which are decreasing. Otherwise, the mobile phone users view mobile advertising numbers are increasing. Broadcast channels as well as whatever is available on their various devices, including computer, mobile devices, gaming devices, time-shifting devices or internet enables devices. As such, it is providing more and more difficult to track the audience and known who they are and the best way to target them. Additionally, the rise of social media adds another dimension to audience research. Social media provides new ways of segmenting audiences that currently can not be done on television. Hence, a national chain of restaurants can get better ways of segmenting its viewers from mobile advertising over a variety of platforms.

So mobile networks can be better
package to the nation chain of restaurants advertising programming and the national chain of restaurants advertiser can make a more effective to attract foreign visitors or domestic visitors to make them to enter its website to view its advertising from their mobiles. For example, car owners, such as those who own a BMW or Audi famous brands cars, which have very homogeneous demographic characteristics, but each car brand has a specific type of owner with a unique personality. A similar look as television audiences could allow advertising of those car brands (who attend the upfront presentations every year) to match their car buyers to specific television shows. Demographics have not caught up with these changes and presume that viewers are still watching in only the conventional way. For instance, there is not yet a way for the networks to get credit for online viewers and it is as more viewers more to

online platforms, like a network in landing site.

Instead, a psychographic profile of the audience, one based on psychological segmentations , such as behaviors, attitudes, interests, values, opinions feelings which is a valid and valuable way of narrowing down the audience into segments for an advertiser. So, psychographic data can measure, such as peoples‘ activities how who spend whose time, their interests what they place importance on in their immediate surroundings, their opinions how their view of themselves and the world around them and some basic characteristics, such as their stage life cycle and income and education and residence location. The result of the research then provides a detailed profile that allows the marketer to be better visualize the target audience.

Psychographics start with people and reveal how the people feel client specific subjects, which can lead to be more effective marketing. When psychographic segmentations are used, the consumers are divided into group based on lifestyle and personality, often with all of this in mind, the research questions proposed here as follows: What psychographic measurements are being used right now to determine the television audience or mobile advertising ?

How are the various branches of the industry , such as restaurant industry adaptive to the new television landscape ,such as mobile advertising and what actions are they taking?

What are some challenges and resistances to psychographic measures between television advertising and mobile advertising?

What incentives or lack are there to change between television and mobile advertising?

What would be helpful for advertisers , such as a national chain of restaurants or networks , such as internet advertising to know or do in order to more towards wider use of psychographics?

A reason behind dividing audiences based on engagement can be illustrated with the Pod mobile phone, such as the national chain of restaurants organization has shown that audiences' attachment to specific the restaurants‘ brand corresponds directly to how much the audience will pay attention to the national restaurant brand's advertisements from mobile and how likely who are the actually to choose to go to the national chain of restaurants to eat lunch or dinner or breakfast more than its other restaurants.

The problem is how the national chain of restaurants to advertise it's foods taste, price and service and locations uniquely to win its other restaurant competitors from mobile specific program, providing the network to be best convenient that it's restaurant brand to advertise on that specific program. Another key problem is trend segments viewers based on domestic and foreign consumers' behavior are more specifically their viewing behavior mixed with their restaurants choosing eating behavior in whose countries, watching the national chain of restaurants television advertising from whose mobile , what who are watching to know its existence and on how to let them to know what their actual eating taste to the national chain of restaurants can provide. Hence, I suggest the national chain of restaurants can attempt to use surveys to carry on researching the different countries foreign visitors and domestic visitors whether what whose tastes are preferable to choose what kinds of foods and drinks who hope to eat in this national chain of restaurants from mobile advertising website. The problem is who may choose not to fill its surveys from its mobile website advertising. If they use computer to fill its surveys at home, it will have more opportunities to gather data from survey due to who can sit down to fill surveys in quiet environment. Hence, I suggest it ought use computer internet to do market research about what whose tastes are preferable to eat in its restaurants. When it estimates whether the foreign visitors and domestic visitors numbers, how many people choose to eat different kinds of foods and drinks to its identifications. After it can achieve mobile advertising to promote its restaurant brand more confidently in this mobile marketing advertising strategy.

2. Discuss methods that could be used to assess the effectiveness of mobile advertising.

Measuring social media marketing , such as mobile advertisement, effectiveness and identifying the target market. The use of social media sites as part of company's marketing strategy has increased significantly. Regardless its popularity, there is still very limited information to answer some of the key issues concerning the effectiveness of social media marketing , ways to measure its return on investment and its target market. The social media was started around ten years ago. It began with linked in, which was launched in 2003 year, followed by both My space and face book in 2004 year. You tube in 2005 year and Twitter in 2006 in year. The popularity of social media sites has also spread to companies as part of their strategies. Executives are concerned with their budget justification for a social media plan in computer or media online advertising, when there is lack of supporting materials to confirm the effectiveness of the social media platform , i.e. conversion rate, the relation between buyer-seller relationship and increase in sales and the rate of return investment that they can earn from this plan. Others also believe that their companies' performance are not affected by their lack of involvement in the social media sites.

Clearly, the fact that social media marketing is still relatively new among business practitioners has raised some major concerns , such as its effectiveness, the main purpose of including social media mobile advertising in a company's media platforms, it's relation to the existing platforms and the target audience of this strategy. The methods to assess effectiveness of mobile advertisement include that marketing research method is about target client segment of respondents' social media activities and buying decisions relationship survey. Survey questions can include whether how long time and how often who turn on mobile phone to use internet, such as a week is less than 20 hours average or a week is between 20 hours and 30 hours average or a week is between 30 hours and 50 hours or a week is more than 50 hours, why who like to use mobile to use internet and not use home computer to use internet, e.g. reducing to use home electricity, interesting, convenience, no computer at home, what who will seek to see from mobile advertisement, e.g. advertisement , news ,email , message, movie, whether who decide to buy products or consume services choice is from which kinds of channel advertisement influence mostly, such as television, radios, newspapers, magazines, computer internet, mobile internet. It aims to gather target client segment of respondents' social media activities and buying decision relationship to estimate whether there are how many numbers of target client will decide to buy the company's product or use it's service from mobile advertisement channel.

Hence, the survey result can indicate these five respondent groups, such as highly affected, somewhat affected, neutral somewhat not affected and not affected at all groups. Mobile phone advertisement is needed to any organizations to use internet to operate. Hence, to access the effectiveness of mobile advertising which may begin by using measures that were very easy to capture and understand, such as the number of website hits or percentage of users who clicked on an advertisement. These measures were very useful fro examining trends in traffic patterns, but the impact of this traffic on sale and other marketing objective was sales and other marketing objectives were little understand. Standardized approaches for capturing and summarizing websites behavior were eventually developed to help make sense of web traffic and patterns. Metrics, such as number of unique visitors and the amount of time who spent viewing web pages provided marketers with new insights into who was assessing the site and how who were using it. But even with a high level of detail about how customers were interacting with the company via the web, marketing manager often lacked the information how user behavior data translates into increased profits and business value. For example, organizations using websites primarily for after sales support have used exactly the same kinds of metrics as these selling directly from the site. This is not due to a lack of available data. Many organizations using web analytics gather and store vast amounts of information and develop large, complex databases to house it. But much of that information is never used. Because organizations who first began to market over the internet often lacked a clearly formulated strategy. In addition, the rapidly changing internet environment made it difficult for marketers to formulate clear expectation about the impact of activities. Both the amount of returns and amount of investments are difficult to measure. I suggest organizations may estimate the value of a visit to a particular web page by estimating the number of visitors who will become customers and then multiplying that number by the average value of all clients to estimate returns. What the 'clicks and hits' and 'measurement driven' approached have in common organization's strategic objectives and provide quantified models that plan and track internet marketing investments from intermediate outcomes to financial results. Hence, it can indicate how marketing expenditures in mobile internet advertising method to lead to increase shareholder value aim. I think investment in internet marketing , organizations will need follow these stages. In the beginning is inputs stage:

Organization and business unit strategy includes structures, systems, resources as well as marketing strategy includes structures, systems as well as information strategy includes structures, systems and market strategy transfers to websites, search marketing , advertisement and public relations, mobile marketing and marketing research. Next, it is outputs stage: It includes intermediate outputs, such as awareness and perceptions, attitudes and intentions, value provisions, channel optimization and market information as well as it includes final outputs, such as marketing assets: customer value, brand equity, knowledge as well as financial flows: increased revenue, cash flows, reduced revenue, lower cost, lower working capital, lower fixed capital and reduced risk. Finally, it is outcomes stage includes shareholder value, return on investment and corporate profitability. For example, Donald restaurant uses its website to promote lower calorie food and fruit options as well as its global campaign tied to the Olympics, nutrition (Business week 8-7-06). Each organization should carefully identify the outputs it seeks to achieve. How can process produce these outputs? Organization can attempt to enhance of website functional or initiation of an email campaign. The final question to organizations which will ask : How outputs contribute to the long term financial performance of the organization from mobile advertising ? Is critical for organizations seeking to enhance return on investment from mobile advertising? In addition, whether mobile advertising can give these benefits to any companies, such as market capitalization and shareholder value can be enhanced by increases in marketing assets (customer value, brand equity and knowledge base) that produce future corporate financial flows from mobile internet advertising method. Hence, marketing assets include customer value, such as using dynamic pricing to manage demand, supporting sales through online information sites, shipping directly to reduce need for inventory possession, shifting in store sales to online sales, eliminating clients with prior post sales problems from promotion lists; brand equity, such as additional revenue through brand premiums, using customer relationship to speed adoption of next generation products target marketing to loyal clients during predicted slow periods, reducing customer turnover and support costs, shifting responsibility and risk for inventory management to major suppliers, pool inventories with suppliers and clients to reduce warehouse space across the supply chain, using trust in brand to reduce unwarranted lawsuits, knowledge base, such as developing mass customization capability, reducing time to market through online concept trials, time promotions to smooth demand, eliminating product features that are not valuable to clients. Watching production timing to demand, direct in store sales to products that generate high contribution margin per square foot of fixed space and anticipating and respond to stakeholder concerns. Finally, customer value and brand equity and knowledge base shall transfer to financial flows aim, such as increased revenue, accelerated cash flow, reduced revenue volatility, lower cost, lower working capital requirement, lower fixed capital requirement and reduced risk.

However, Metrics can be used to access effectiveness of mobile advertising, both financial and non financial metrics are needed to effectively measure performance. Some non financial items , such as market research activities are difficult to measure and companies often avoid measuring those items. However, if the item plays a critical role in delivering organizational value. Measuring it, preferably in quantifiable terms, such as monetary changes or percentages. Even when such measures are difficult to obtain or depend a rough estimates, they provide a basis for examining trends over time and can provide useful information to managers. For example, two metrics for the output awareness are: The number of emails opened recipients and the number of clients that clicked on a promotional mobile advertising. Those two metrics can provide different perspectives on the meaning of awareness, thus the choice of metrics helps clarify the objectives, just as clear objectives can help in identifying specific and to be relevant must be specific and to be relevant they must be customized to meet the unique dynamics of the organization . It aims to achieve the best to capture and reflect the organization's unique sets of activities and results some may be relevant to all organizations and many can be readily adopted to be useful for decision making.

3. Discuss the relationship between mobile advertising and other elements of the promotion in campaign planning.

Mobile advertisement defines as the use of the mobile medium, it is as a communications and entertainment channel between a brand and an end user. In basic terms, it is the process of planning and execution conception, pricing, promotion and distribution of products and services through the mobile channel. Advertising is a form of communication intended to convince an audience (viewers, readers or listeners) to purchase or take some action upon products, information or services etc. The relationship between independent variables elements and mobile advertising which are environmental response and emotional response with behavioral aspect of consumer buying behavior with mobile advertising. It is time that people purchase those brands with which who are emotionally attached elements. Almost every one grows up in the world which is flooded with the mass media, e.g. television, films, videos, magazines, movies advertising and internet channel is either mobile advertising or computer advertising. Advertising is a subset of promotion mix which is one of the 4'p in the marketing mix, i.e. product, price, place and promotion. As a promotional strategy, advertising serve as a major tool in creating product awareness in the mind of a potential consumer to take eventual purchase decision. Advertising, sales promotion and public relations are mass communication tools available to marketers.

Telecommunication technology, such as mobile advertising enables business and industry to grow at a faster pace when contributing to the economic development and at the same time telecommunication infrastructure can be reliable. Cellular phone industry has been one of the profitable businesses in Asian. The country's growing population and huge demand potential have always been an attraction for many high-technological multinational companies. Societies used symbols and pictorial signs to attract their produce users. There elements were used for promotion of products. A company can't make dream to be a well known brand until which invests in their promotional activities for which consumer market have been dominating through advertisements. As the primary mission of advertiser is to reach prospective customers and influence their awareness, attitudes and buying behavior.

The major aim of advertising is to impact on buying behavior, however this impact about brand is changes or strengthened frequently in peoples' memories. Memories about the brand consist of their associations that are related to brand name in consumer mind. These brand cognition influence consideration, evaluation and finally purchases. The promotion in campaign planning to mobile advertising focuses on young people because who choose advertising information and characters as whose role models, who may not only identify with them but also intend to copy them in terms of how who dress and what who are going to buy. As the market is surplus with several products or services, so many companies make similar functional claim, so it has became extremely difficult for companies to differentiate their products or services based on functional attributes alone. Differentiations based on functional attributed, which are shown in advertisement, are never long lasting as the competitors could copy the same. Mobile advertising may differentiate companies' products or services promotion channel to attract client's attention, e.g. the company can use movable product images on internet video to show on mobile. However, mobile advertising time ought depend on the business nature, e.g. facial health products target segment is female, so it's mobile advertising time ought choose form 9:00 AM to 6:00 PM working time between Monday to Sunday, due to housewives or working women shall go back home to cook, who shall not turn on mobile phones at home. Hence, if the company had differentiated which brand and it had chose what time is the more popular to accept to let mobile users to turn on their mobile from mobile advertising. The company mobile advertising will have more promotion effort. For example, if the company sold toys, it's target segment would be 3 ages to 10 ages old. It's mobile advertising ought let every family to find its company website easily. If the family didn't know it's brand, but is was difficult to let the family to find what its toys sale from whose mobile phone because there are many toy companies were using internet advertising to promote which toys. So, it might let every family types " toy" word on yahoo, Google websites, then this toy company name would appear on their websites, the family only clicked its name on their mobile phone, it could show it' toys images, prices, which country manufacturing and which year manufacturing different kind of toys, sale payment and delivery method, e.g. visa card payment, air or land or shipping transportation flight delivery, toys manufacturing ingredients indication from website advertising and it's toys advertising time ought to choose family working time, such as between 9:00 and 6:00 PM , due to who shall bring their mobile to work usually. Hence, the toy company needs to consider family will choose what time to use mobile phone. It ought not choose night time to advertise its toy products from mobile due to family would not turn on whose mobile at home at night time usually. Economic theory has sought to establish relationships between selling prices, sales achieved and consumer's income, similarly before the company chooses to spend mobile advertising expenditure, it ought frequently compared it with sales actual income each month.

Social media marketing, such as mobile advertising effectiveness is highly influenced by three aspects: content quality, involvement and integration with the other media platforms methods to assess whether effectiveness of mobile advertising.

On the first aspect, content quality isn't quantity. It shows that managers should not totally reply on the monitoring software to measure and analyze their social media campaign. For example, the twitter website analysis show that some brands/companies, e.g. Microsoft used their Twitter account to connect and to

communicate with customers . Their Tweets were about communicating and connecting with their follows, through some personal conversations in subjects. That were relevant to their customers . As a results, Microsoft clients were able to

beat their main competitors in financial performances and Twitter activities. So, Microsoft can use twitter website to assess whether how many numbers of people use internet service to enter phone, then who decide to buy its software products . If Microsoft found the result of the number of buyers who decide to buy its software from mobile phone Twitter website advertisement channel which is more than mobile phone Yahoo or Google websites advertisement channel after who turn on mobile to see advertising. On the another aspect, building trust and long term relationship to mobile advertising to indicate to how to persuade to increase many shippers to decide to buy any products or seek service, e.g. travel tickets booking service after who use mobile to seek advertising habitually. Today, media marketing is about building relationship and trust through effective two way communications , e.g. talk about something that customers are interested in and creating products or service that will help to solve customers' problems from mobile advertising. Some of today's social media marketing campaigns are still driven by the old fashioned marketing and focus on short-term effect sales, which is also known as incentive induced behavior. To assess trust and genuine buyer/seller relationships achieved through consistent and engaging conversation will increase the messages (SMM) level of influence. Trust is the key factor to get the followers to actually to something , i.e. change in buying decisions influence their peers and turn it into revenue for the companies. It is crucial to build a strong relationship with customers and enhance brand loyalty. Hence, it implies mobile phone companies need to build trust relationship to let them to pay extract internet charges to aim to read email, news, watch movie habitually. Then, it will increase chance to let potential buyers to prefer to seek advertisement to choose to buy and products or consume service from mobile websites habitually. Hence, assessment of mobile internet habitual users who use mobile internet time per week from survey is one effective method. Also, firms should start their involvement by inviting their customers or prospects to join their social media community. For example, firms can post the icons of the social media main websites or giving some special deals to customers who become their fans or followers . In the online community, firms should start writing more effective posts. An effective post should reflect honesty and conciseness, it is as key elements of an effective post. It should also be informative to satisfy clients' need for information and experts; opinions. Effective contents should be able to actions from the audience (conversion) so that by the end of this process. Followers will place on order, subscribe newsletter or participate on online surveys. In the offline community, managers should share expertise with their speaker in the local community, which will help to attract more followers or fans and to strength connection with the community. A debate has been going on whether or not consumers are willing to receive mobile advertising. America consumers seem to willing to accept mobile advertising to subsidize the cost of other mobile services , such as email and news services.

A study conducted by HRI Research on behalf of Nokia brand found that the core mobile phone subscriber market (16 to 45 year old) is not only receptive to experiencing mobile advertising, but also actively welcoming mobile advertising in the form of electronic coupons promotion. The relationship between mobile advertising and the four key elements contributing to mobile advertising's acceptance of the promotion in campaign planning. There were mobile advertising should allow users to decide whether or not to receive messages, users could bypass sales messages easily, users should be filter the message received and users want to get mutual benefits of something back. The SMA advertising campaigns of mobile advertising industry plays and consumers have been made afraid of the spam phenomenon deriving from negative email spamming experiences. The personal nature of the website phone markets spamming especially invasive compared to spam received via other channels and devices. Mobile advertising has the potential to be one of the most powerful one to one digital advertising mediums of utilized in the right manner. SMS trials across the would have show the power of mobile advertising in building direct one to one relationship. The online companies like AT&T, AOC wireless, Microsoft and Nokia to mention few companies that are focused on the potential of mobile marketing via mobile handsets. Factors contributing to the success of mobile advertising include that ability, setting up research. measurement, tracking systems, availability of specialist expertise in agency, service provide and establishing consistent rate mobile cards. Other factors impact of drivers on the development of mobile advertising include that personalized medium, users able to opt in , call to action , i.e. immediate response possible , location specific, interactive profiling, appeals to younger customers , one to many communication.

In conclusion, the relatively between mobile advertising and other elements of the promotion in campaign planning include as below: The first element is by utilizing mobile advertising, companies can run marketing campaigns targeted to tens of thousands of people with a fragment of the costs compared to other direct marketing mediums, such as direct mail or telephone and this in just few seconds of line. The advertising industry uses two types of cost calculation cost per thousand impressions (CPM) and cost per rating point (CPP). CPM is used for both print and electronic media when CPP is more popular for electronic media. For instance, if an advertising campaign costs US$5,000 and has an audience of 300,000 consumers, the CPM will be approximately to the initial CPM measure in media selection , such as quality of the audience, audience attention probability and believability of media selection when the CPM for direct mail is between UA$500 to US$700. For email the CPM ranges from US$5 to US$7. However when email marketing is losing its efficiency, mobile advertising offers new ways to promote products and services. A significant factor contributing to consumers' willingness to accept mobile advertisement is the capability of mobile handsets to service certain type of messages , such as multimedia messages. Evidently, most consumers in the future will carry on smart phone with them. The smart phones allow advertisers to reach consumers in different locations with personalize messages at a given time. Another element is the industry of SG or 4G network service is faster connection speed is a obvious enables users to receive digital photographs, moving wide images, high quality sound for their mobile handsets. From advertisers; perspective this opens various opportunities to plan and implement more advance m-advertising campaigns and integrate those with existing marketing channels. However, to develop and provide applications, for example, interfaces to the carrier's wireless network need to be provided in multiple areas: location, presence, billing, personalization, provisioning, packet network, transport and messaging systems. Next element is location awareness cab be seen as the driving force of many wireless applications and suits also well types of mobile advertising. When mobile phones are almost always carried with and intelligent location awareness technical solution are available. The final element is personalization means building customer loyalty by building a meaningful one to one relatively by understanding the needs to each individual and helping to satisfy a goal that efficiently and knowledgeably addresses each.

Personalization is about mapping and satisfying of client's goal in specific contest with a business's goal in its respective context. Personalization means understanding different kinds of individual preferences , needs, mindsets and lifestyles and cultural as well as geographical differences. Mobile are already equipment with a profiting options, e.g. silent, meeting, outdoors. For example, the utilization of time and location awareness as personalization variables has the benefit that mobile advertising is a marketing medium has features that other marketing channels lack. Hence, email advertising needs to keep every mobile users' personal information to be confidential, solicited message, relevance to users need and the right frequency.

Reference

Adrian, P. (2012). Introduction to marketing theory & practice, 3 rd edition, London: Oxford press.

Couper, M.P. J. Blair and T. Triplet (1999). A Comparison Of Mail And E-mail For a Survey Of Employees In USA Statistical Agencies. Journal Of Official Statistics, 15, 39-56.

Data monitor (2008). The proctor and gamble company. Retrieved Nov. 15 2009 from http://www.datamonitor.com/

Dyer, D., F. Dalzell & R. Olegario (2004). Rising tide. Lessons learned from 165 years of brand building at Procter and Gamble. Boston, MA: Havard Business School Press.

Priesnitz, W. (2007) Counting Our Food Miles. Natural Life, 1 July.

Sullivan, Nicholas P(2007). You can hear me now: How Micro loans and cell phones are connecting the world, San Francisco, CA: John Wilsey & Sans, 2007.

CHAPTER XXXIV

CHAPTER XXXV

A national chain of restaurant mobile advertising strategy

Critically assess the likely opportunities and problems
of mobile advertising for a national chain of restaurants.

A global crisis in the advertising industry largely linked to the impact of the internet is transforming the business models of media industries, the content they create and distribute, and the audiences who consume that contents. Such as consumers can use whose mobiles to find where the chain of restaurants are located and meal and drink prices and meal and drink types and

restaurant opening and closing time etc. information for the national chain of restaurants from internet advertising when who leave at home conveniently. The opportunity to mobile advertising for a national chain of restaurants, it can expand its national chain of restaurants brand to different countries visitors and instead of its self country visitors to let them to know whether where its chain of restaurants can provide what kinds of food or drink to serve to them to eat before they prepare to go to any one of the national chain of restaurants immediately. Hence, when visitors travel to its country, it will be more easy to let them to remember where any one of the national chain restaurants are located in the nation when who enter the national chain restaurants website or enter yahoo website to type" national chain restaurants" word, then who can seek any one of the national chain restaurants from whose mobiles easily.

In fact, if a national chain of restaurants chose to use television advertising, due to the national chain of restaurants which locate at itself country locally. It is only concentrate on promoting it's country's domestic eating consumers target to know it's existence when its country's domestic eating consumers are watching television at homes. Usually, working people need to work and students need to go to school to study from morning 9:00AM to 6:00 PM at night. Hence, the national chain of restaurants can only advertise at night time. Furthermore, the overseas travelers watch the nation's television when who are staying in the nation's hotels at night time. Hence, the national chain of restaurants can only use television to advertise to attract the largest numbers of local and foreign visitors to watch its advertisement at night time possibly.

Due to mobile advertising exists, television advertising is more difficult to attract the durability of audience segmentation models to build upon demographic and it also lacks new opportunities to implement psychographic and behavioral models for understanding audiences. Such as, many young people who accept to use mobile to communicate, so it implies every family usually has a mobile to use and mobile advertising also have much opportunity to help any businesses to promote whose services or products to let many families to know whose advertising. In fact, mobile users can use mobile to watch movies or news, so who ought to link internet to watch during who are sitting on any transportations or walking, so when the nation's people who feel hungry, who can use their mobiles to link to internet to seek any restaurants to decide which restaurants are the most close to their locations to choose. As a national chain of restaurants, it is more effective to advertise it's different chain of restaurants' locations to let any it's different locations of national mobile users to seek its any one of chain restaurant conveniently when who are walking on the street if who feel hungry who can turn on mobile to find map to seek the national chain of restaurants immediately. In fact, the global households who the average viewing audience composition, the number of global households using the television set and the various times it is in use, the average audience (home viewing during an average minute of a

program) and the total audiences (homes viewing the program in excess of minutes) which are decreasing. Otherwise, the mobile phone users view mobile advertising numbers are increasing. Broadcast channels as well as whatever is available on their various devices, including computer, mobile devices, gaming devices, time-shifting devices or internet enables devices. As such, it is providing more and more difficult to track the audience and known who they are and the best way to target them. Additionally, the rise of social media adds another dimension to audience research. Social media provides new ways of segmenting audiences that currently can not be done on television. Hence, a national chain of restaurants can get better ways of segmenting its viewers from mobile advertising over a variety of platforms.

So mobile networks can be better

package to the nation chain of restaurants advertising programming and the national chain of restaurants advertiser can make a more effective to attract foreign visitors or domestic visitors to make them to enter its website to view its advertising from their mobiles. For example, car owners, such as those who own a BMW or Audi famous brands cars, which have very homogeneous demographic characteristics, but each car brand has a specific type of owner with a unique personality. A similar look as television audiences could allow advertising of those car brands (who attend the upfront presentations every year) to match their car buyers to specific television shows. Demographics have not caught up with these changes and presume that viewers are still watching in only the conventional way. For instance, there is not yet a way for the networks to get credit for online viewers and it is as more viewers more to online platforms, like a network in landing site.

Instead, a psychographic profile of the audience, one based on psychological segmentations , such as behaviors, attitudes, interests, values, opinions feelings which is a valid and valuable way of narrowing down the audience into segments for an advertiser. So, psychographic data can measure, such as peoples' activities how who spend whose time, their interests what they place importance on in their immediate surroundings, their opinions how their view of themselves and the world around them and some basic characteristics, such as their stage life cycle and income and education and residence location. The result of the research then provides a detailed profile that allows the marketer to be better visualize the target audience.

Psychographics start with people and reveal how the people feel client specific subjects, which can lead to be more effective marketing. When psychographic segmentations are used, the consumers are divided into group based on lifestyle and personality, often with all of this in mind, the research questions proposed here as follows: What

psychographic measurements are being used right now to determine the television audience or mobile advertising ?
How are the various branches of the industry , such as restaurant industry adaptive to the new television landscape ,such as mobile advertising and what actions are they taking?
What are some challenges and resistances to psychographic measures between television advertising and mobile advertising?
What incentives or lack are there to change between television and mobile advertising?
What would be helpful for advertisers , such as a national chain of restaurants or networks , such as internet advertising to know or do in order to more towards wider use of psychographics?
A reason behind dividing audiences based on engagement can be illustrated with the Pod mobile phone, such as the national chain of restaurants organization has shown that audiences' attachment to specific the restaurants' brand corresponds directly to how much the audience will pay attention to the national restaurant brand's advertisements from mobile and how likely who are the actually to choose to go to the national chain of restaurants to eat lunch or dinner or breakfast more than its other restaurants.

The problem is how the national chain of restaurants to advertise it's foods taste, price and service and locations uniquely to win its other restaurant competitors from mobile specific program, providing the network to be best convenient that it's restaurant brand to advertise on that specific program. Another key problem is trend segments viewers based on domestic and foreign consumers' behavior are more specifically their viewing behavior mixed with their restaurants choosing eating behavior in whose countries, watching the national chain of restaurants television advertising from whose mobile , what who are watching to know its existence and on how to let them to know what their actual eating taste to the national chain of restaurants can provide. Hence, I suggest the national chain of restaurants can attempt to use surveys to carry on researching the different countries foreign visitors and domestic visitors whether what whose tastes are preferable to choose what kinds of foods and drinks who hope to eat in this national chain of restaurants from mobile advertising website. The problem is who may choose not to fill its surveys from its mobile website advertising. If they use computer to fill its surveys at home, it will have more opportunities to gather data from survey due to who can sit down to fill surveys in quiet environment. Hence, I suggest it ought use computer internet to do market research about what whose tastes are preferable to eat in its restaurants. When it estimates whether the foreign visitors and domestic visitors numbers, how many people choose to eat different kinds of foods and drinks to its identifications. After it can achieve mobile advertising to promote its restaurant brand more confidently in this mobile marketing advertising strategy.

2. Discuss methods that could be used to assess the effectiveness of mobile advertising.

Measuring social media marketing , such as mobile advertisement, effectiveness and identifying the target market. The use of social media sites as part of company's marketing strategy has increased significantly. Regardless its popularity, there is still very limited information to answer some of the key issues concerning the effectiveness of social media marketing , ways to measure its return on investment and its target market. The social media was started around ten years ago. It began with linked in, which was launched in 2003 year, followed by both My space and face book in 2004 year. You tube in 2005 year and Twitter in 2006 in year. The popularity of social media sites has also spread to companies as part of their strategies. Executives are concerned with their budget justification for a social media plan in computer or media online advertising, when there is lack of supporting materials to confirm the effectiveness of the social media platform , i.e. conversion rate, the relation between buyer-seller relationship and increase in sales and the rate of return investment that they can earn from this plan. Others also believe that their companies' performance are not affected by their lack of involvement in the social media sites.

Clearly, the fact that social media marketing is still relatively new among business practitioners has raised some major concerns , such as its effectiveness, the main purpose of including social media mobile advertising in a company's media platforms, it's relation to the existing platforms and the target audience of this strategy. The methods to assess effectiveness of mobile advertisement include that marketing research method is about target client segment of respondents' social media activities and buying decisions relationship survey. Survey questions can include whether how long time and how often who turn on mobile phone to use internet, such as a week is less than 20 hours average or a week is between 20 hours and 30 hours average or a week is between 30 hours and 50 hours or a week is more than 50 hours, why who like to use mobile to use internet and not use home computer to use internet, e.g. reducing to use home electricity, interesting, convenience, no computer at home, what who will seek to see from mobile advertisement, e.g. advertisement , news ,email , message, movie, whether who decide to buy products or consume services choice is from which kinds of channel advertisement influence mostly, such as television, radios, newspapers, magazines, computer internet, mobile internet. It aims to gather target client segment of respondents' social media activities and buying decision relationship to estimate whether there are how many numbers of target client will decide to buy the company's product or use it's service from mobile advertisement channel.

Hence, the survey result can indicate these five respondent groups, such as highly affected, somewhat affected, neutral somewhat not affected and not affected at all groups. Mobile phone advertisement is needed to any organizations to use internet to operate. Hence, to access the effectiveness of mobile advertising which may begin by using measures that were very easy to capture and understand, such as the number of website hits or percentage of users who clicked on an advertisement. These measures were very useful fro examining trends in traffic patterns, but the impact of this traffic on sale and other marketing objective was sales and other marketing objectives were little understand. Standardized approaches for capturing and summarizing websites behavior were eventually developed to help make sense of web traffic and patterns. Metrics, such as number of unique visitors and the amount of time who spent viewing web pages provided marketers with new insights into who was assessing the site and how who were using it. But even with a high level of detail about how customers were interacting with the company via the web, marketing manager often lacked the information how user behavior data translates into increased profits and business value. For example, organizations using websites primarily for after sales support have used exactly the same kinds of metrics as these selling directly from the site. This is not due to a lack of available data. Many organizations using web analytics gather and store vast amounts of information and develop large, complex databases to house it. But much of that information is never used. Because organizations who first began to market over the internet often lacked a clearly formulated strategy. In addition, the rapidly changing internet environment made it difficult for marketers to formulate clear expectation about the impact of activities. Both the amount of returns and amount of investments are difficult to measure. I suggest organizations may estimate the value of a visit to a particular web page by estimating the number of visitors who will become customers and then multiplying that number by the average value of all clients to estimate returns. What the ‘clicks and hits’ and ‘measurement driven’ approached have in common organization’s strategic objectives and provide quantified models that plan and track internet marketing investments from intermediate outcomes to financial results. Hence, it can indicate how marketing expenditures in mobile internet advertising method to lead to increase shareholder value aim. I think investment in internet marketing , organizations will need follow these stages. In the beginning is inputs stage:

Organization and business unit strategy includes structures, systems, resources as well as marketing strategy includes structures, systems as well as information strategy includes structures, systems and market strategy transfers to websites, search marketing , advertisement and public relations, mobile marketing and marketing research. Next, it is outputs stage: It includes intermediate outputs, such as awareness and perceptions, attitudes and intentions, value provisions, channel optimization and market information as well as it includes final outputs, such as marketing assets: customer value, brand equity, knowledge as well as financial flows: increased revenue, cash flows, reduced revenue, lower cost, lower working capital, lower fixed capital and reduced risk. Finally, it is outcomes stage includes shareholder value, return on investment and corporate profitability. For example, Donald restaurant uses its website to promote lower calorie food and fruit options as well as its global campaign tied to the Olympics, nutrition (Business week 8-7-06). Each organization should carefully identify the outputs it seeks to achieve. How can process produce these outputs? Organization can attempt to enhance of website functional or initiation of an email campaign. The final question to organizations which will ask : How outputs contribute to the long term financial performance of the organization from mobile advertising ? Is critical for organizations seeking to enhance return on investment from mobile advertising? In addition, whether mobile advertising can give these benefits to any companies, such as market capitalization and shareholder value can be enhanced by increases in marketing assets (customer value, brand equity and knowledge base) that produce future corporate financial flows from mobile internet advertising method. Hence, marketing assets include customer value, such as using dynamic pricing to manage demand, supporting sales through online information sites, shipping directly to reduce need for inventory possession, shifting in store sales to online sales, eliminating clients with prior post sales problems from promotion lists; brand equity, such as additional revenue through brand premiums, using customer relationship to speed adoption of next generation products target marketing to loyal clients during predicted slow periods, reducing customer turnover and support costs, shifting responsibility and risk for inventory management to major suppliers, pool inventories with suppliers and clients to reduce warehouse space across the supply chain, using trust in brand to reduce unwarranted lawsuits, knowledge base, such as developing mass customization capability, reducing time to market through online concept trials, time promotions to smooth demand, eliminating product features that are not valuable to clients. Watching production timing to demand, direct in store sales to products that generate high contribution margin per square foot of fixed space and anticipating and respond to stakeholder concerns. Finally, customer value and brand equity and knowledge base shall transfer to financial flows aim, such as increased revenue, accelerated cash flow, reduced revenue volatility, lower cost, lower working capital requirement, lower fixed capital requirement and reduced risk.

However, Metrics can be used to access effectiveness of mobile advertising, both financial and non financial metrics are needed to effectively measure performance. Some non financial items , such as market research activities are difficult to measure and companies often avoid measuring those items. However, if the item plays a critical role in delivering organizational value. Measuring it, preferably in quantifiable terms, such as monetary changes or percentages. Even when such measures are difficult to obtain or depend a rough estimates, they provide a basis for examining trends over time and can provide useful information to managers. For example, two metrics for the output awareness are: The number of emails opened recipients and the number of clients that clicked on a promotional mobile advertising. Those two metrics can provide different perspectives on the meaning of awareness, thus the choice of metrics helps clarify the objectives, just as clear objectives can help in identifying specific and to be relevant must be specific and to be relevant they must be customized to meet the unique dynamics of the organization . It aims to achieve the best to capture and reflect the organization's unique sets of activities and results some may be relevant to all organizations and many can be readily adopted to be useful for decision making.

3. Discuss the relationship between mobile advertising and other elements of the promotion in campaign planning.

Mobile advertisement defines as the use of the mobile medium, it is as a communications and entertainment channel between a brand and an end user. In basic terms, it is the process of planning and execution conception, pricing, promotion and distribution of products and services through the mobile channel. Advertising is a form of communication intended to convince an audience (viewers, readers or listeners) to purchase or take some action upon products, information or services etc. The relationship between independent variables elements and mobile advertising which are environmental response and emotional response with behavioral aspect of consumer buying behavior with mobile advertising. It is time that people purchase those brands with which who are emotionally attached elements. Almost every one grows up in the world which is flooded with the mass media, e.g. television, films, videos, magazines, movies advertising and internet channel is either mobile advertising or computer advertising. Advertising is a subset of promotion mix which is one of the 4'p in the marketing mix, i.e. product, price, place and promotion. As a promotional strategy, advertising serve as a major tool in creating product awareness in the mind of a potential consumer to take eventual purchase decision. Advertising, sales promotion and public relations are mass communication tools available to marketers.

Telecommunication technology, such as mobile advertising enables business and industry to grow at a faster pace when contributing to the economic development and at the same time telecommunication infrastructure can be reliable. Cellular phone industry has been one of the profitable businesses in Asian. The country's growing population and huge demand potential have always been an attraction for many high-technological multinational companies. Societies used symbols and pictorial signs to attract their produce users. There elements were used for promotion of products. A company can't make dream to be a well known brand until which invests in their promotional activities for which consumer market have been dominating through advertisements. As the primary mission of advertiser is to reach prospective customers and influence their awareness, attitudes and buying behavior.

The major aim of advertising is to impact on buying behavior, however this impact about brand is changes or strengthened frequently in peoples' memories. Memories about the brand consist of their associations that are related to brand name in consumer mind. These brand cognition influence consideration, evaluation and finally purchases. The promotion in campaign planning to mobile advertising focuses on young people because who choose advertising information and characters as whose role models, who may not only identify with them but also intend to copy them in terms of how who dress and what who are going to buy. As the market is surplus with several products or services, so many companies make similar functional claim, so it has became extremely difficult for companies to differentiate their products or services based on functional attributes alone. Differentiations based on functional attributed, which are shown in advertisement, are never long lasting as the competitors could copy the same. Mobile advertising may differentiate companies‘ products or services promotion channel to attract client's attention, e.g. the company can use movable product images on internet video to show on mobile. However, mobile advertising time ought depend on the business nature, e.g. facial health products target segment is female, so it's mobile advertising time ought choose form 9:00 AM to 6:00 PM working time between Monday to Sunday, due to housewives or working women shall go back home to cook, who shall not turn on mobile phones at home. Hence, if the company had differentiated which brand and it had chose what time is the more popular to accept to let mobile users to turn on their mobile from mobile advertising. The company mobile advertising will have more promotion effort. For example, if the company sold toys, it's target segment would be 3 ages to 10 ages old. It's mobile advertising ought let every family to find its company website easily. If the family didn't know it's brand, but is was difficult to let the family to find what its toys sale from whose mobile phone because there are many toy companies were using internet advertising to promote which toys. So, it might let every family types " toy" word on yahoo, Google websites, then this toy company name would appear on their websites, the family only clicked its name on their mobile phone, it could show it' toys images, prices, which country manufacturing and which year manufacturing different kind of toys, sale payment and delivery method, e.g. visa card payment, air or land or shipping transportation flight delivery, toys manufacturing ingredients indication from website advertising and it's toys advertising time ought to choose family working time, such as between 9:00 and 6:00 PM , due to who shall bring their mobile to work usually. Hence, the toy company needs to consider family will choose what time to use mobile phone. It ought not choose night time to advertise its toy products from mobile due to family would not turn on whose mobile at home at night time usually. Economic theory has sought to establish relationships between selling prices, sales achieved and consumer's income, similarly before the company chooses to spend mobile advertising expenditure, it ought frequently compared it with sales actual income each month.

Social media marketing, such as mobile advertising effectiveness is highly influenced by three aspects: content quality, involvement and integration with the other media platforms methods to assess whether effectiveness of mobile advertising.

On the first aspect, content quality isn't quantity. It shows that managers should not totally reply on the monitoring software to measure and analyze their social media campaign. For example, the twitter website analysis show that some brands/companies, e.g. Microsoft used their Twitter account to connect and to communicate with customers . Their Tweets were about communicating and connecting with their follows, through some personal conversations in subjects. That were relevant to their customers . As a results, Microsoft clients were able to beat their main competitors in financial performances and Twitter activities. So, Microsoft can use twitter website to assess whether how many numbers of people use internet service to enter phone, then who decide to buy its software products . If Microsoft found the result of the number of buyers who decide to buy its software from mobile phone Twitter website advertisement channel which is more than mobile phone Yahoo or Google websites advertisement channel after who turn on mobile to see advertising. On the another aspect, building trust and long term relationship to mobile advertising to indicate to how to persuade to increase many shippers to decide to buy any products or seek service, e.g. travel tickets booking service after who use mobile to seek advertising habitually. Today, media marketing is about building relationship and trust through effective two way communications , e.g. talk about something that customers are interested in and creating products or service that will help to solve customers' problems from mobile advertising. Some of today's social media marketing campaigns are still driven by the old fashioned marketing and focus on short-term effect sales, which is also known as incentive induced behavior. To assess trust and genuine buyer/seller relationships achieved through consistent and engaging conversation will increase the messages (SMM) level of influence. Trust is the key factor to get the followers to actually to something , i.e. change in buying decisions influence their peers and turn it into revenue for the companies. It is crucial to build a strong relationship with customers and enhance brand loyalty. Hence, it implies mobile phone companies need to build trust relationship to let them to pay extract internet charges to aim to read email, news, watch movie habitually. Then, it will increase chance to let potential buyers to prefer to seek advertisement to choose to buy and products or consume service from mobile websites habitually. Hence, assessment of mobile internet habitual users who use mobile internet time per week from survey is one effective method. Also, firms should start their involvement by inviting their customers or prospects to join their social media community. For example, firms can post the icons of the social media main websites or giving some special deals to customers who become their fans or followers . In the online community, firms should start writing more effective posts. An effective post should reflect honesty and conciseness, it is as key elements of an effective post. It should also be informative to satisfy clients' need for information and experts; opinions. Effective contents should be able to actions from the audience (conversion) so that by the end of this process. Followers will place on order, subscribe newsletter or participate on online surveys. In the offline community, managers should share expertise with their speaker in the local community, which will help to attract more followers or fans and to strength connection with the community. A debate has been going on whether or not consumers are willing to receive mobile advertising. America consumers seem to willing to accept mobile advertising to subsidize the cost of other mobile services , such as email and news services.

A study conducted by HRI Research on behalf of Nokia brand found that the core mobile phone subscriber market (16 to 45 year old) is not only receptive to experiencing mobile advertising, but also actively welcoming mobile advertising in the form of electronic coupons promotion. The relationship between mobile advertising and the four key elements contributing to mobile advertising's acceptance of the promotion in campaign planning. There were mobile advertising should allow users to decide whether or not to receive messages, users could bypass sales messages easily, users should be filter the message received and users want to get mutual benefits of something back. The SMA advertising campaigns of mobile advertising industry plays and consumers have been made afraid of the spam phenomenon deriving from negative email spamming experiences. The personal nature of the website phone markets spamming especially invasive compared to spam received via other channels and devices. Mobile advertising has the potential to be one of the most powerful one to one digital advertising mediums of utilized in the right manner. SMS trials across the would have show the power of mobile advertising in building direct one to one relationship. The online companies like AT&T, AOC wireless, Microsoft and Nokia to mention few companies that are focused on the potential of mobile marketing via mobile handsets. Factors contributing to the success of mobile advertising include that ability, setting up research. measurement, tracking systems, availability of specialist expertise in agency, service provide and establishing consistent rate mobile cards. Other factors impact of drivers on the development of mobile advertising include that personalized medium, users able to opt in , call to action , i.e. immediate response possible , location specific, interactive profiling, appeals to younger customers , one to many communication.

In conclusion, the relatively between mobile advertising and other elements of the promotion in campaign planning include as below: The first element is by utilizing mobile advertising, companies can run marketing campaigns targeted to tens of thousands of people with a fragment of the costs compared to other direct marketing mediums, such as direct mail or telephone and this in just few seconds of line. The advertising industry uses two types of cost calculation cost per thousand impressions (CPM) and cost per rating point (CPP). CPM is used for both print and electronic media when CPP is more popular for electronic media. For instance, if an advertising campaign costs US$5,000 and has an audience of 300,000 consumers, the CPM will be approximately to the initial CPM measure in media selection , such as quality of the audience, audience attention probability and believability of media selection when the CPM for direct mail is between UA$500 to US$700. For email the CPM ranges from US$5 to US$7. However when email marketing is losing its efficiency, mobile advertising offers new ways to promote products and services. A significant factor contributing to consumers‘ willingness to accept mobile advertisement is the capability of mobile handsets to service certain type of messages , such as multimedia messages. Evidently, most consumers in the future will carry on smart phone with them. The smart phones allow advertisers to reach consumers in different locations with personalize messages at a given time. Another element is the industry of SG or 4G network service is faster connection speed is a obvious enables users to receive digital photographs, moving wide images, high quality sound for their mobile handsets. From advertisers; perspective this opens various opportunities to plan and implement more advance m-advertising campaigns and integrate those with existing marketing channels. However, to develop and provide applications, for example, interfaces to the carrier's wireless network need to be provided in multiple areas: location, presence, billing, personalization, provisioning, packet network, transport and messaging systems. Next element is location awareness cab be seen as the driving force of many wireless applications and suits also well types of mobile advertising. When mobile phones are almost always carried with and intelligent location awareness technical solution are available. The final element is personalization means building customer loyalty by building a meaningful one to one relatively by understanding the needs to each individual and helping to satisfy a goal that efficiently and knowledgeably addresses each.

Personalization is about mapping and satisfying of client's goal in specific contest with a business's goal in its respective context. Personalization means understanding different kinds of individual preferences , needs, mindsets and lifestyles and cultural as well as geographical differences. Mobile are already equipment with a profiting options, e.g. silent, meeting, outdoors. For example, the utilization of time and location awareness as personalization variables has the benefit that mobile advertising is a marketing medium has features that other marketing channels lack. Hence, email advertising needs to keep every mobile users' personal information to be confidential, solicited message, relevance to users need and the right frequency.

9 798886 848663

Printed by Libri Plureos GmbH in Hamburg,
Germany